AFFAIRS OF STATE

AFFAIRS OF STATE

Bob Gorrell

Foreword by Lawrence Douglas Wilder

PELICAN PUBLISHING COMPANY
Gretna 1995

For Pat and my four favorite doodles—Rob, Sarah, Teddy, and PJ

Special thanks for help in producing this collection go to Ross Mackenzie, Gary Brookins, Todd Culbertson, and Kathy Barnes

The word "Pelican" and the depiction of a pelican are trademarks of Pelican Publishing Company, Inc., and are registered in the U.S. Patent and Trademark Office.

Manufactured in the United States of America
Published by Pelican Publishing Company, Inc.
1101 Monroe Street, Gretna, Louisiana 70053

Contents

Foreword

When I was a teen-ager and first starting to pay attention to editorial pages, it was the cartoons that attracted me. Fred Seibel of the *Richmond Times-Dispatch*, with his ubiquitous crow, and Herblock of *The Washington Post* seemed to capture the essence of the news in eloquent yet tasteful depictions of newsmakers and events through their cartoons.

Dabbling as I did as one of my high-school paper's cartoonists, I was struck by the seeming ease of these accomplishments. I say "seeming ease," for I have come to know and appreciate the enormous talent required for someone to be able to produce at a level of excellence on a regular, even daily, basis.

In this collection Bob Gorrell displays why his generation of news junkies relies on the visual "byte." It becomes clear that one could not produce these pictures without himself having digested and synthesized events in rapid turn-around time. The mixture of national, state, and regional issues here makes this collection all the more appealing.

If there is truth in the adage "a picture is worth a thousand words," then this collection serves to enlarge one's library regarding government and political figures. And in this era of "political correctness," those who write or portray the news are ever mindful of the need for sensitivity. Without sacrificing the fullest of expression or kowtowing to those winds, but nevertheless projecting a keen sense of what a discerning public demands and expects, this collection represents the total gamut of approbation or criticism: the good, the bad, and the ugly.

A test of relevance might be whether, if the cartoon is seen in Albuquerque or Arlington, Boise or Baltimore, Portland or Philadelphia, the reader relates to a cartoonist's effort. There can be no question that Bob Gorrell's understated simplicity projects images that transcend region, class, race, and party. This invaluable contribution to the comprehension of government serves to help stem the tide of creeping cynicism and should help to reawaken public interest.

Looking at the evolution of cartoons in this country as a form of expression, one is struck by their combination of humor, satire, wit, and erudition. All of this would be of no avail if the artist could not bring "mind to pen" to effect this. Bob Gorrell's artistic talents are the ultimate release valve for this expression. We are here treated to some of his finest.

LAWRENCE DOUGLAS WILDER

Clinton and Company

GORRELL

THE LIBERAL PRESS

SEPTEMBER 1992

115TH YEAR   No 281

Prices May Vary in Areas Outside
Metropolitan Washington (*See Box on A3)   25¢

WEATHER
Ozone hole expands.
Bush held responsible.

ELECT BILL CLINTON!

Inept Bush Panics —
Accuses Media of Bias

Clinton Correctly Views Coverage as Fair

In an effort to revive his falter-
ing re-election campaign,
George Bush today whined
about the media and its coverage
of his presidency. Looking silly
and frenetic, he claimed
reporters tend to favor the dis-
tinguished Governor of
Arkansas, whose insightful
analysis of current affairs has

Clinton appeared totally in con-
trol and in charge of the facts
as he disputed the soon to be
ex-President's charges of unbal-
anced reporting. "I think the
press coverage of this campaign has been just fine," said

See GEORGE, A4, Col. 1

Clinton

Sections

A News/Editorials
B Metro/Obituaries
C Style/Television

Voting for
GOP Linked
To Cancer

Many people who vote
Republican wind up con-
tracting cancer, according to
a recent medical survey
conducted by the non-parti-
san Democratic Medical
Doctors for Clinton
Association. While no clear

See GEORGE, A4, Col. 1

Inept Bush

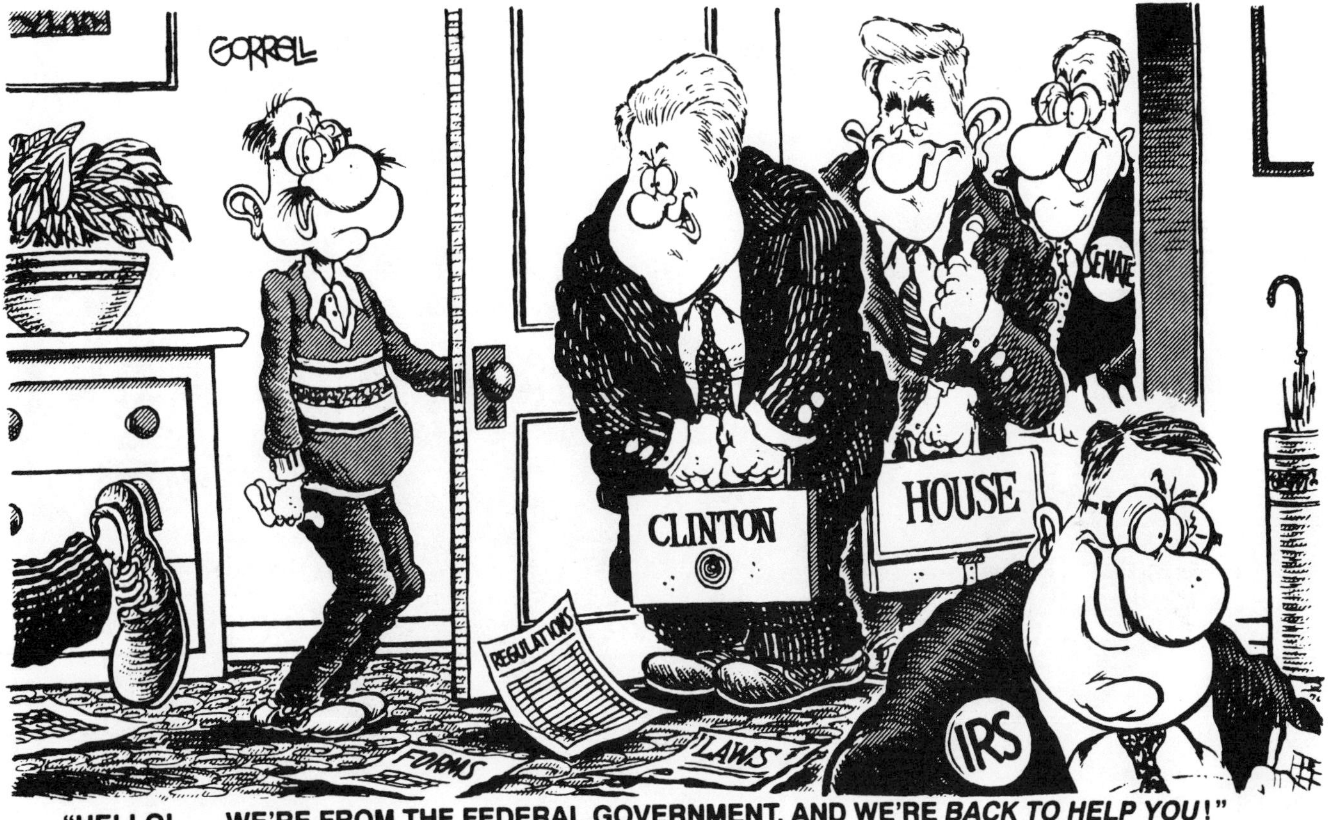
GORRELL
CLINTON
HOUSE
SENATE
IRS
REGULATIONS
FORMS
LAWS

"HELLO! . . . WE'RE FROM THE FEDERAL GOVERNMENT, AND WE'RE *BACK TO HELP YOU*!"

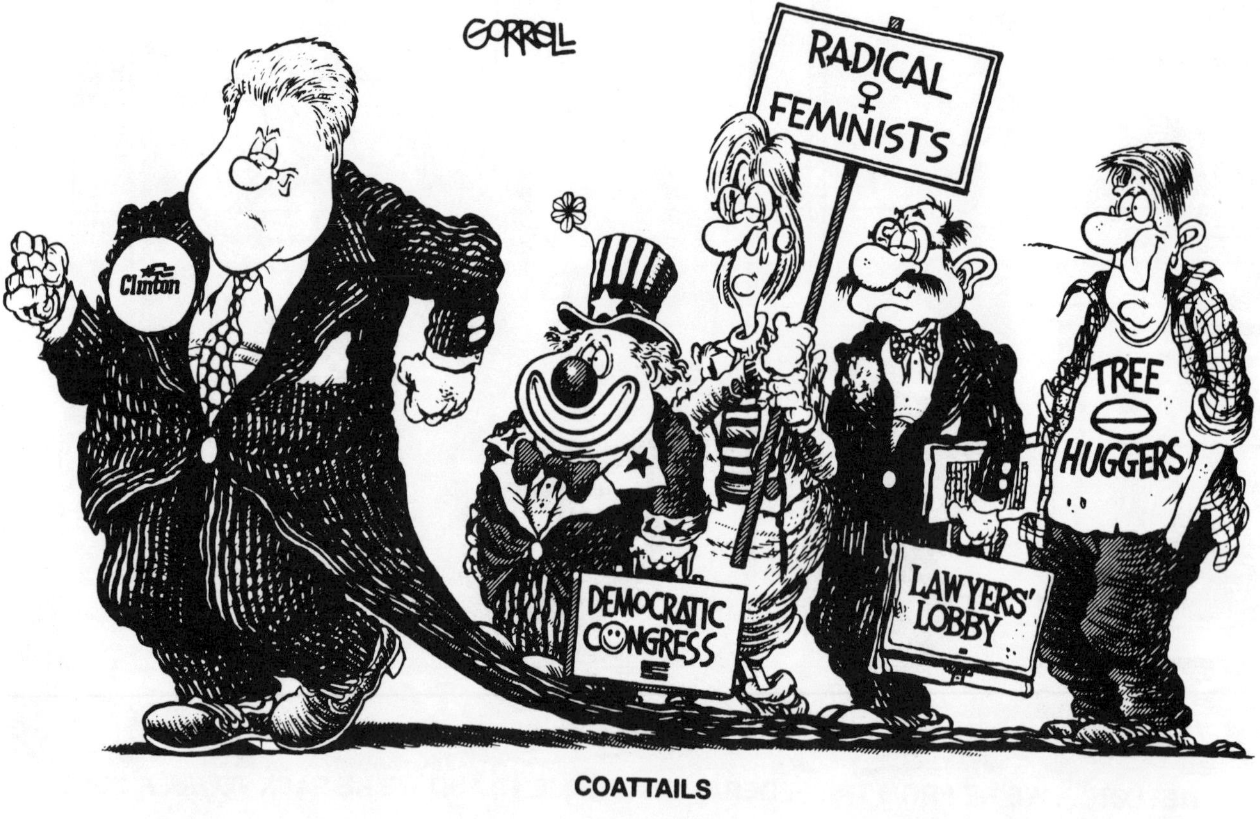
GORRELL
Clinton
RADICAL
FEMINISTS
DEMOCRATIC
CONGRESS
LAWYERS'
LOBBY
TREE
HUGGERS

COATTAILS

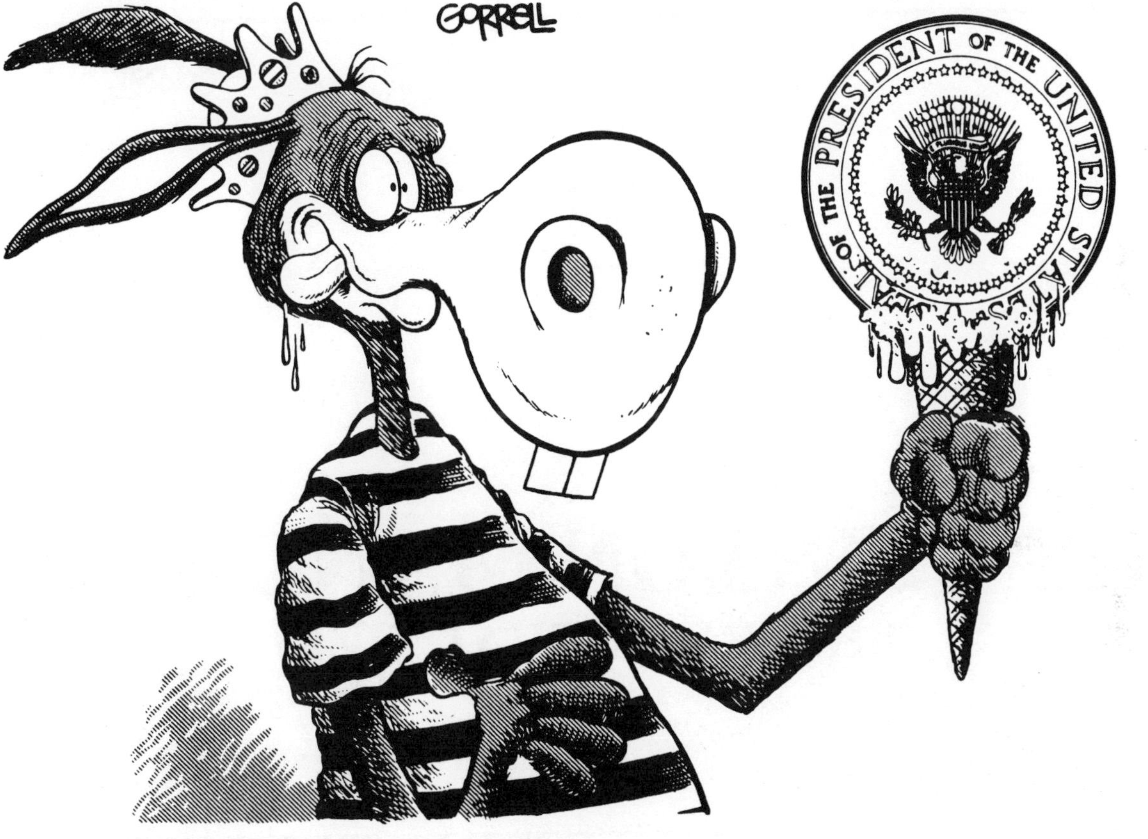
GORRELL
SEAL OF THE PRESIDENT OF THE UNITED STATES

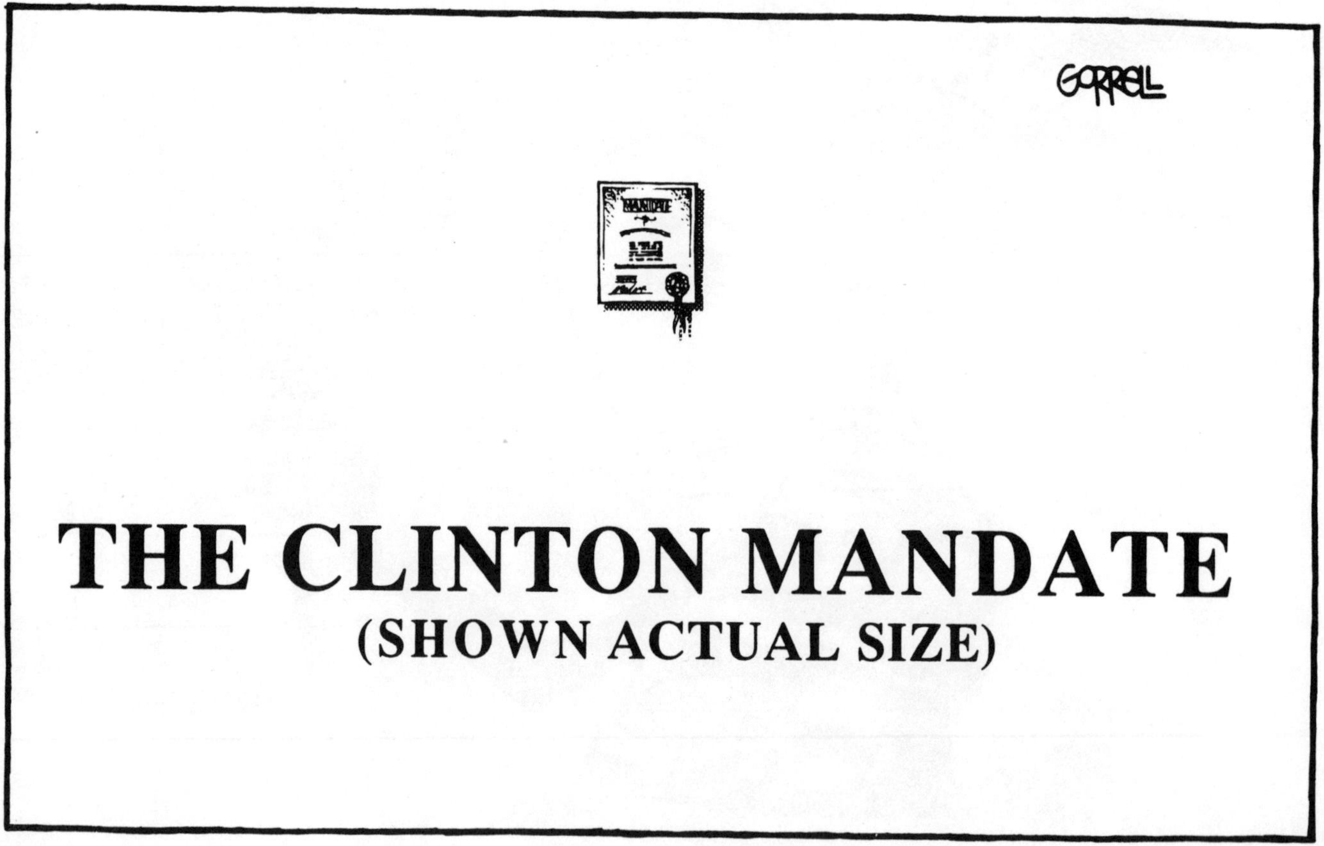
GORRELL
MANDATE
THE CLINTON MANDATE
(SHOWN ACTUAL SIZE)

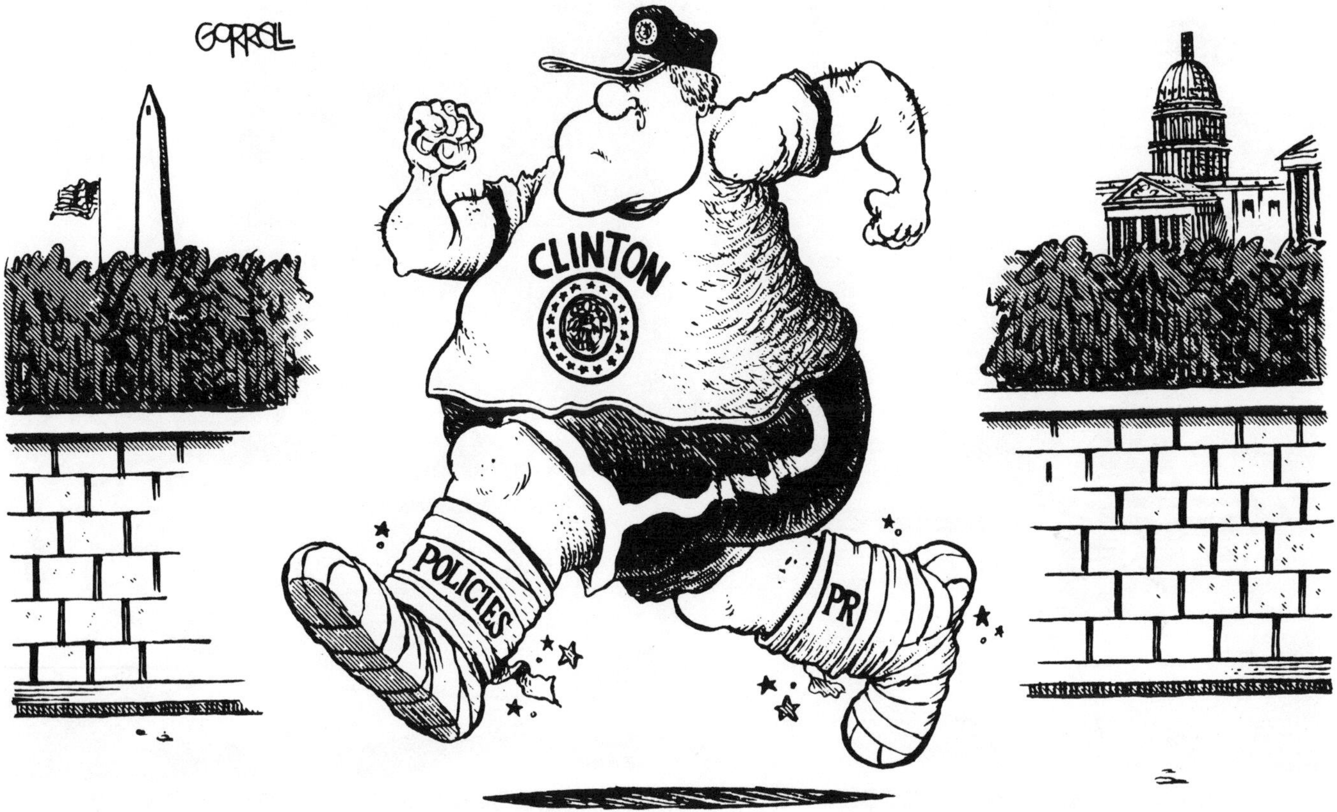
GORRELL
CLINTON
POLICIES
PR

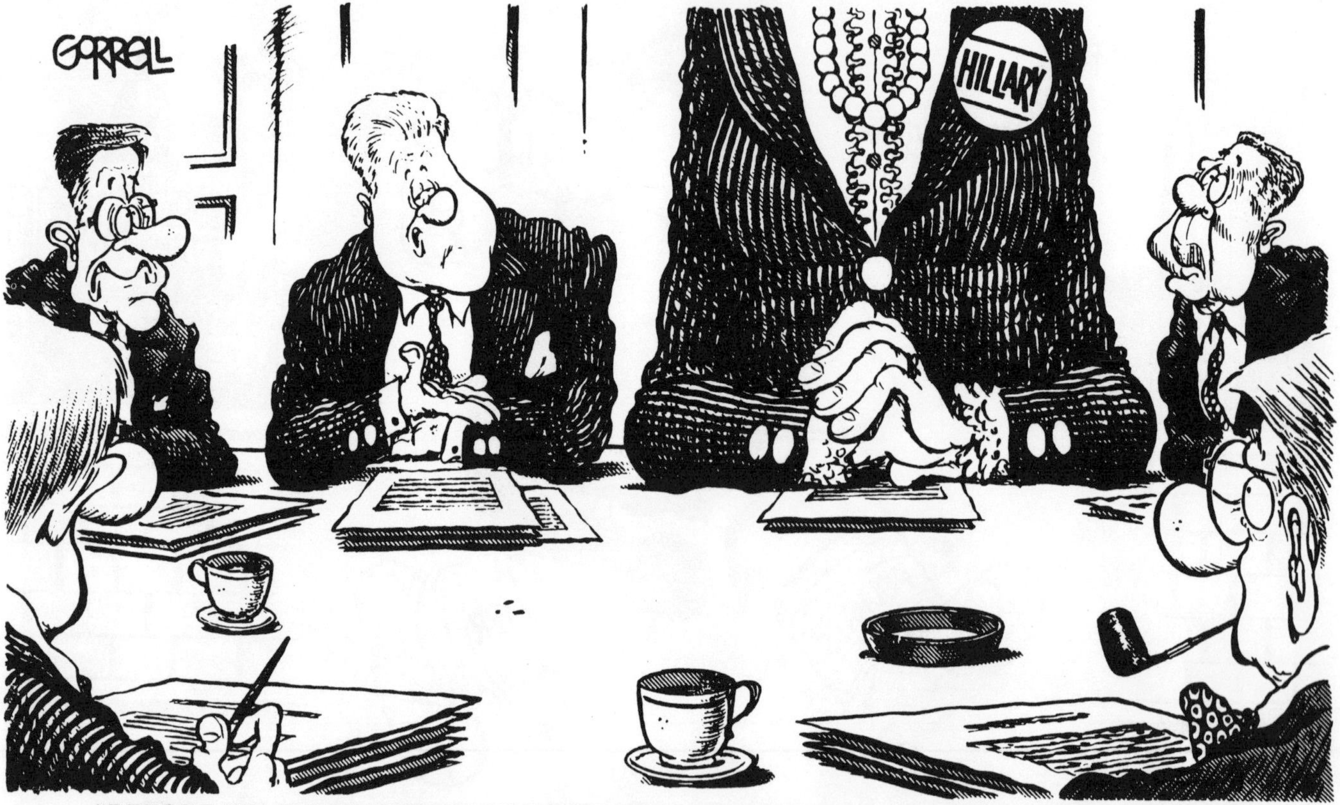
GORRELL
HILLARY
"BEFORE WE START THIS POLICY MEETING, HAS EVERYBODY MET THE *LITTLE WOMAN*?"

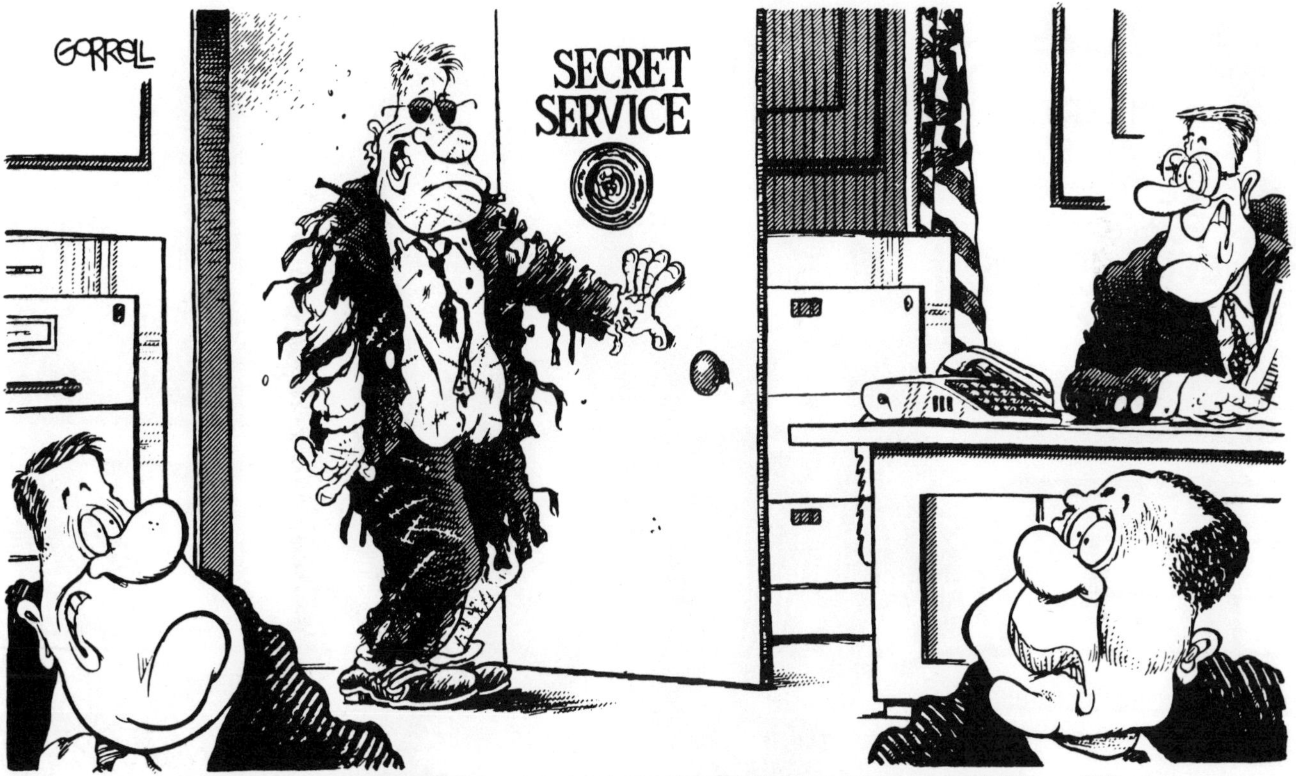
GORRELL
SECRET SERVICE

"REQUEST PERMISSION TO BE RELIEVED FROM GUARDING *SOCKS* . . . ?!"

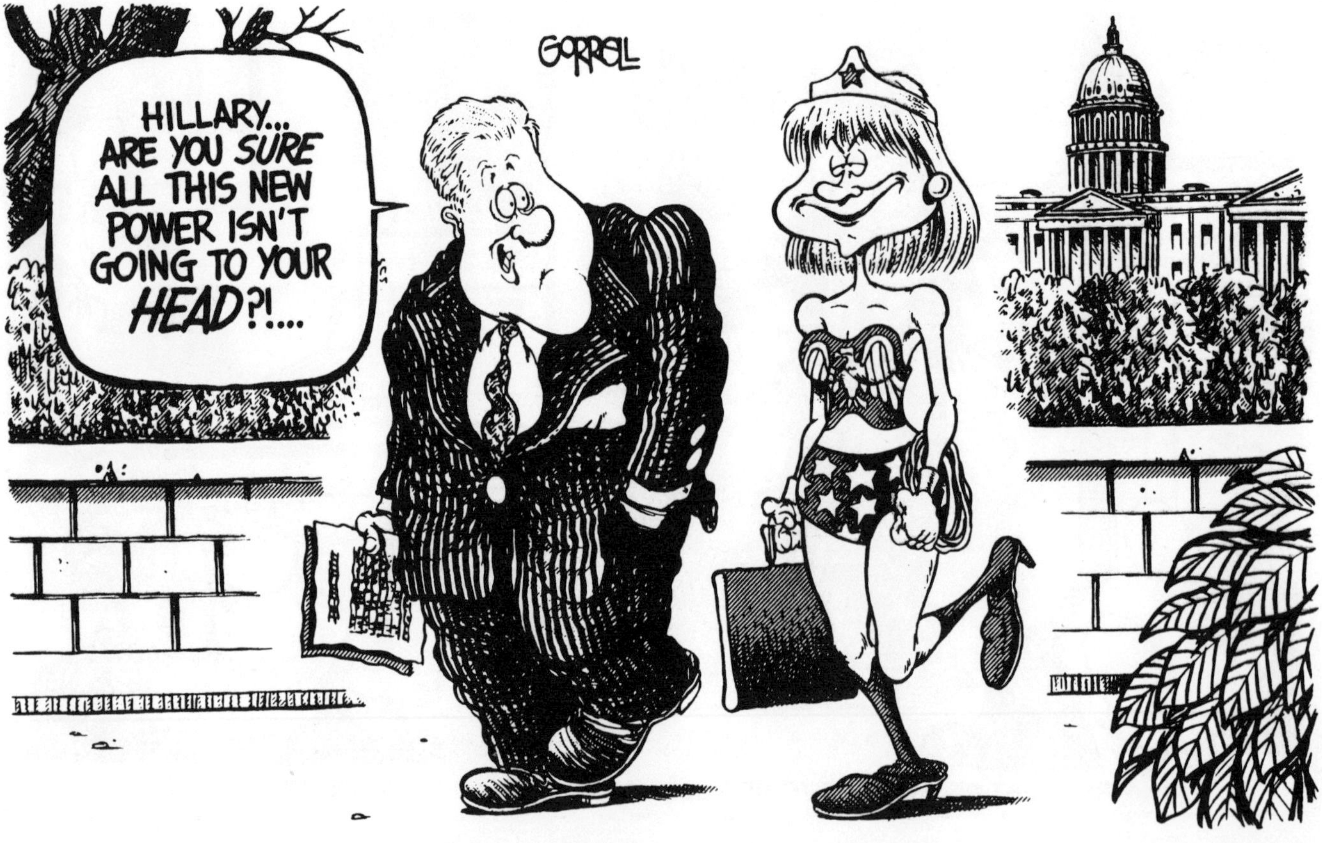
GORRELL
HILLARY... ARE YOU SURE ALL THIS NEW POWER ISN'T GOING TO YOUR HEAD?!....

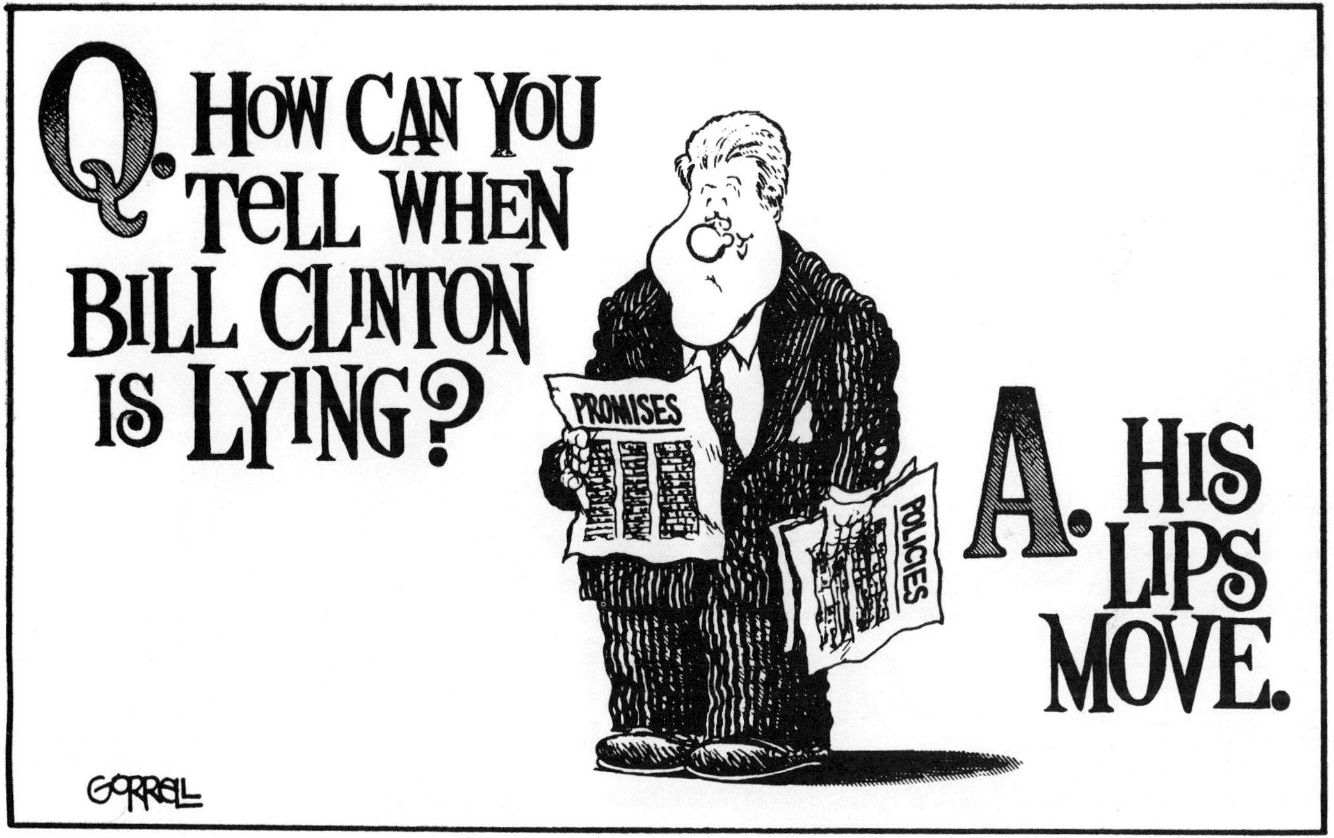

Q. HOW CAN YOU TELL WHEN BILL CLINTON IS LYING?
PROMISES
POLICIES
A. HIS LIPS MOVE.
GORRELL

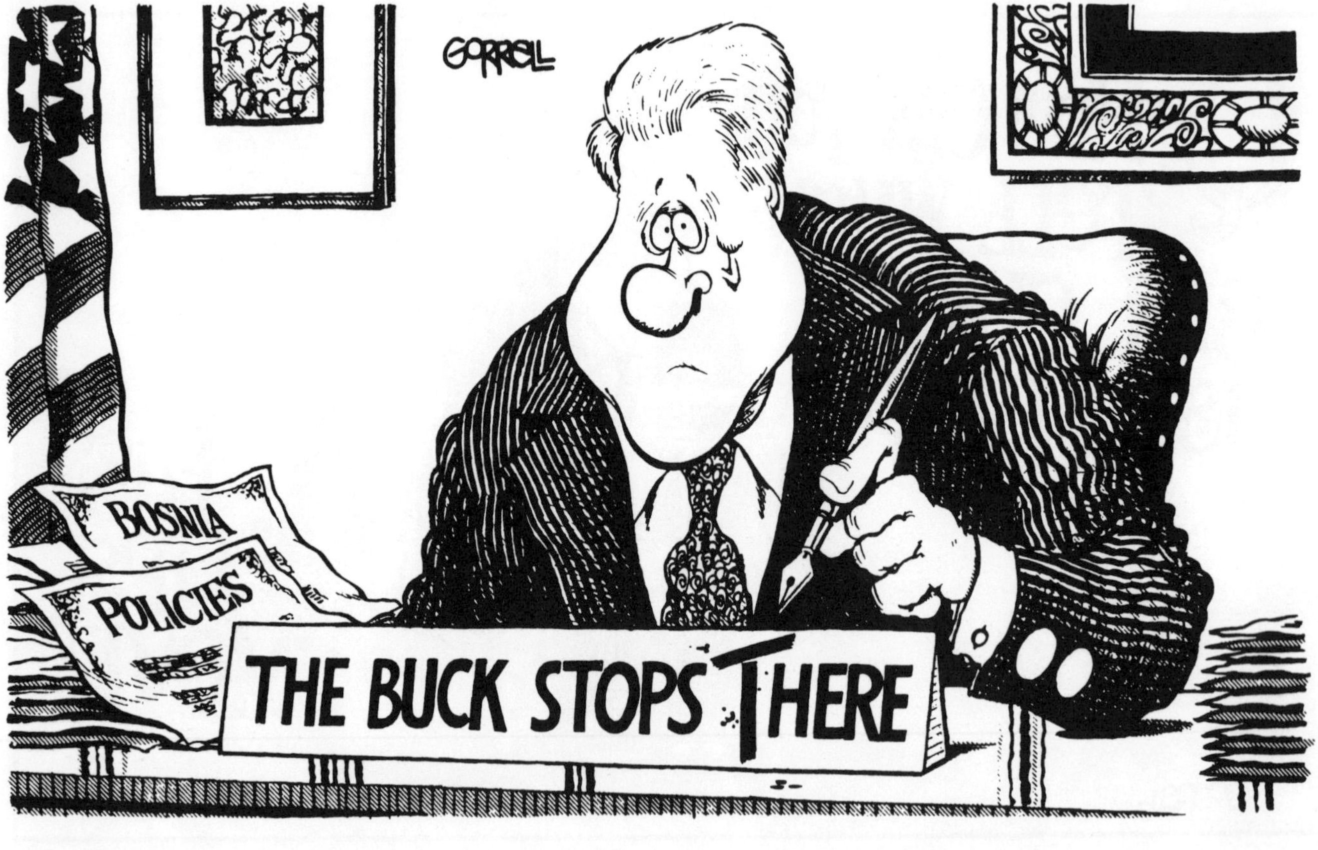
GORRELL
BOSNIA
POLICIES
THE BUCK STOPS THERE

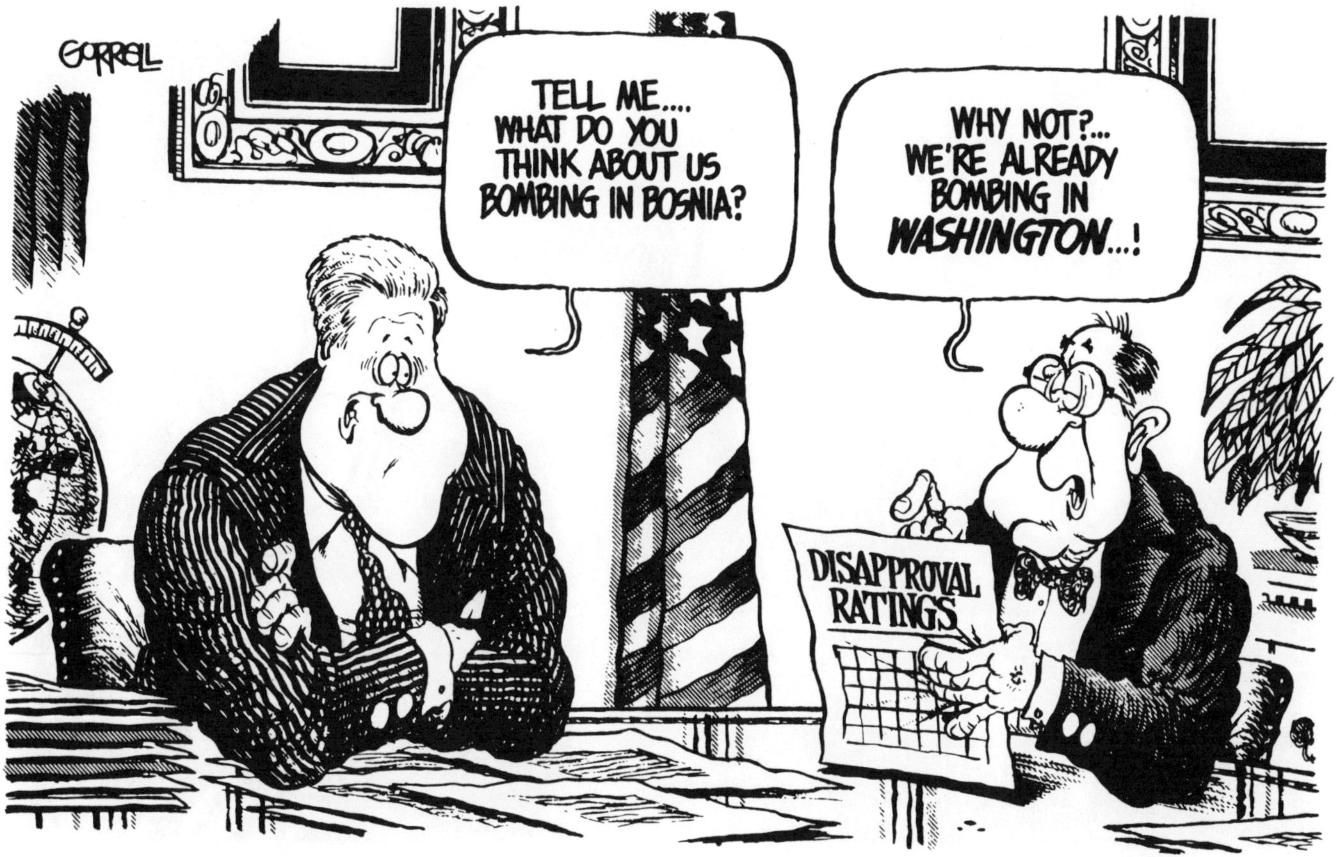
GORRELL
TELL ME.... WHAT DO YOU THINK ABOUT US BOMBING IN BOSNIA?
WHY NOT?... WE'RE ALREADY BOMBING IN WASHINGTON...!
DISAPPROVAL RATINGS

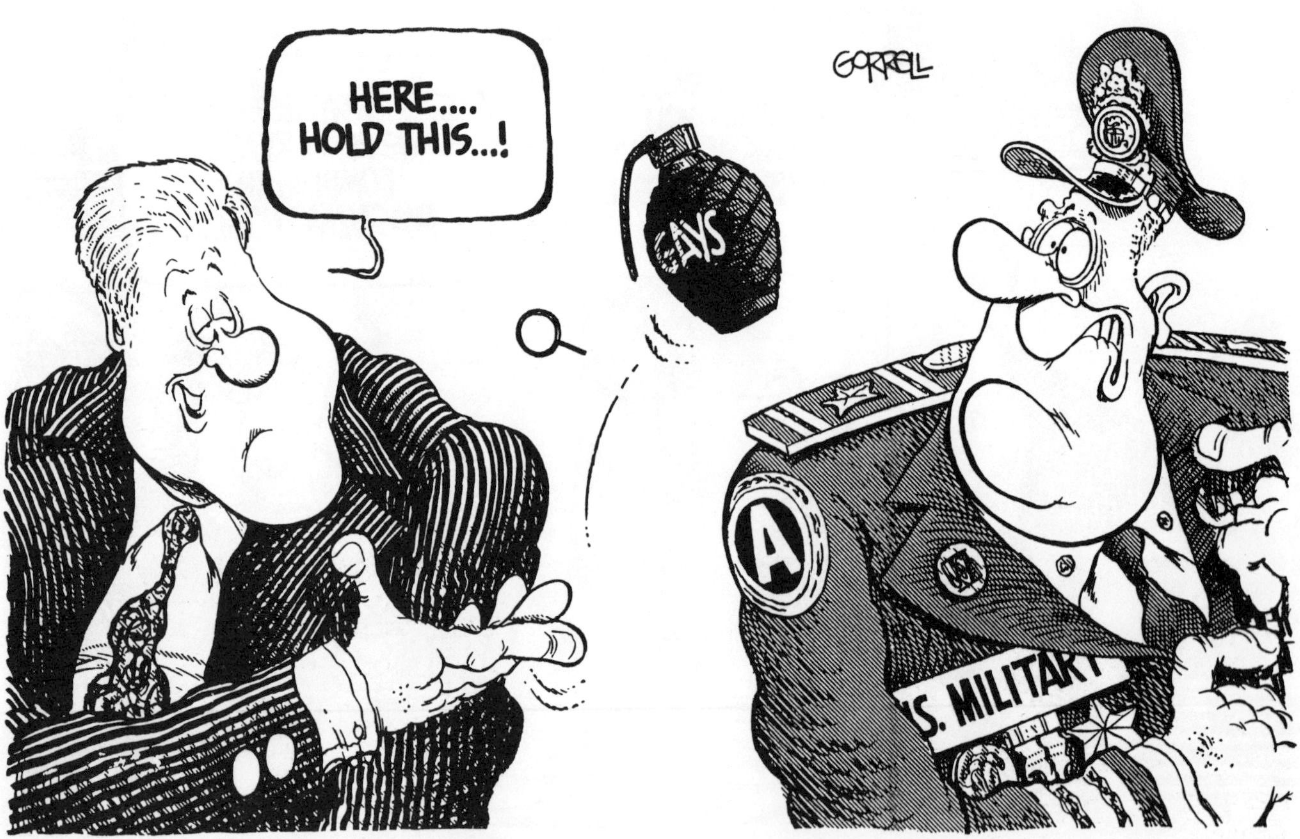
HERE.... HOLD THIS...!
GORRELL
GAYS
A
S. MILITARY

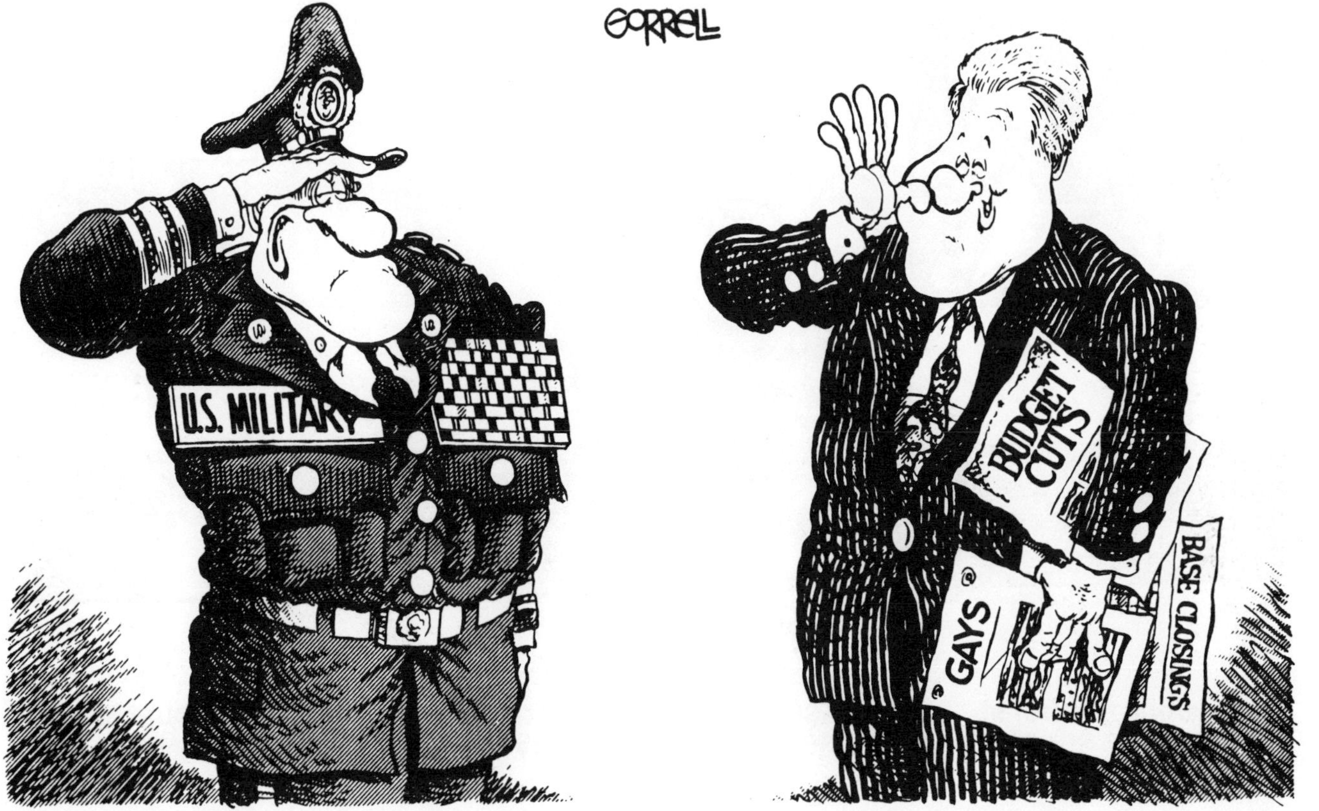
GORRELL
U.S. MILITARY
BUDGET CUTS
GAYS
BASE CLOSINGS

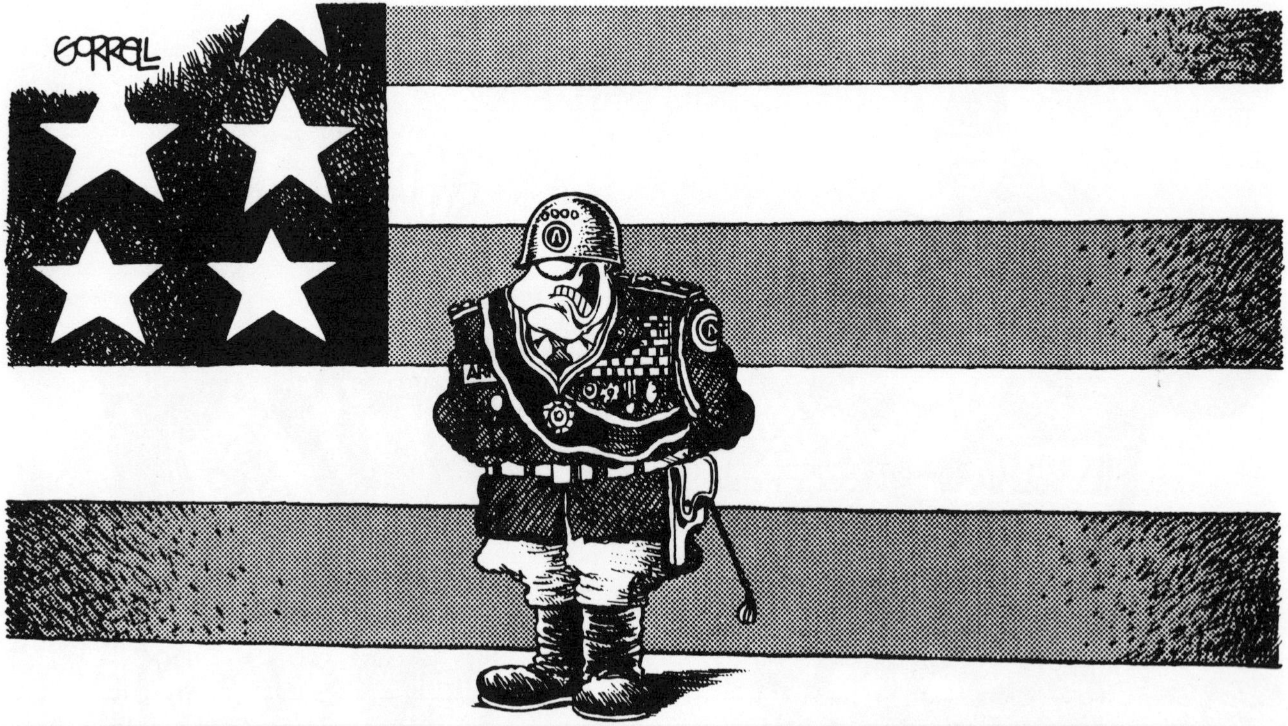
GORRELL

"AWRIGHT, TROOPS! . . . WE ATTACK IMMEDIATELY AFTER OUR GAY-STRAIGHT ENCOUNTER GROUP, BUT DIRECTLY BEFORE OUR SEXUAL HARASSMENT AWARENESS SEMINAR!"

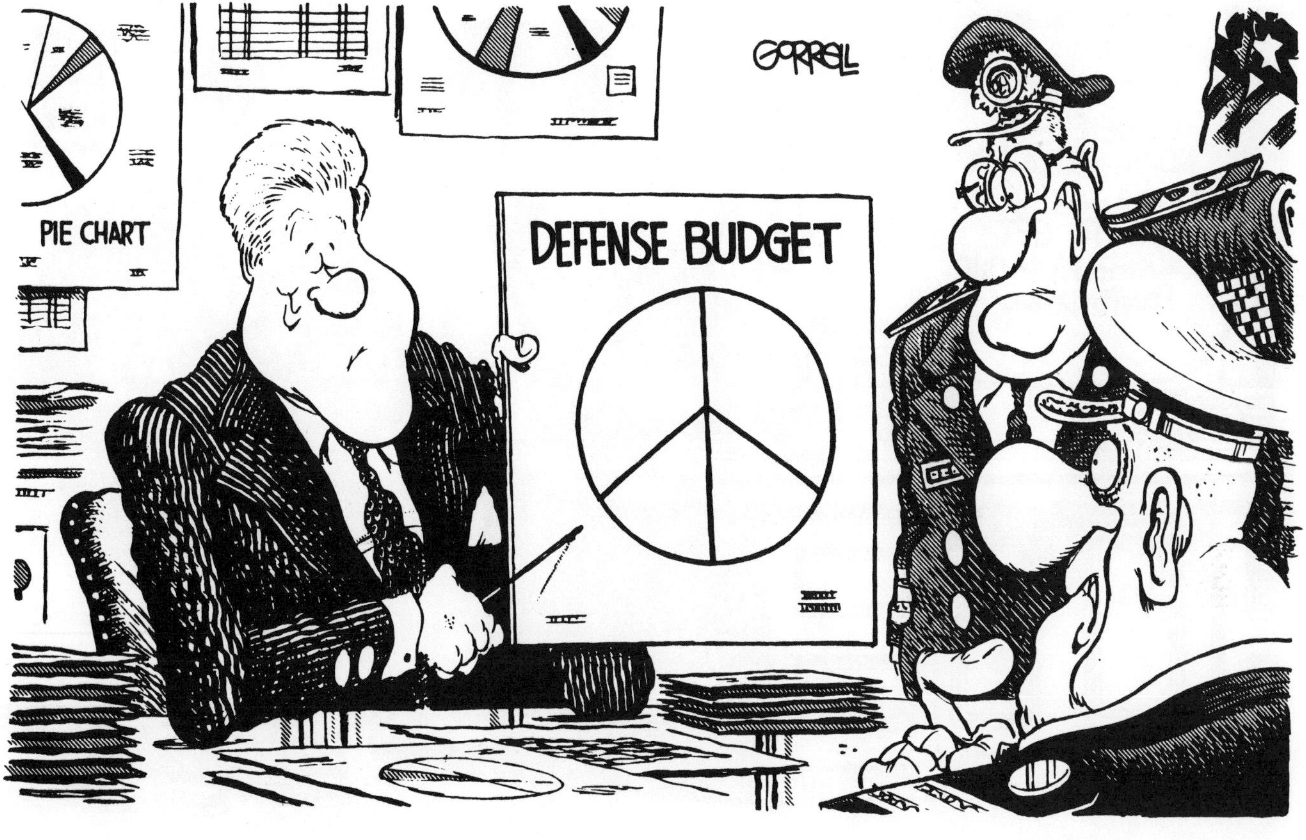
PIE CHART
GORRELL
DEFENSE BUDGET

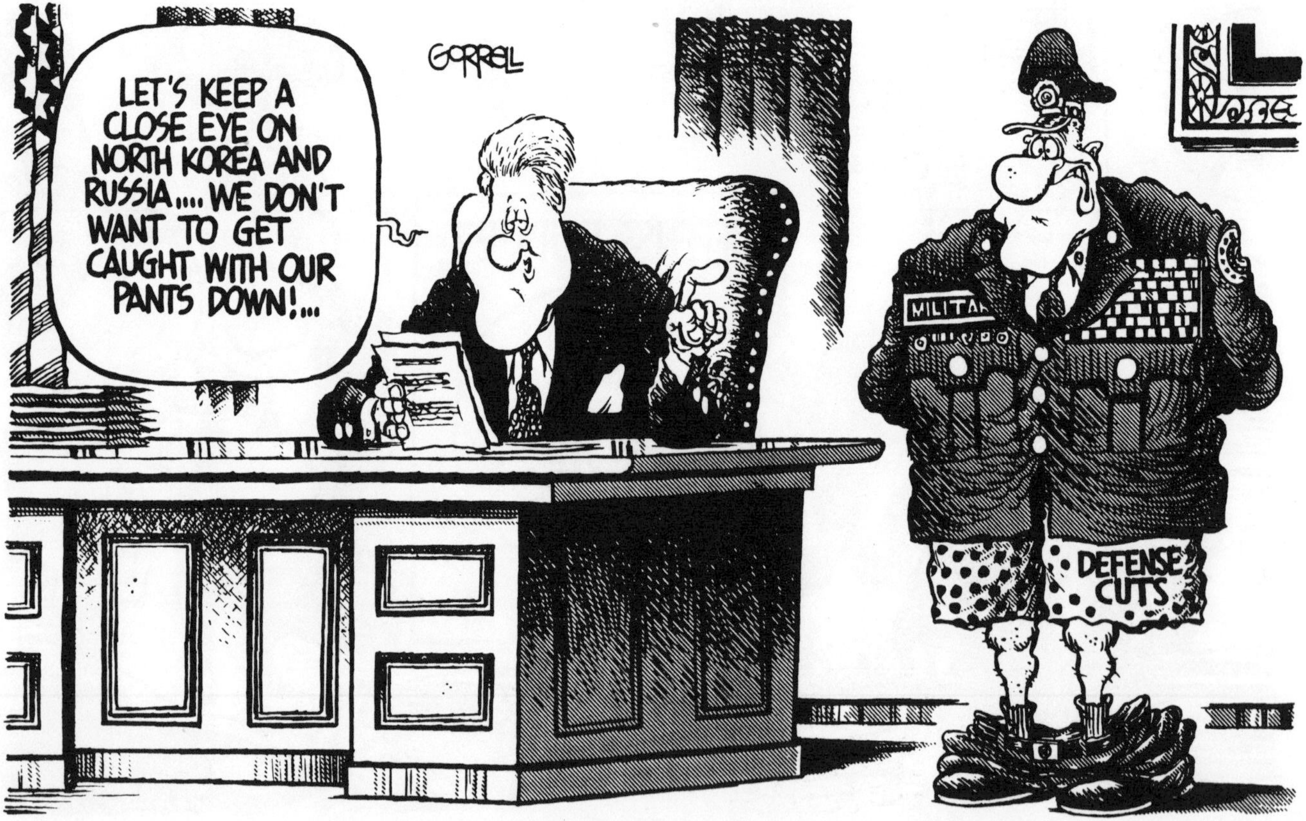
GORRELL
LET'S KEEP A CLOSE EYE ON NORTH KOREA AND RUSSIA.... WE DON'T WANT TO GET CAUGHT WITH OUR PANTS DOWN!...
MILITA
DEFENSE CUTS

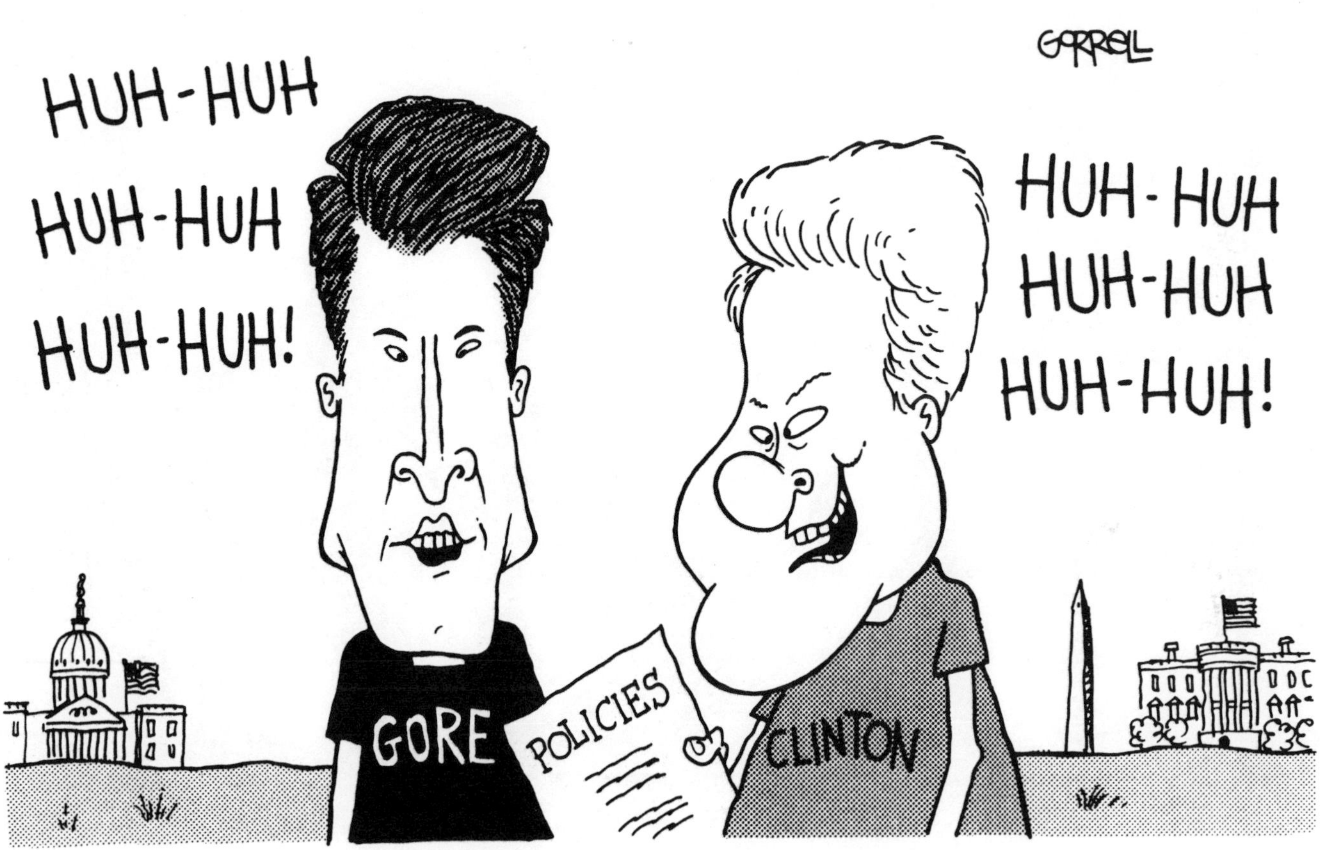
GORRELL
HUH-HUH
HUH-HUH
HUH-HUH!
HUH-HUH
HUH-HUH
HUH-HUH!
GORE
POLICIES
CLINTON

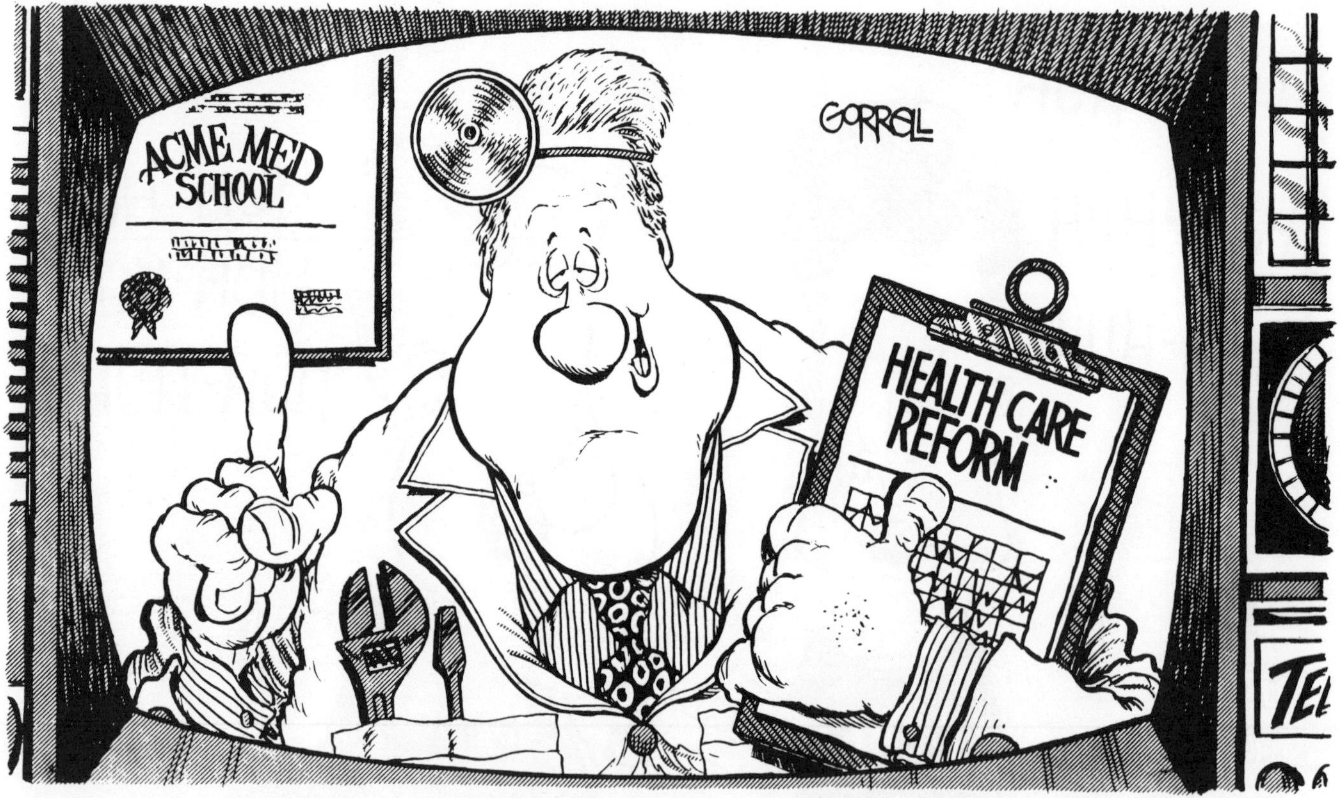
ACME MED SCHOOL
GORRELL
HEALTH CARE REFORM

"HELLO. . . . I'M NOT A DOCTOR, BUT I PLAY ONE ON TELEVISION!"

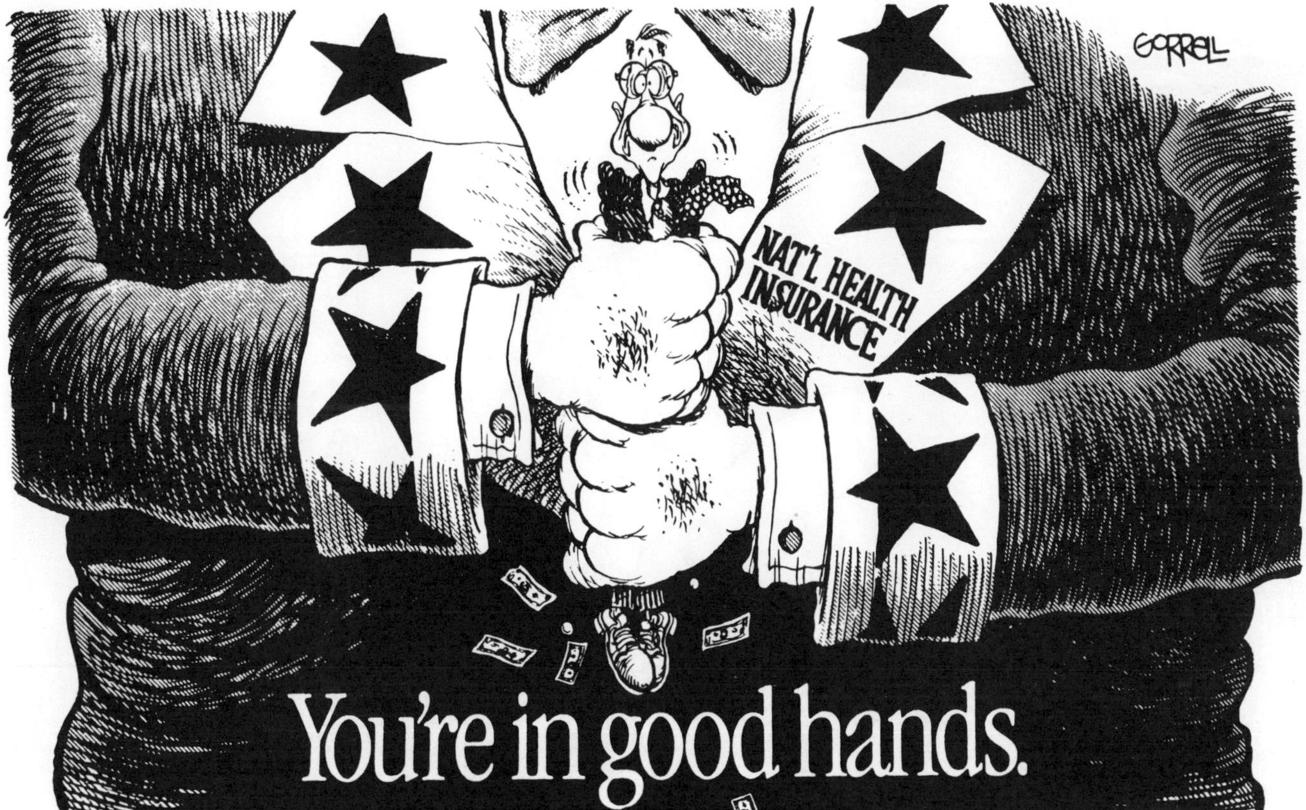
GORRELL
NAT'L HEALTH INSURANCE
You're in good hands.

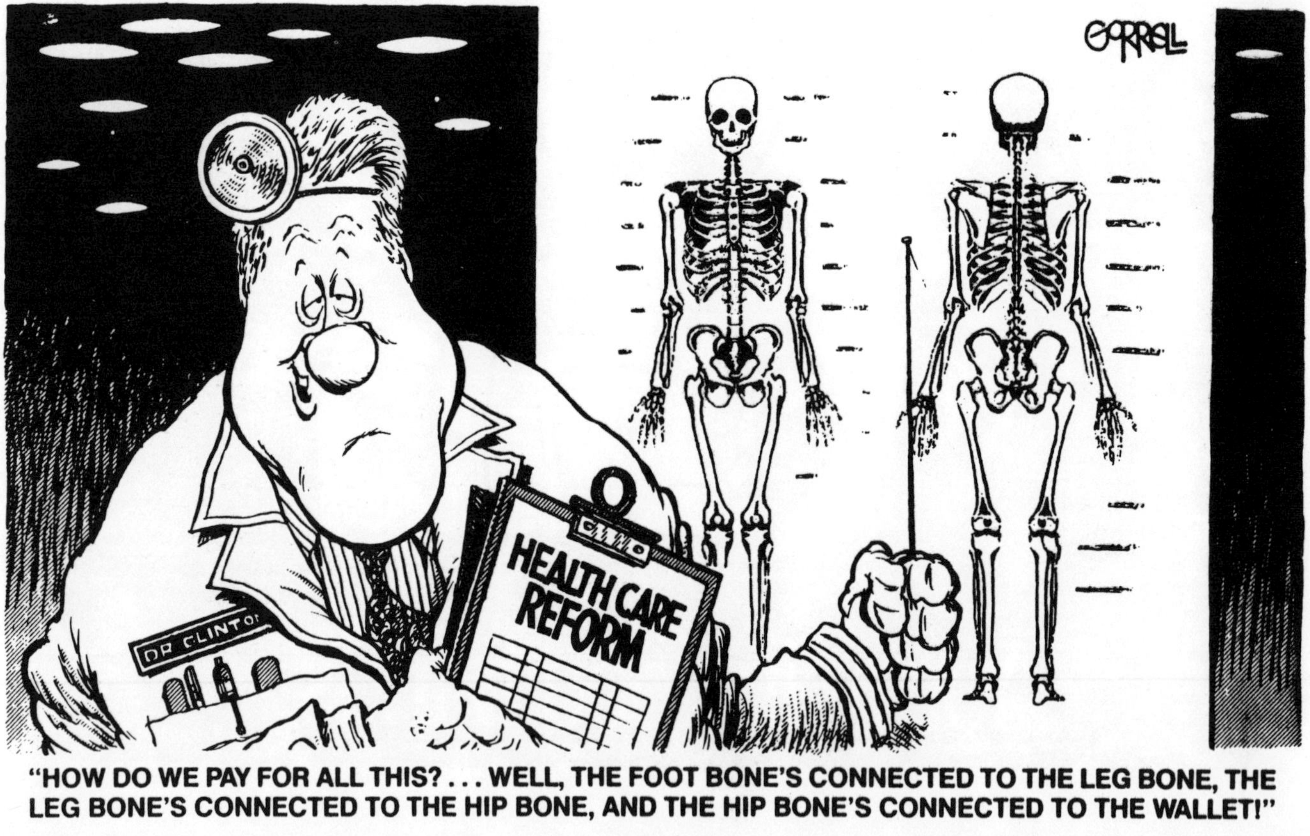
GORRELL
HEALTH CARE REFORM
DR CLINTON

"HOW DO WE PAY FOR ALL THIS? . . . WELL, THE FOOT BONE'S CONNECTED TO THE LEG BONE, THE LEG BONE'S CONNECTED TO THE HIP BONE, AND THE HIP BONE'S CONNECTED TO THE WALLET!"

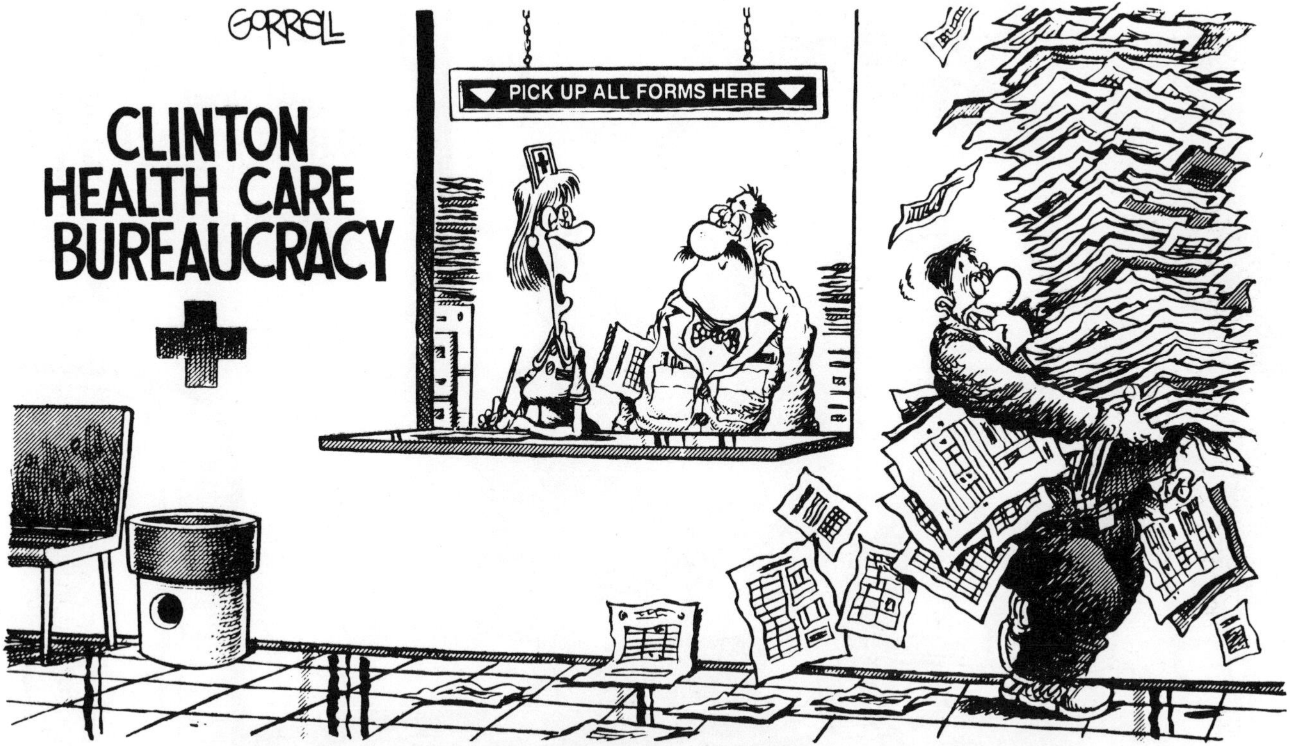
GORRELL
CLINTON HEALTH CARE BUREAUCRACY
PICK UP ALL FORMS HERE

"ODD . . . . EVER SINCE WE CHANGED TO THIS SYSTEM, HERNIA CLAIMS ARE UP TWO HUNDRED PERCENT!"

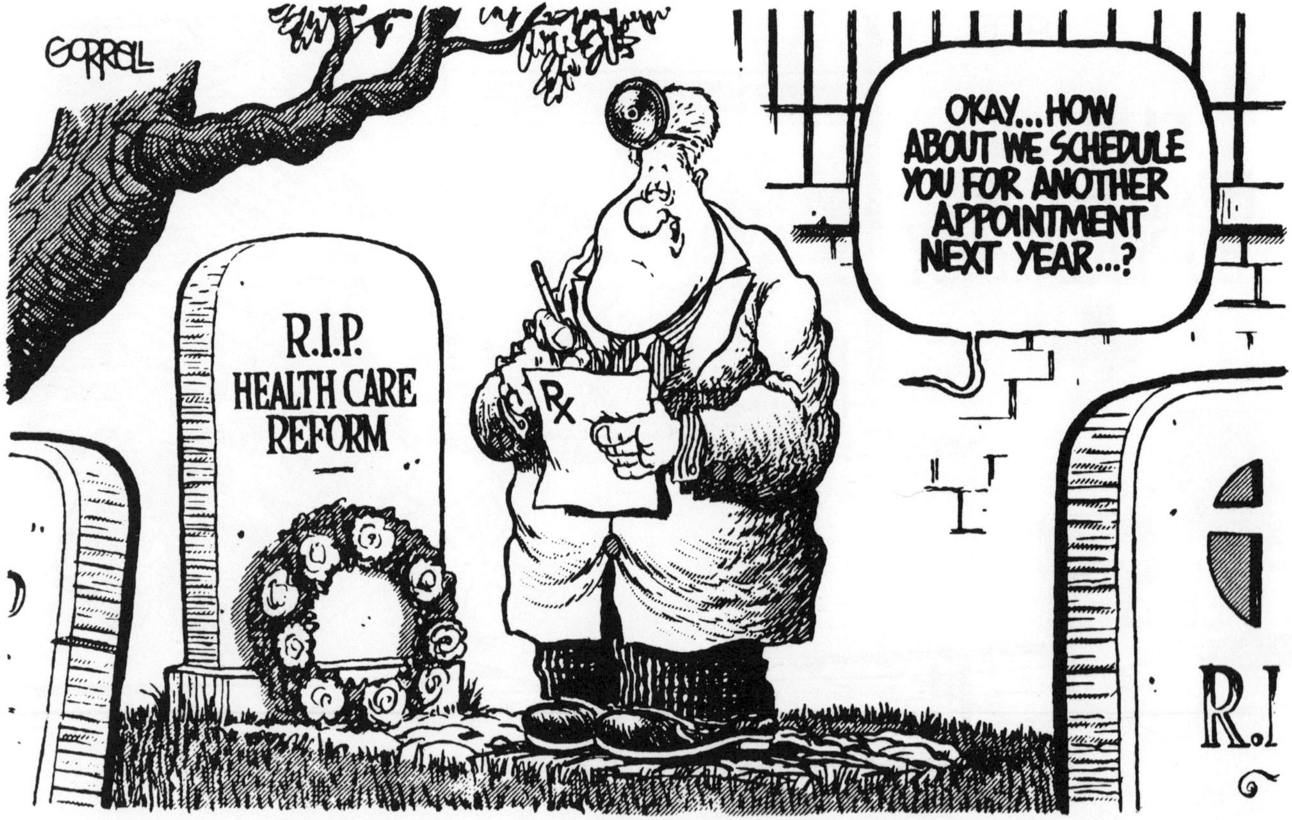
GORRELL
OKAY... HOW ABOUT WE SCHEDULE YOU FOR ANOTHER APPOINTMENT NEXT YEAR...?
R.I.P. HEALTH CARE REFORM
Rx
R.I

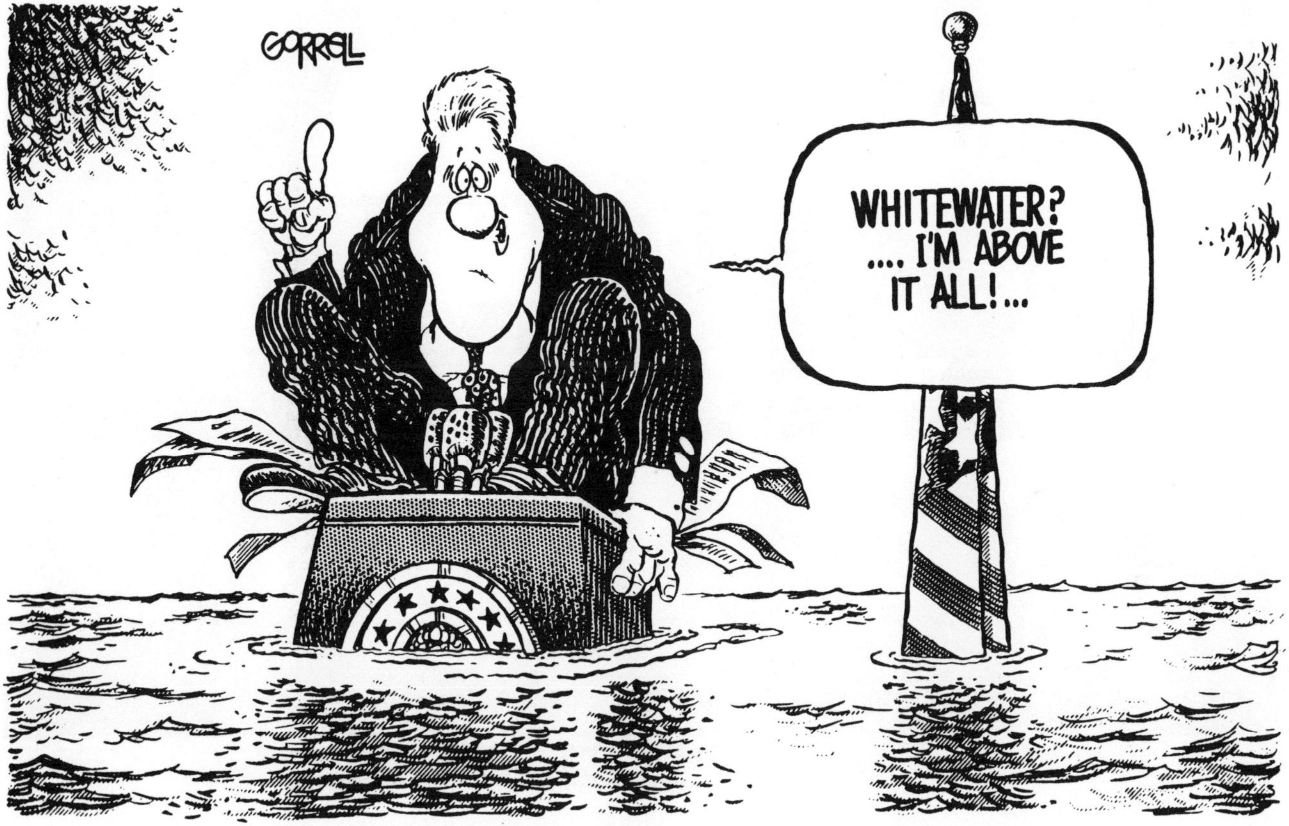
GORRELL
WHITEWATER? .... I'M ABOVE IT ALL!...

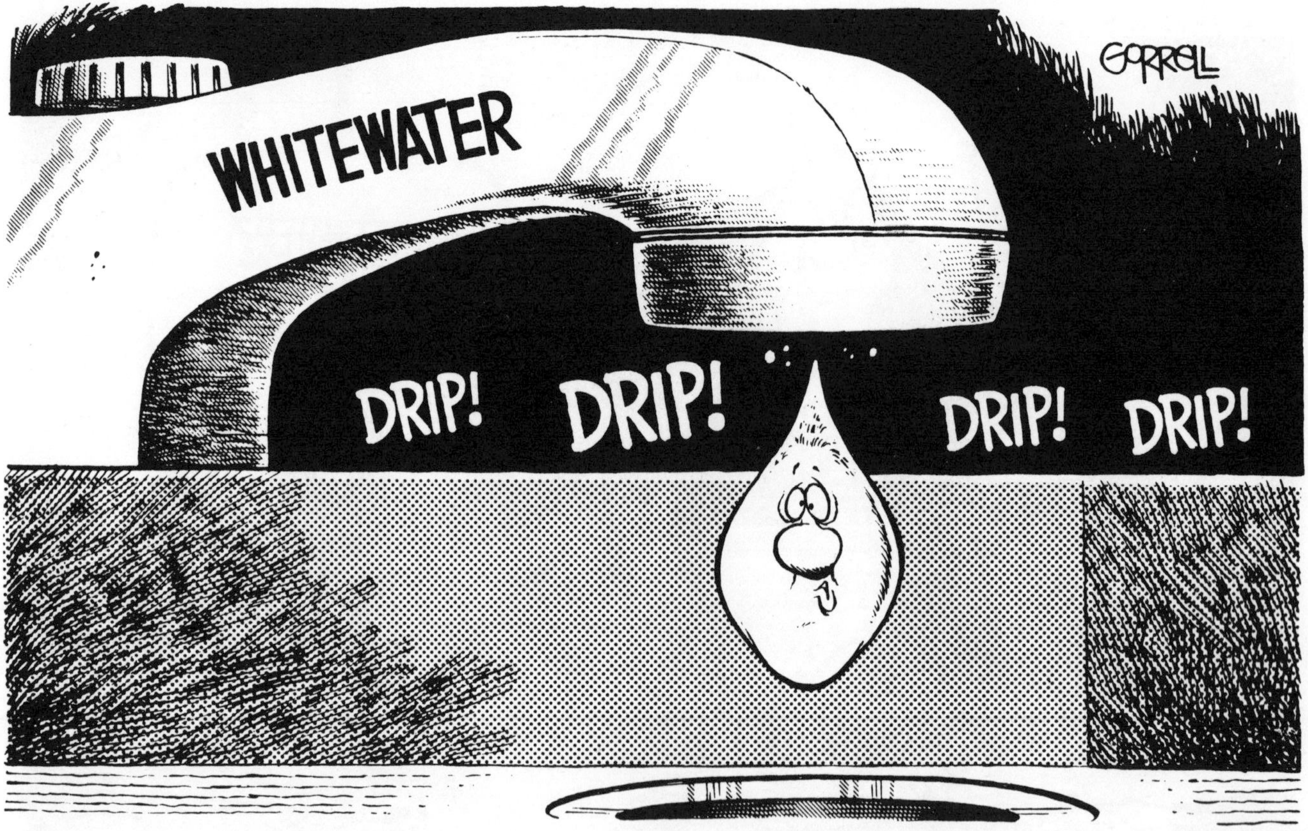

GORRELL
WHITEWATER
DRIP!
DRIP!
DRIP!
DRIP!

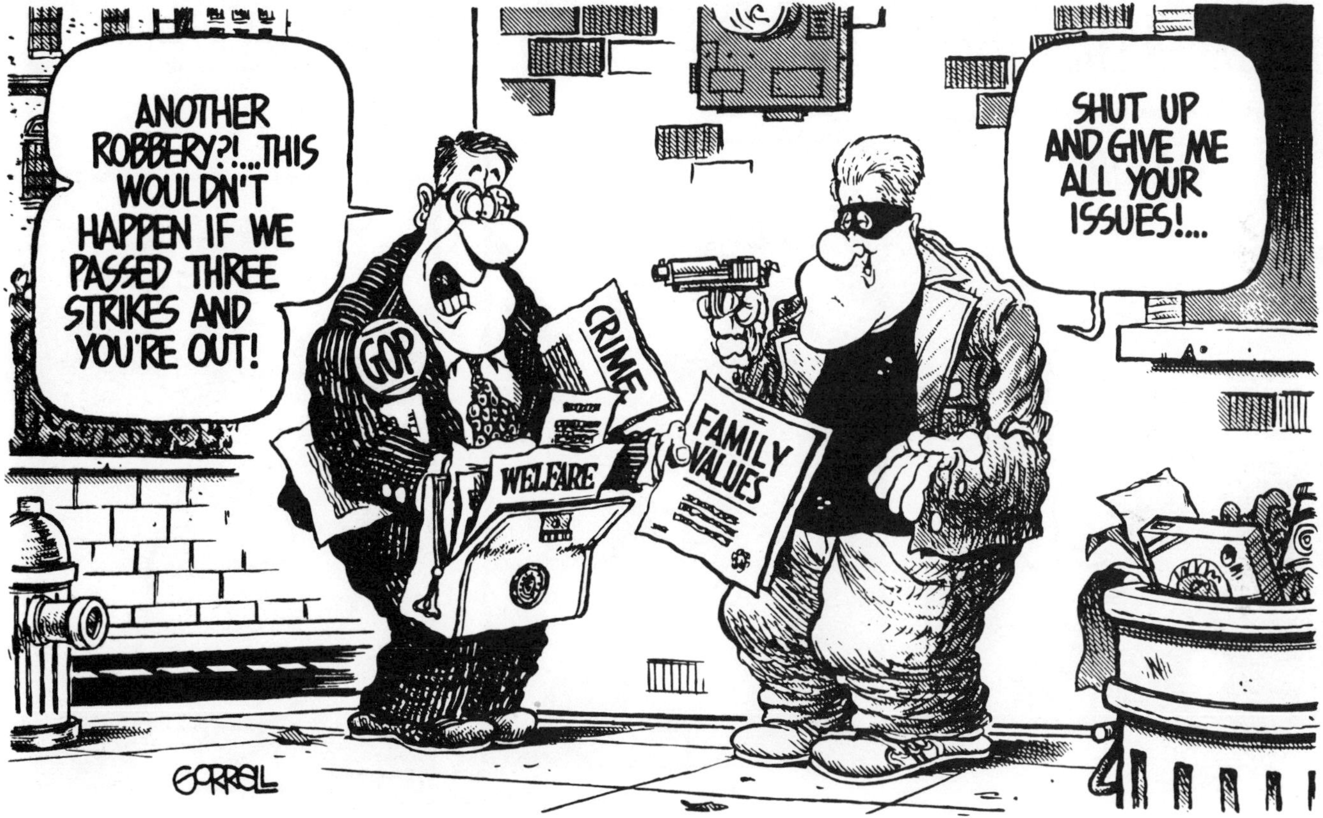
ANOTHER ROBBERY?!...THIS WOULDN'T HAPPEN IF WE PASSED THREE STRIKES AND YOU'RE OUT!
SHUT UP AND GIVE ME ALL YOUR ISSUES!...
GOP
CRIME
WELFARE
FAMILY VALUES
GORRELL

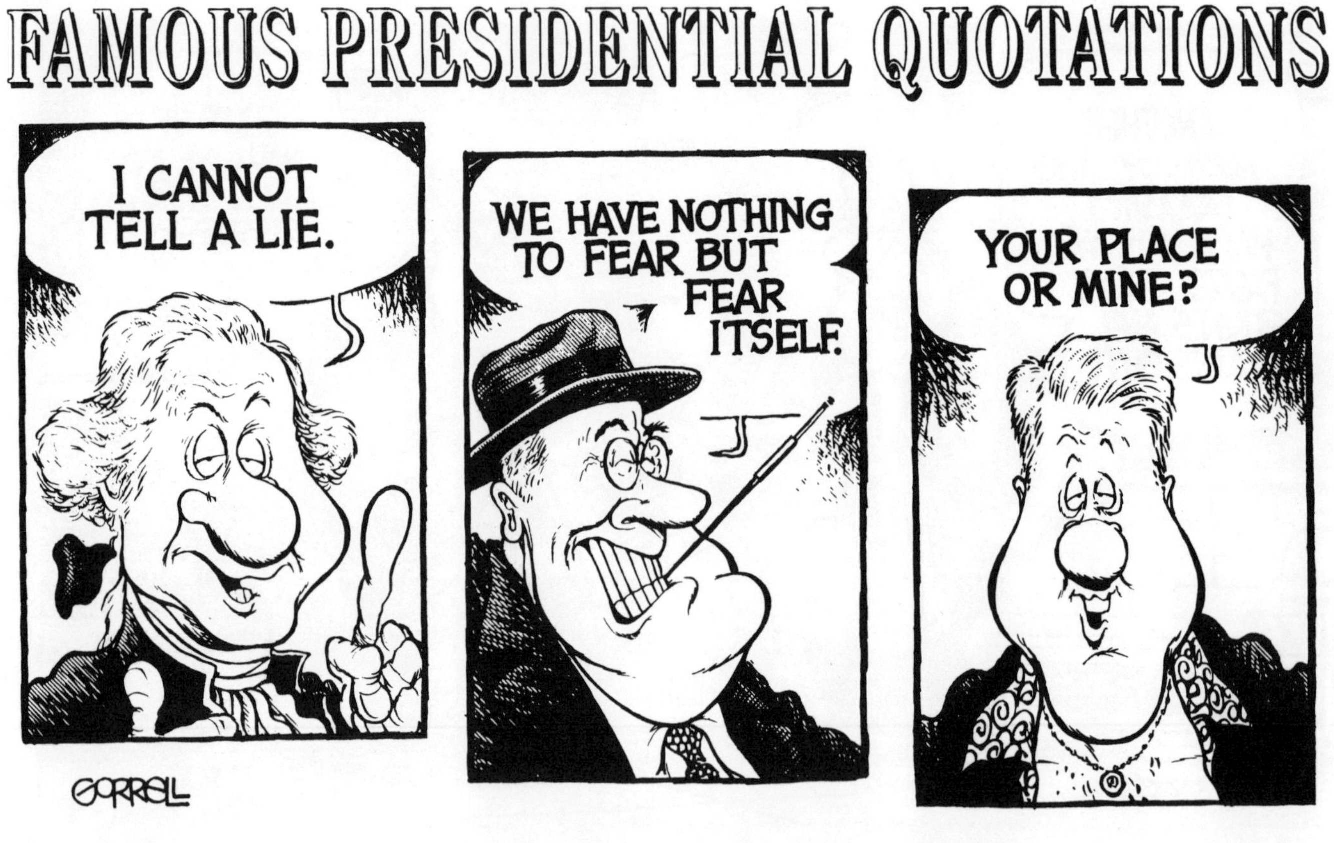
FAMOUS PRESIDENTIAL QUOTATIONS
I CANNOT TELL A LIE.
WE HAVE NOTHING TO FEAR BUT FEAR ITSELF.
YOUR PLACE OR MINE?
GORRELL

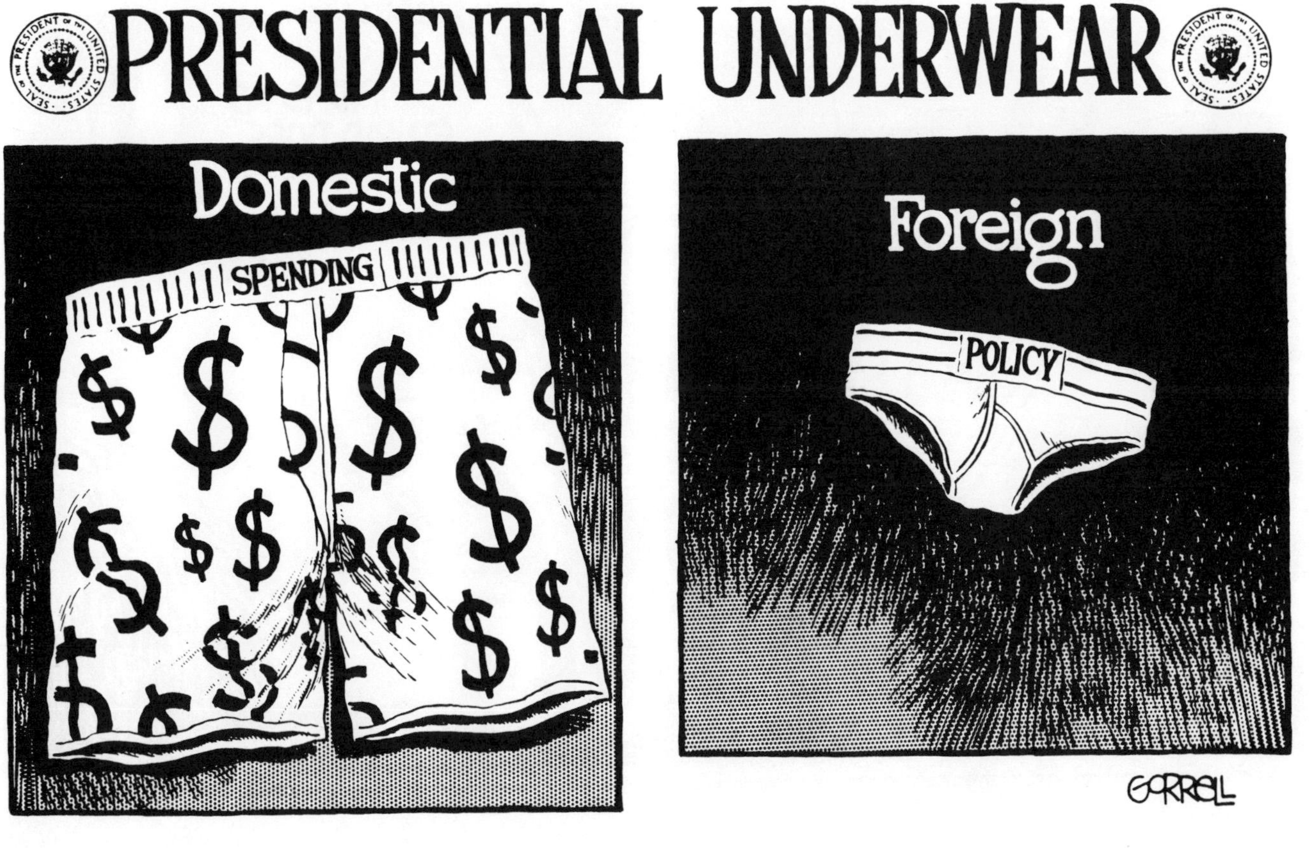
PRESIDENTIAL UNDERWEAR
Domestic
SPENDING
Foreign
POLICY
GORRELL

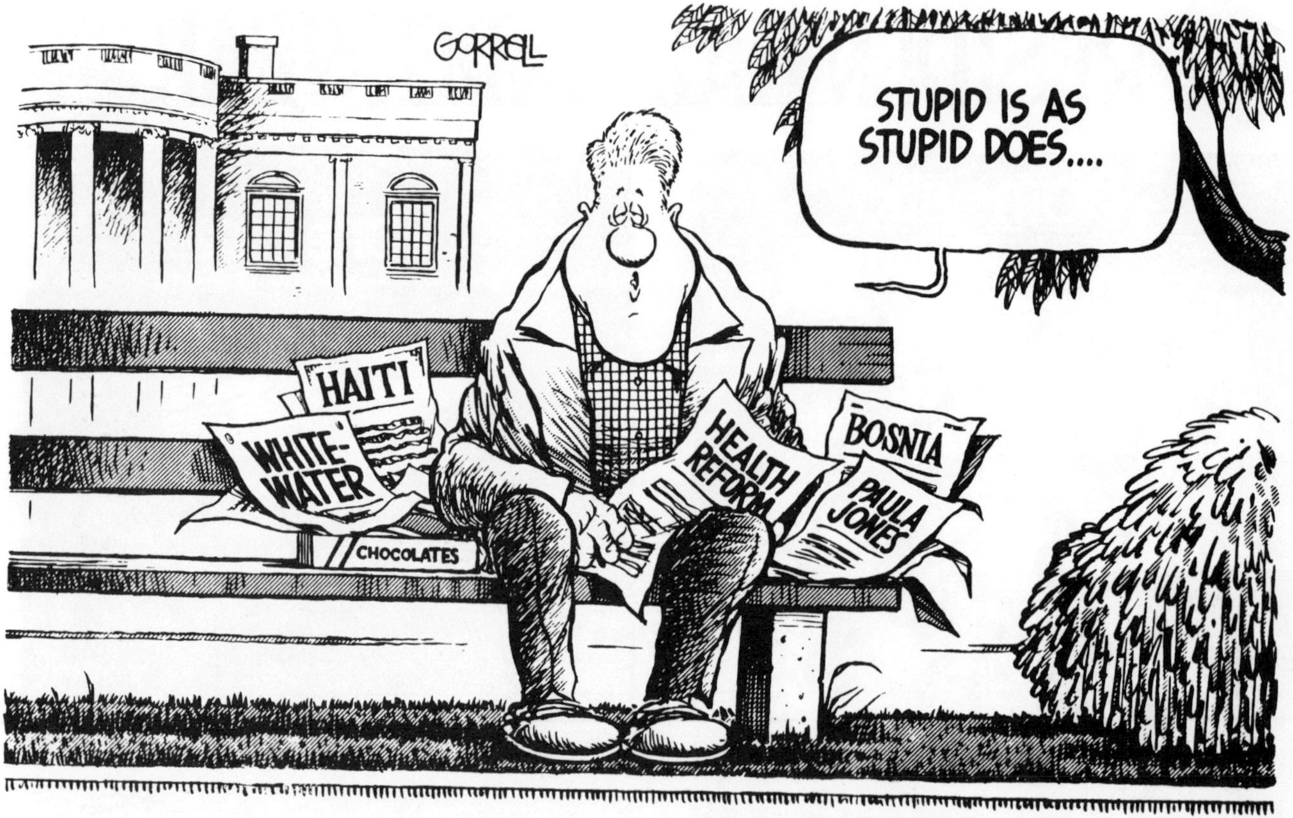
GORRELL
STUPID IS AS STUPID DOES....
HAITI
WHITE-WATER
CHOCOLATES
HEALTH REFORM
BOSNIA
PAULA JONES

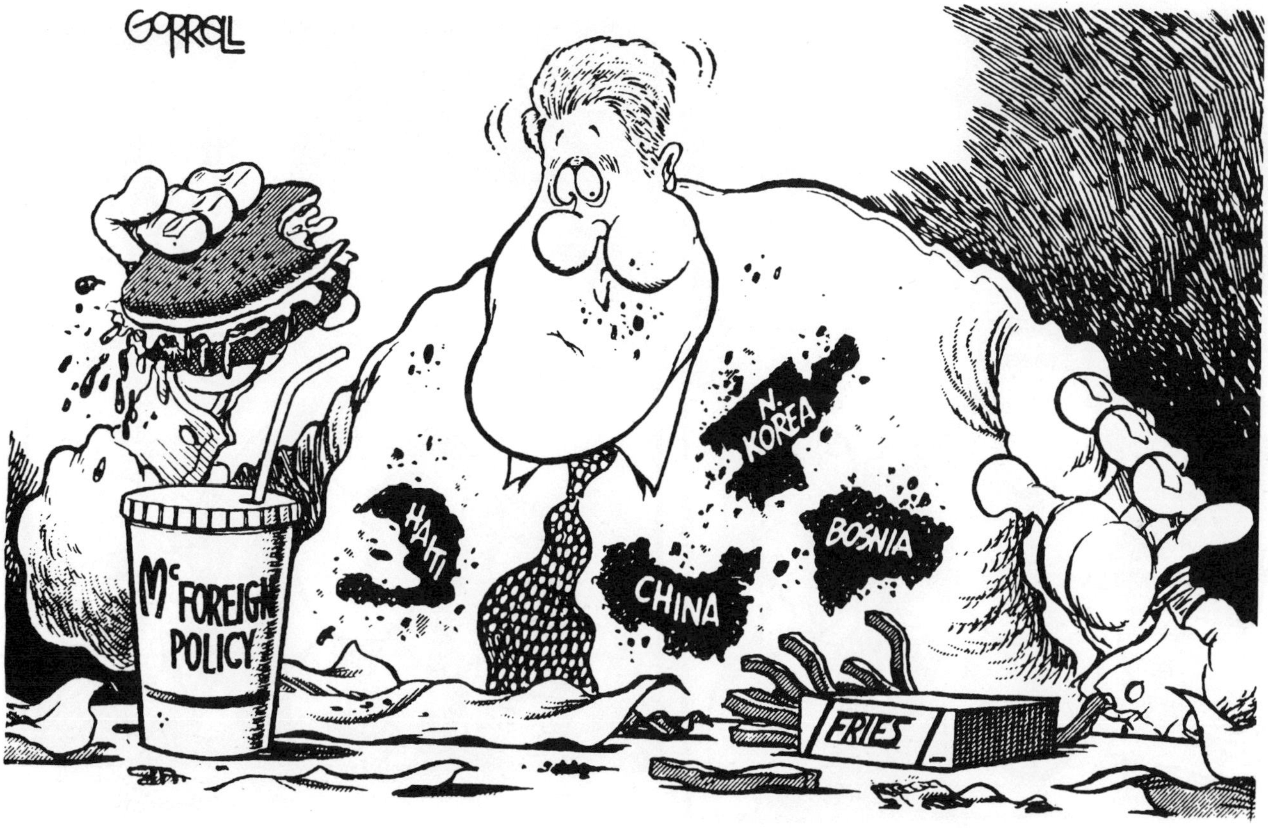

GORRELL
N. KOREA
HAITI
BOSNIA
CHINA
Mc FOREIGN POLICY
FRIES

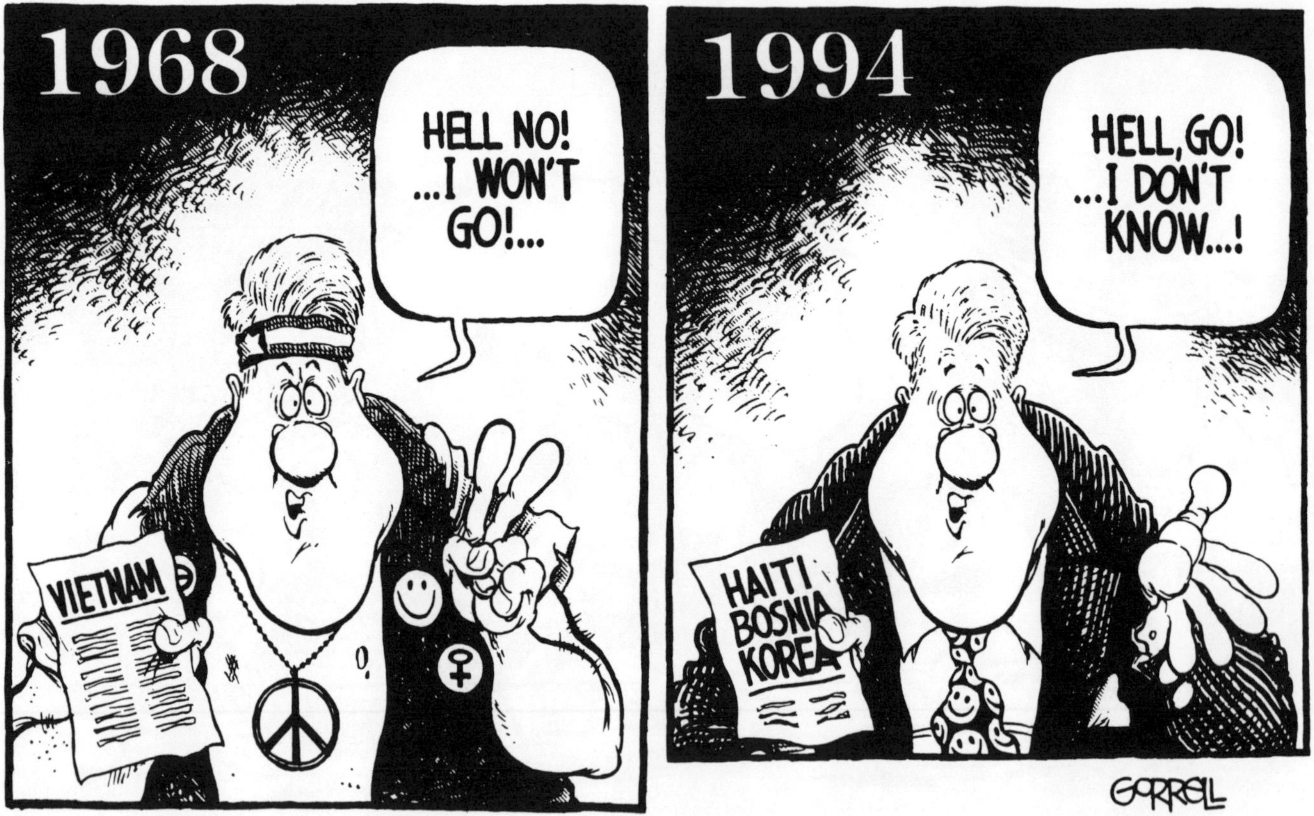
1968
HELL NO! ...I WON'T GO!...
VIETNAM
1994
HELL, GO! ...I DON'T KNOW...!
HAITI BOSNIA KOREA
GORRELL

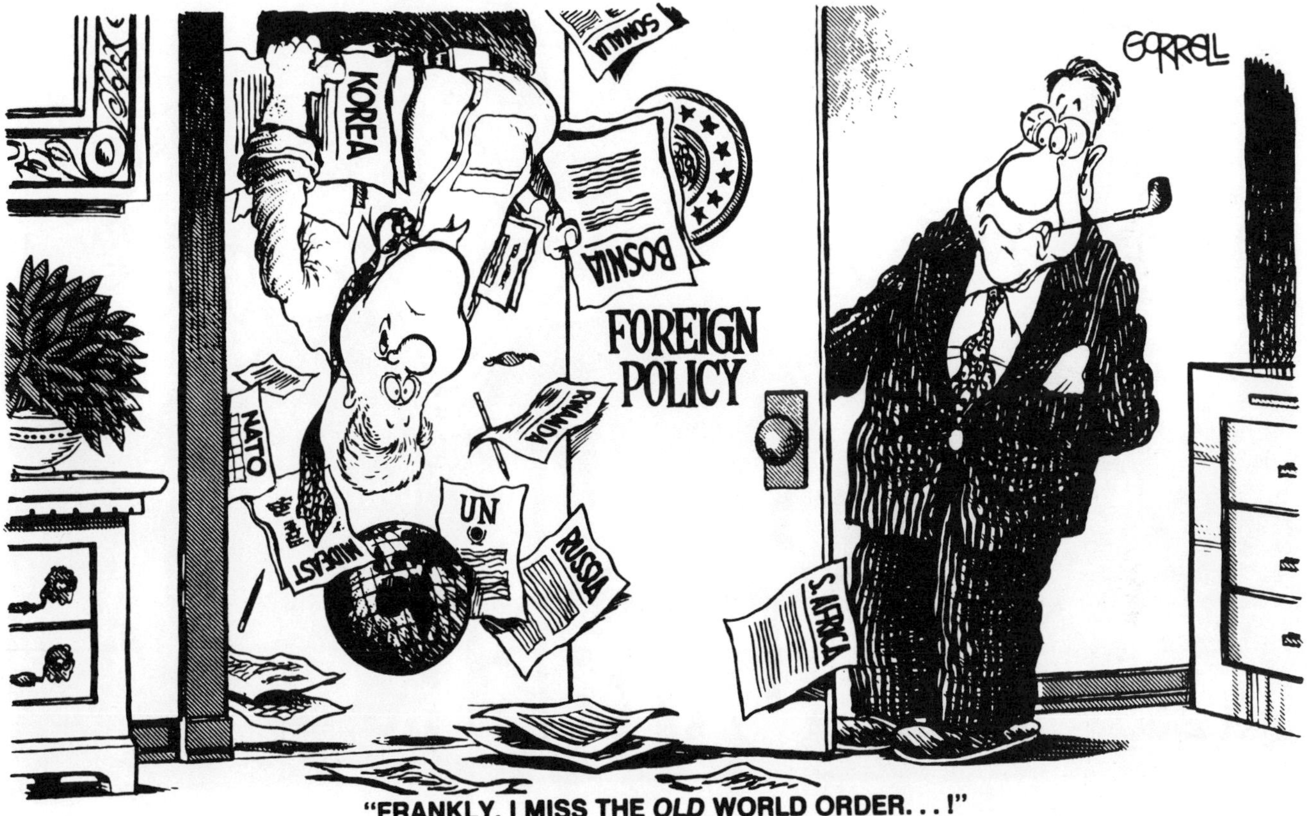
GORRELL
SOMALIA
KOREA
BOSNIA
FOREIGN POLICY
NATO
RWANDA
UN
MIDEAST
RUSSIA
S. AFRICA

"FRANKLY, I MISS THE *OLD* WORLD ORDER. . . !"

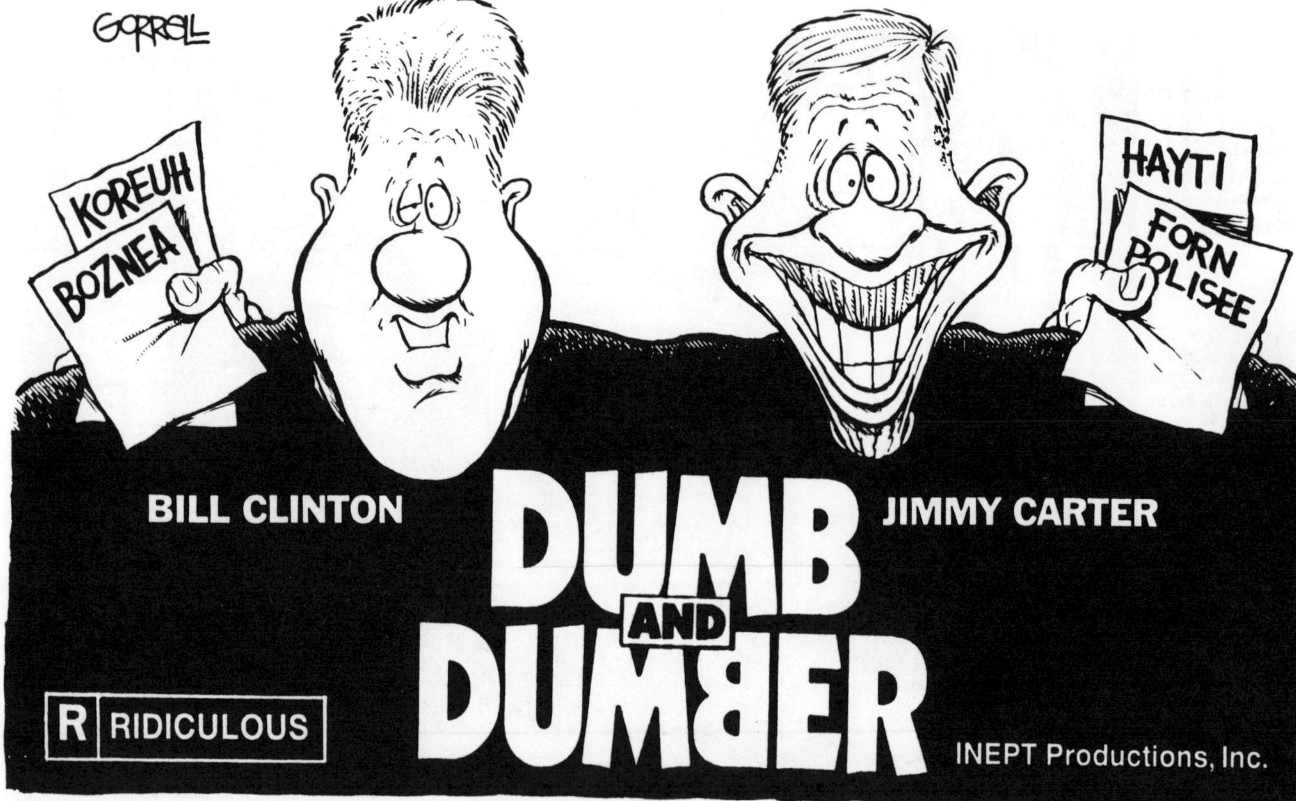
GORRELL
KOREUH
BOZNEA
HAYTI
FORN POLISEE
BILL CLINTON
JIMMY CARTER
DUMB AND DUMBER
R RIDICULOUS
INEPT Productions, Inc.

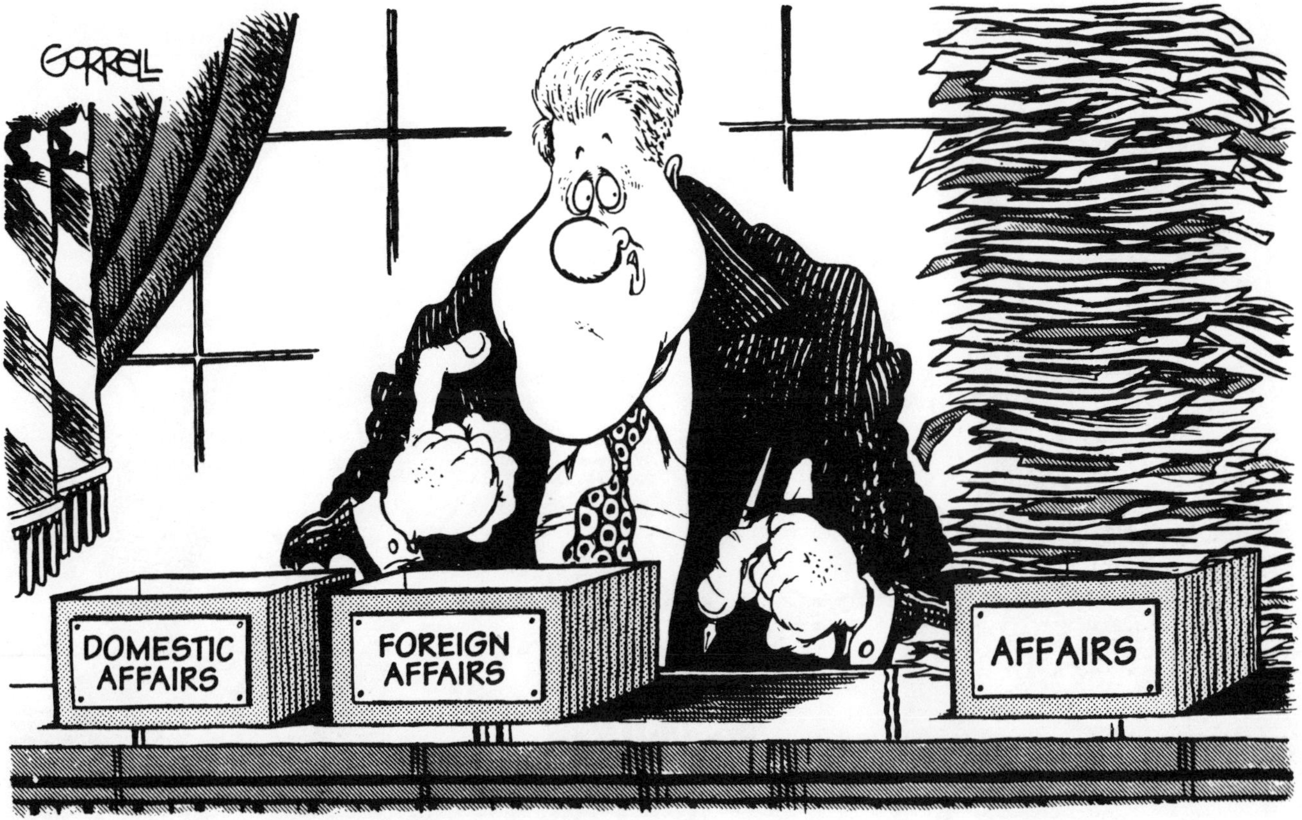
GORRELL
DOMESTIC AFFAIRS
FOREIGN AFFAIRS
AFFAIRS

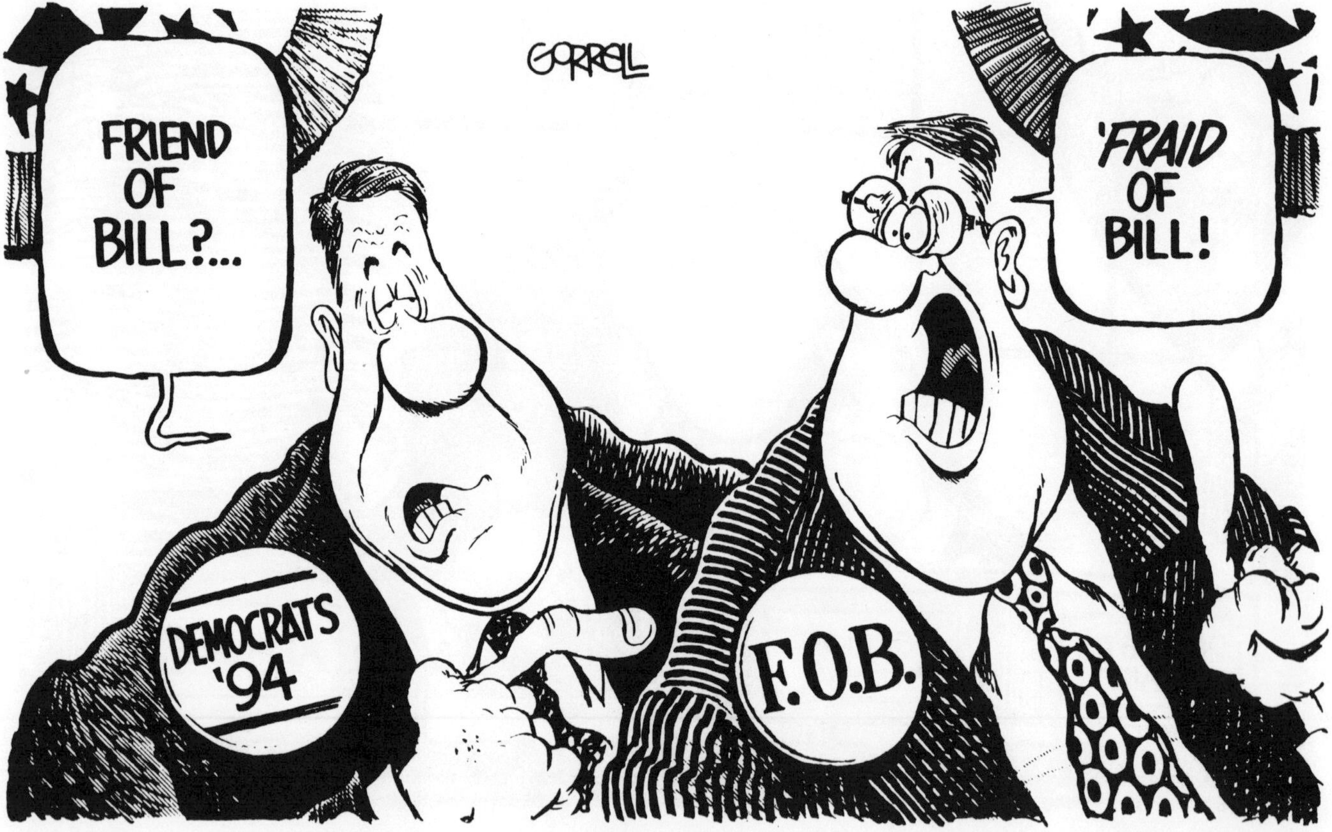
GORRELL
FRIEND OF BILL?...
'FRAID OF BILL!
DEMOCRATS '94
F.O.B.

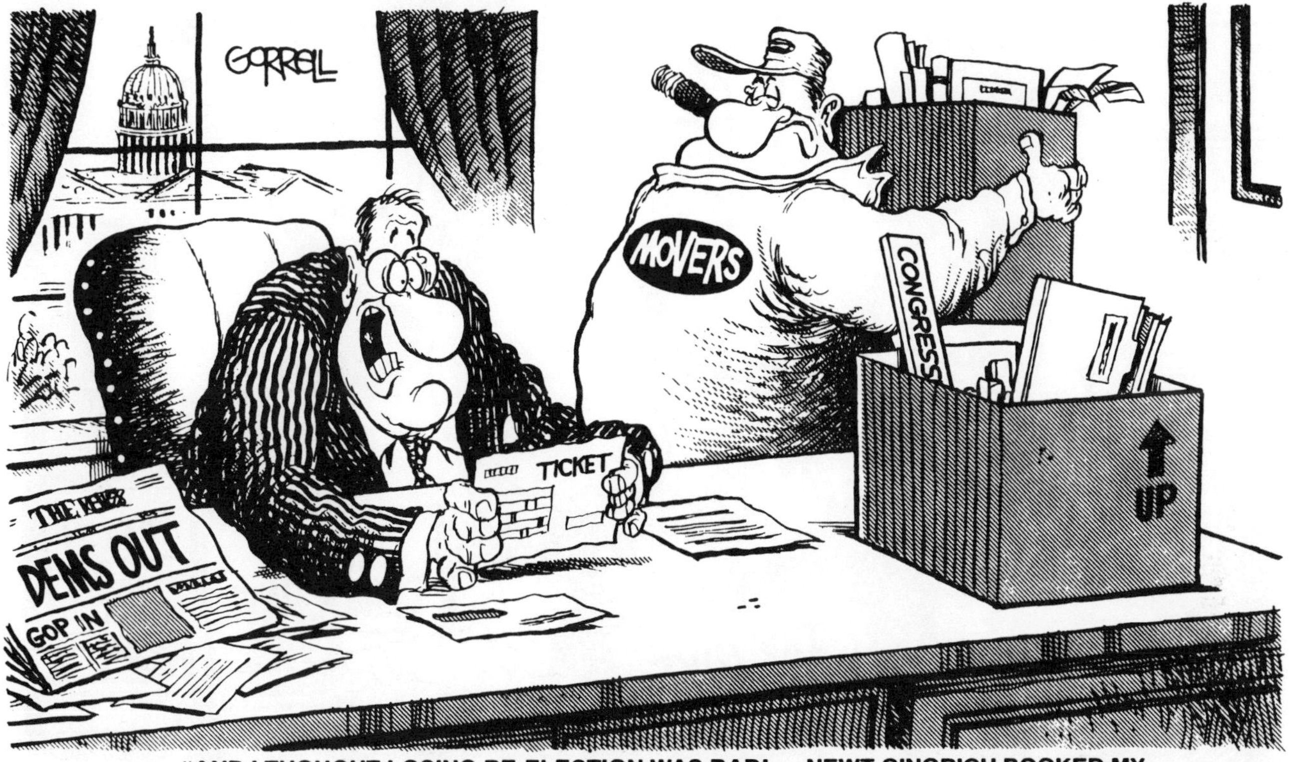
GORRELL
MOVERS
CONGRESS
TICKET
UP
DEMS OUT
GOP IN

"AND I THOUGHT LOSING RE-ELECTION WAS BAD! . . . NEWT GINGRICH BOOKED MY FLIGHT HOME ON A SMALL COMMUTER AIRLINE!"

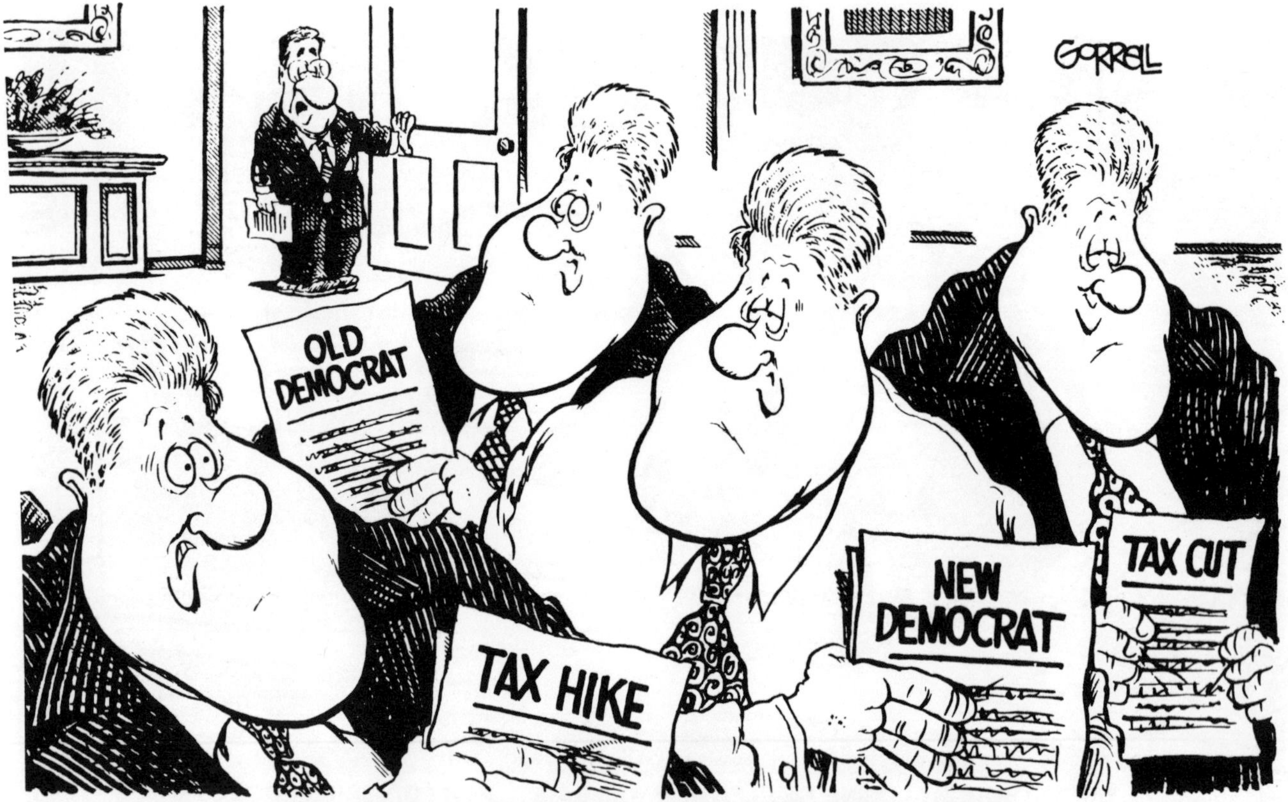
GORRELL
OLD DEMOCRAT
TAX HIKE
NEW DEMOCRAT
TAX CUT

"EXCUSE ME . . . . WHICH BILL CLINTON IS PRESIDENT TODAY?"

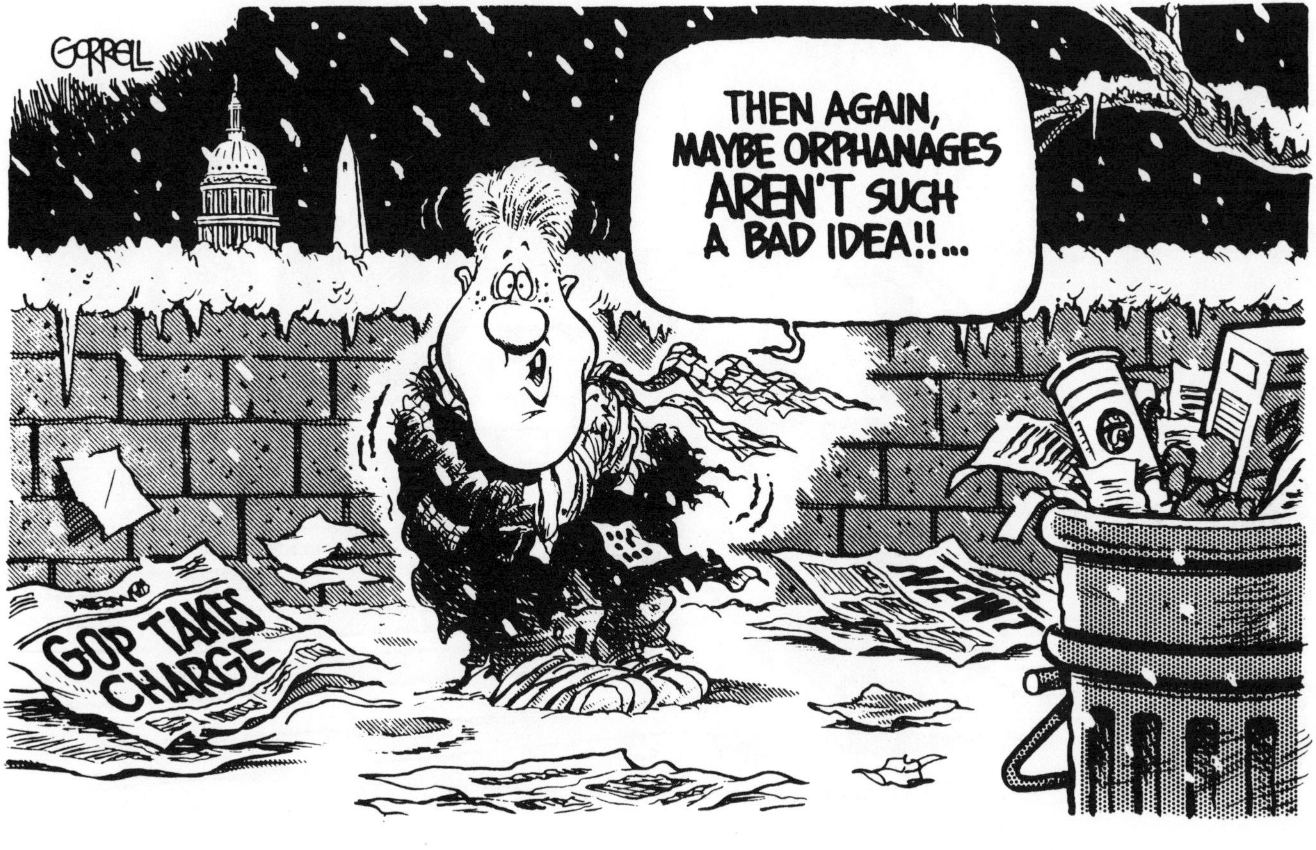
GORRELL
THEN AGAIN, MAYBE ORPHANAGES AREN'T SUCH A BAD IDEA!!...
GOP TAKES CHARGE
NEWS

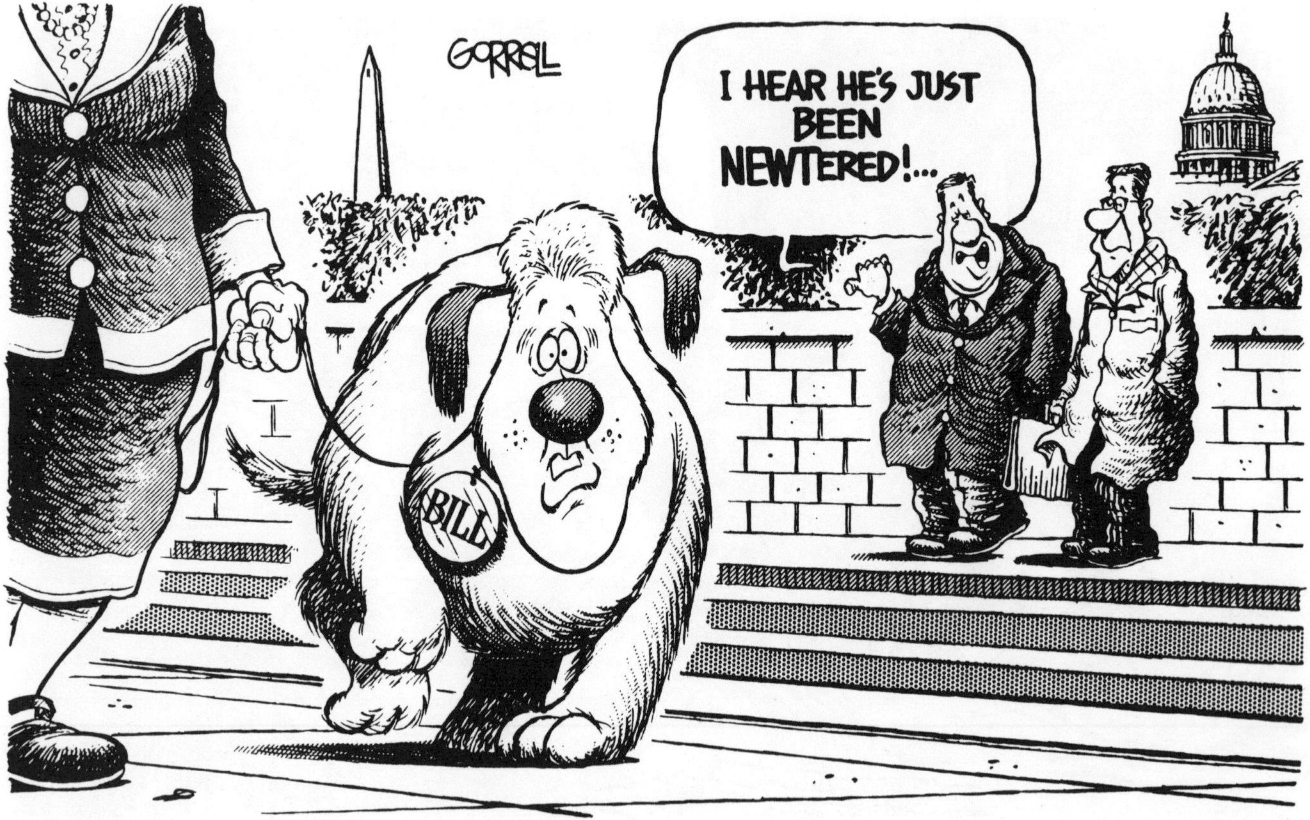
GORRELL
I HEAR HE'S JUST BEEN NEWTERED!...
BILL

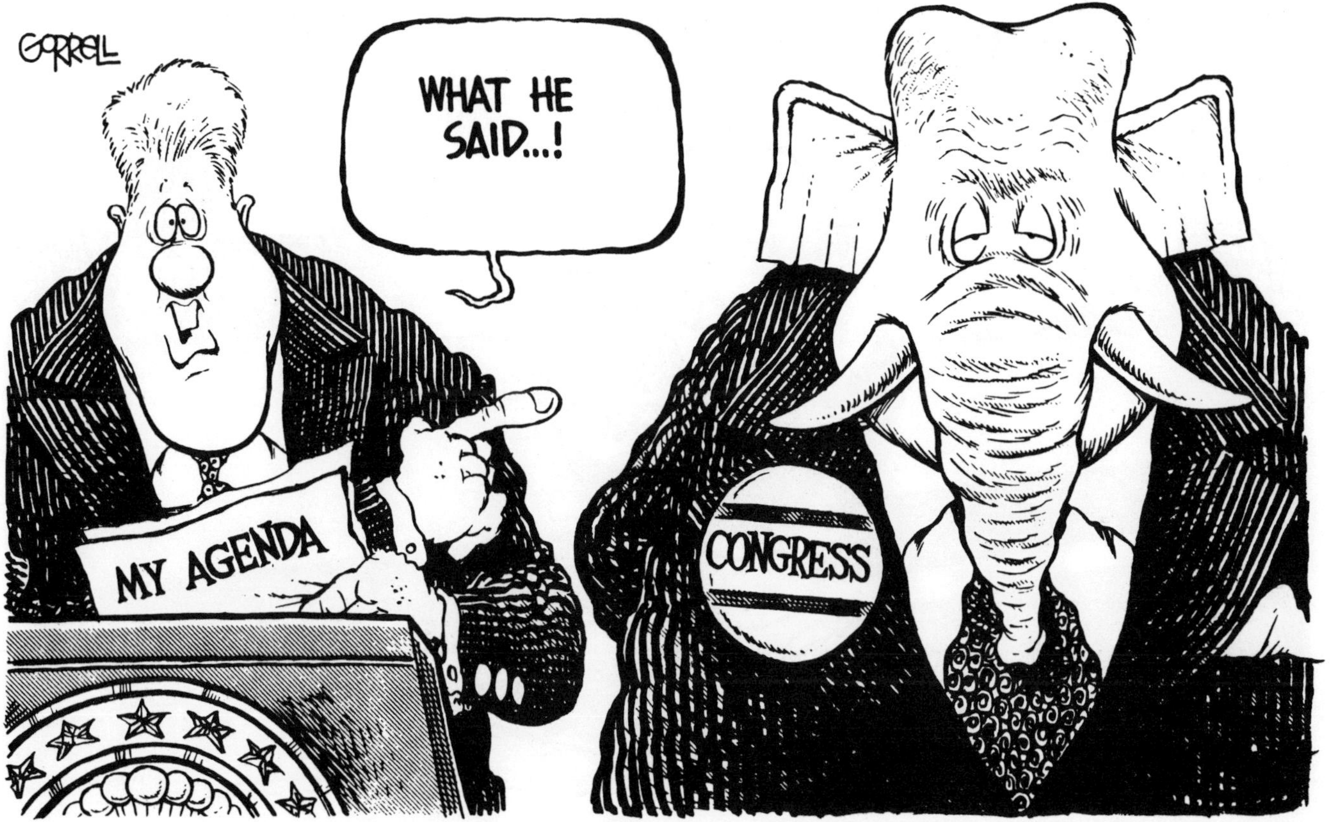
GORRELL
WHAT HE SAID...!
MY AGENDA
CONGRESS

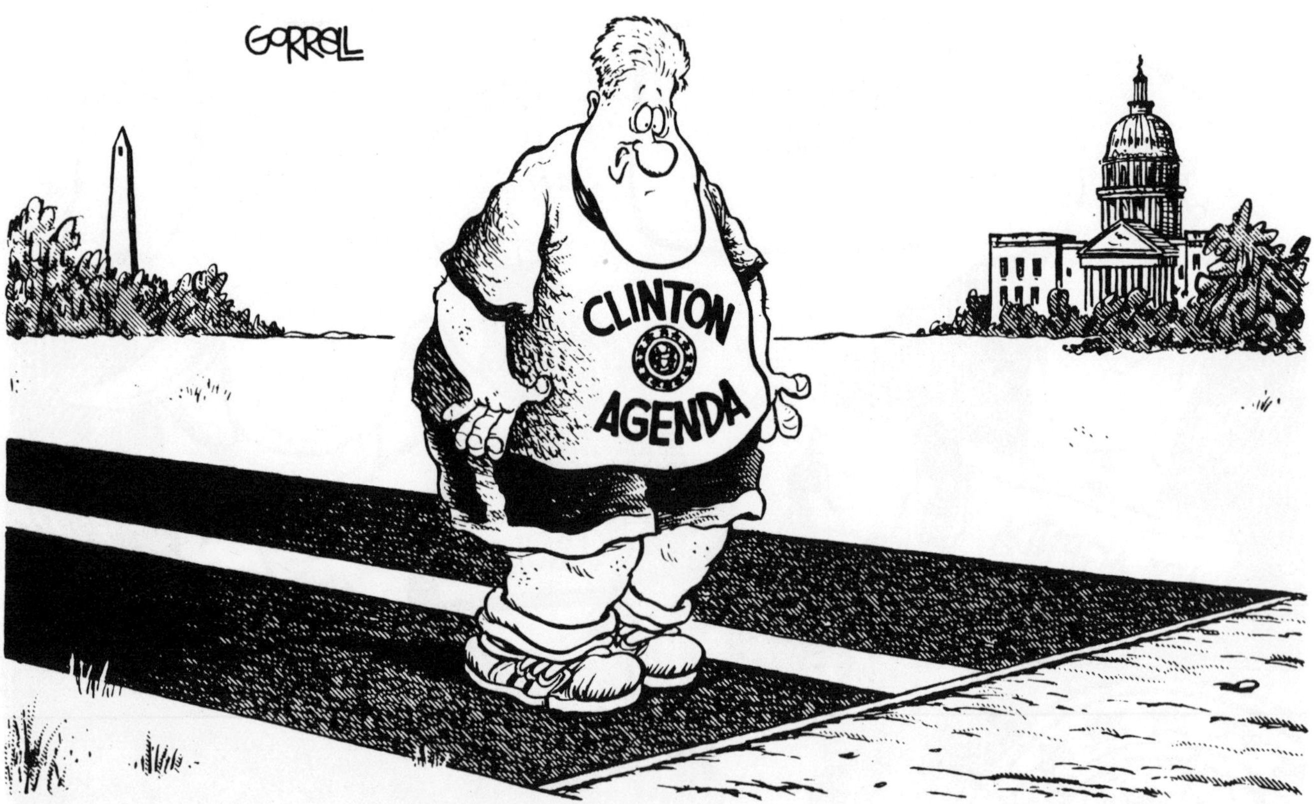
GORRELL
CLINTON
AGENDA

Domestic Concerns

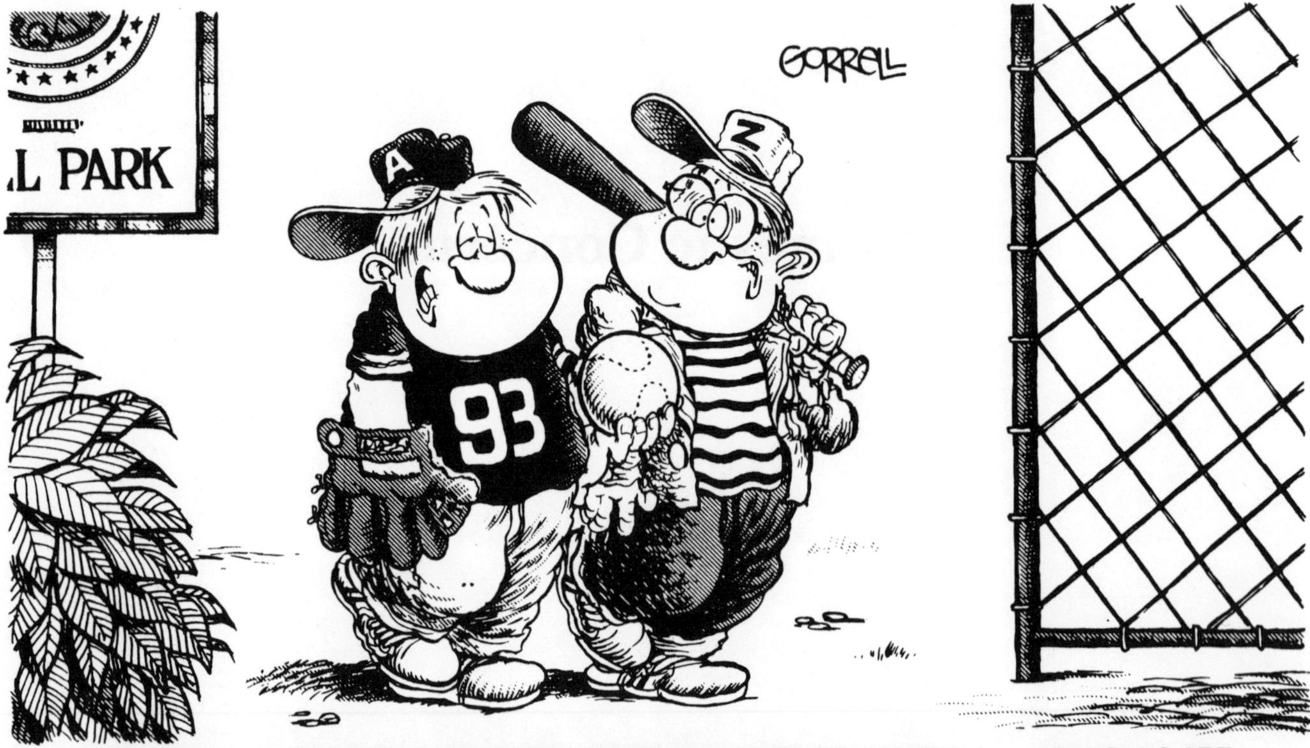
L PARK
GORRELL
A
Z
93

"WHAT'S ALL THIS ABOUT THE BREAK-UP OF THE *AMERICAN FAMILY* ? . . . MY FOLKS ARE *ALWAYS* THERE FOR ME WHEN I FAX MOM AT WORK OR SEE DAD ON VISITATION DAYS!"

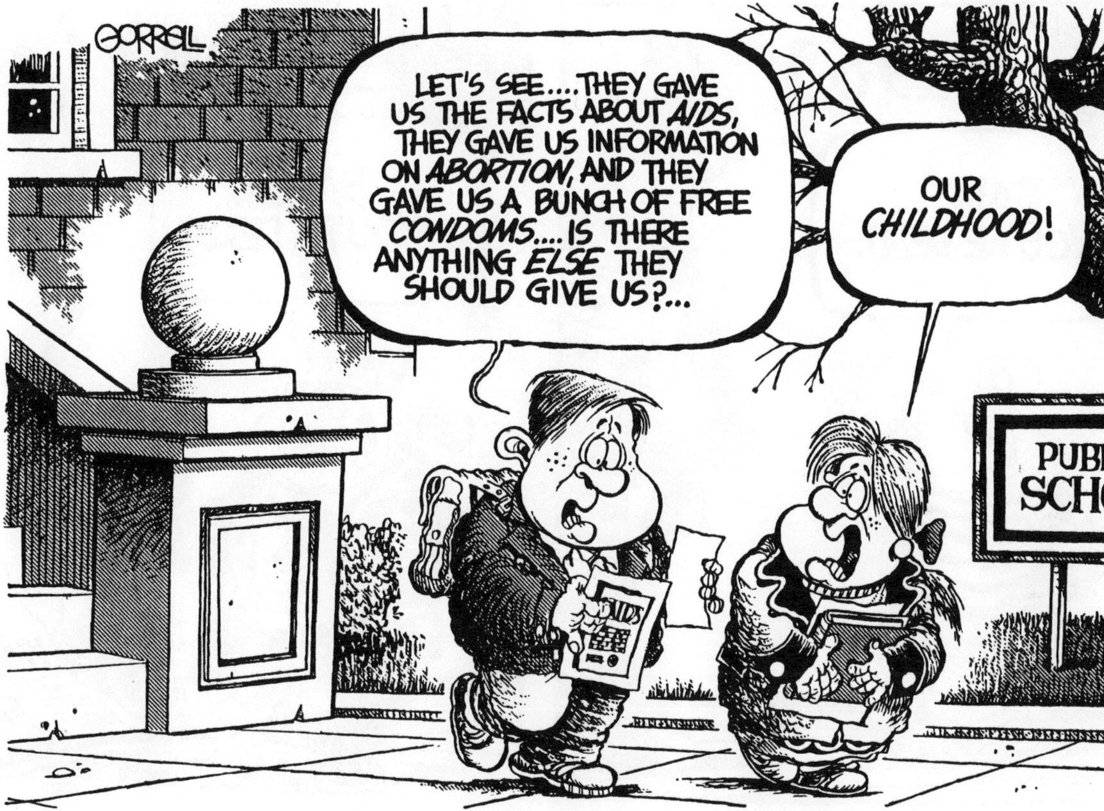
GORRELL
LET'S SEE.... THEY GAVE US THE FACTS ABOUT *AIDS*, THEY GAVE US INFORMATION ON *ABORTION*, AND THEY GAVE US A BUNCH OF FREE *CONDOMS*.... IS THERE ANYTHING *ELSE* THEY SHOULD GIVE US?...
OUR *CHILDHOOD*!
AIDS
PUBL
SCHO

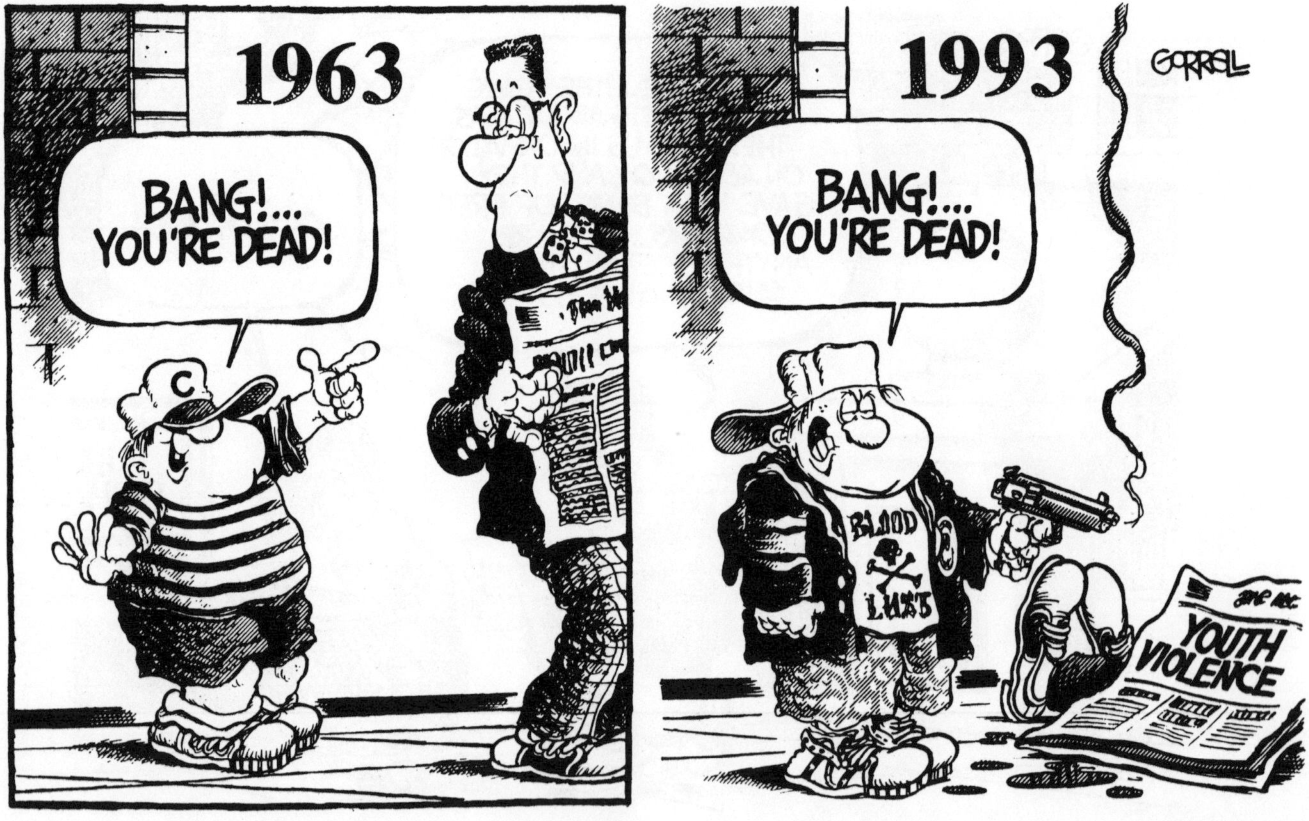
1963
BANG!... YOU'RE DEAD!
1993
GORRELL
BANG!... YOU'RE DEAD!
BLOOD LUST
YOUTH VIOLENCE

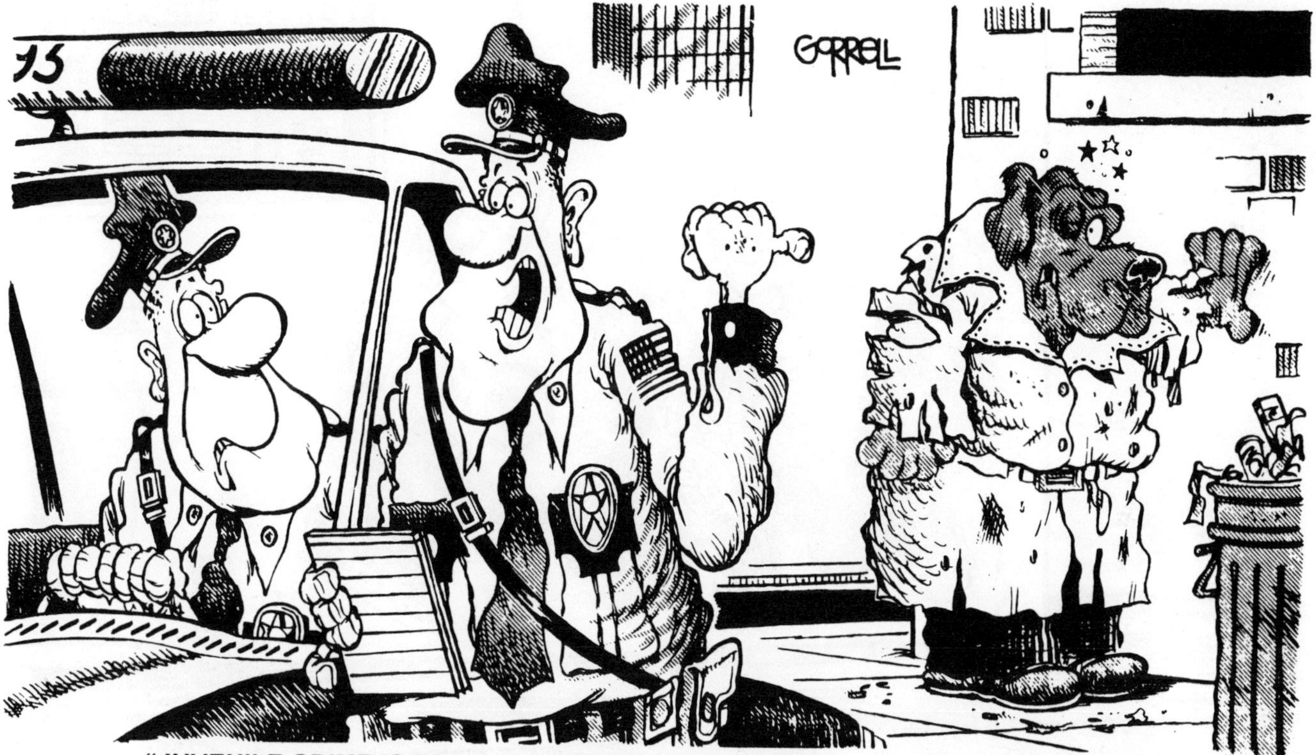
GORRELL
15

"JUVENILE CRIME IS REALLY GETTING OUT OF HAND! . . . SOME KIDS JUST TOOK A BITE OUT OF MCGRUFF!"

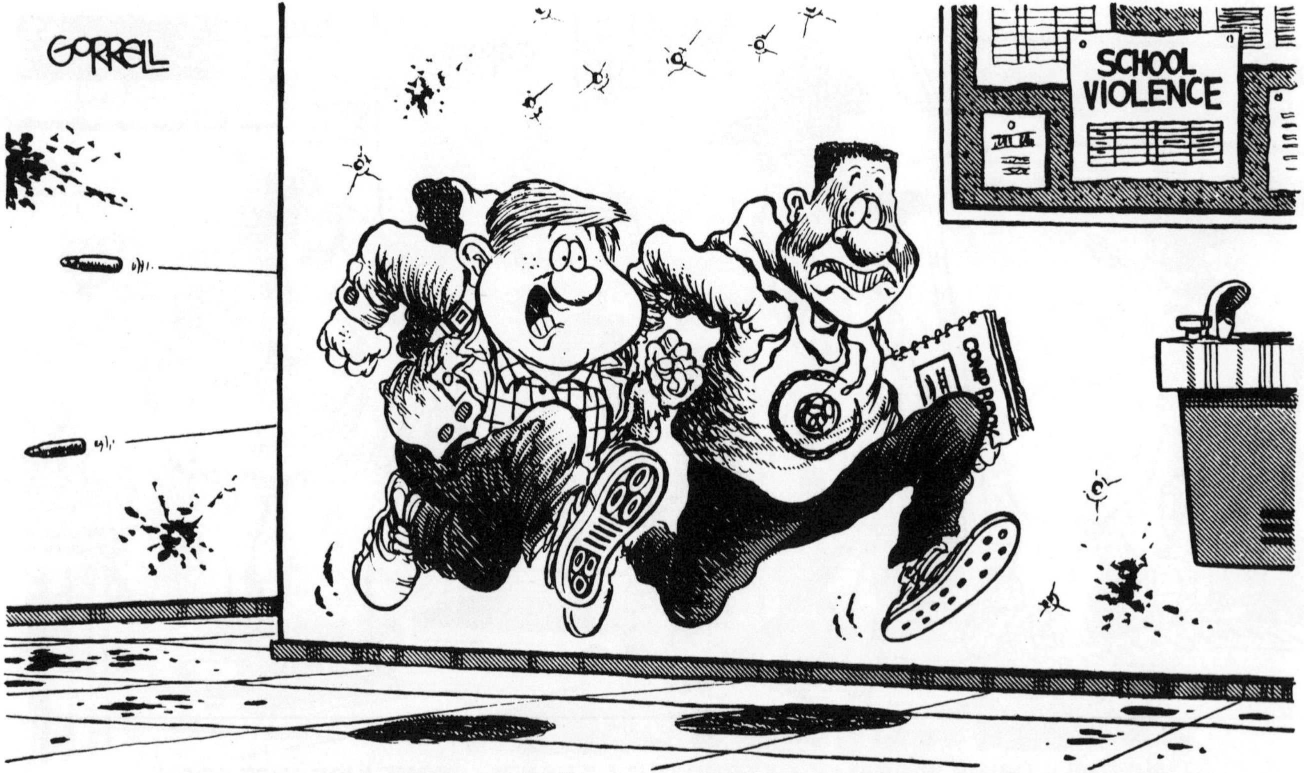
GORRELL
SCHOOL VIOLENCE
COMP BOOK

"IF CONGRESS GOES AHEAD WITH SCHOOL PRAYER, WILL THAT INCLUDE LAST RITES?"

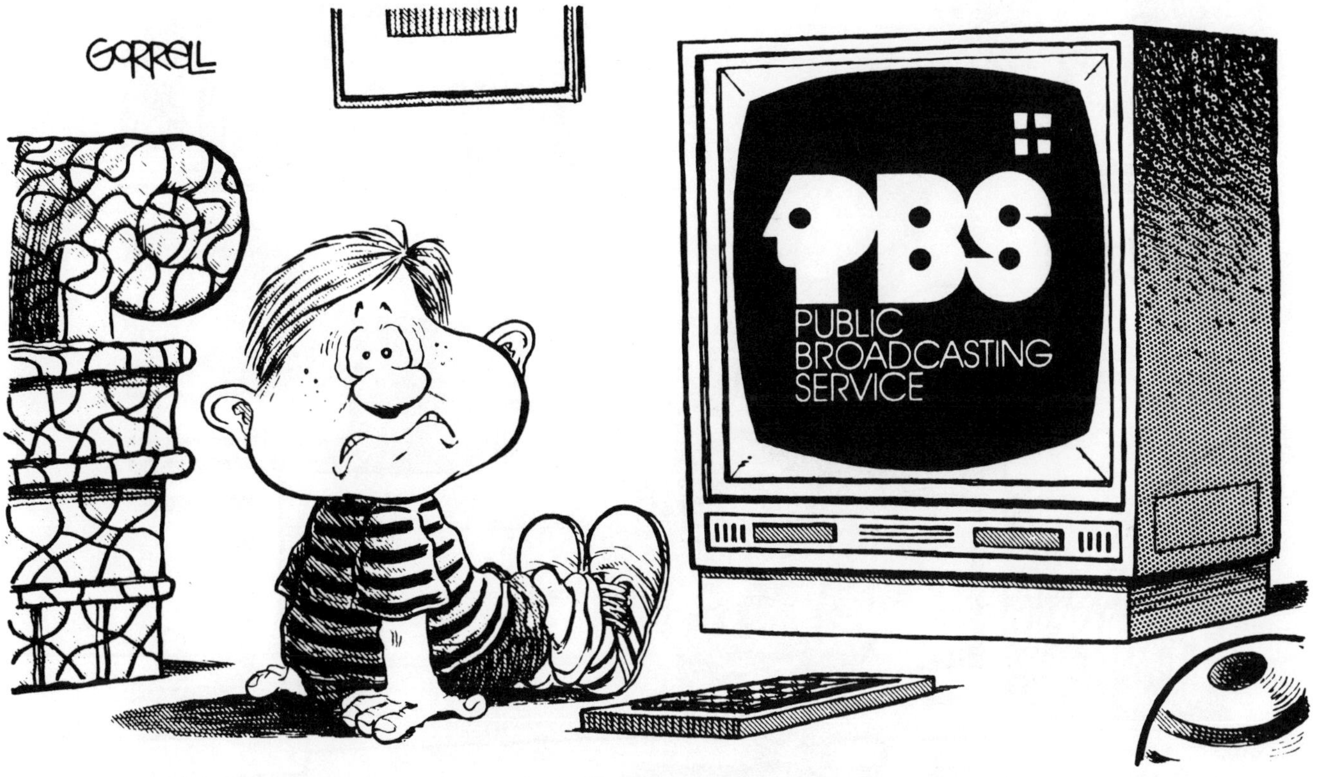
GORRELL
PBS
PUBLIC
BROADCASTING
SERVICE

"SESAME STREET HAS BEEN BROUGHT TO YOU TODAY BY THE LETTERS T, A, X, E, AND S."

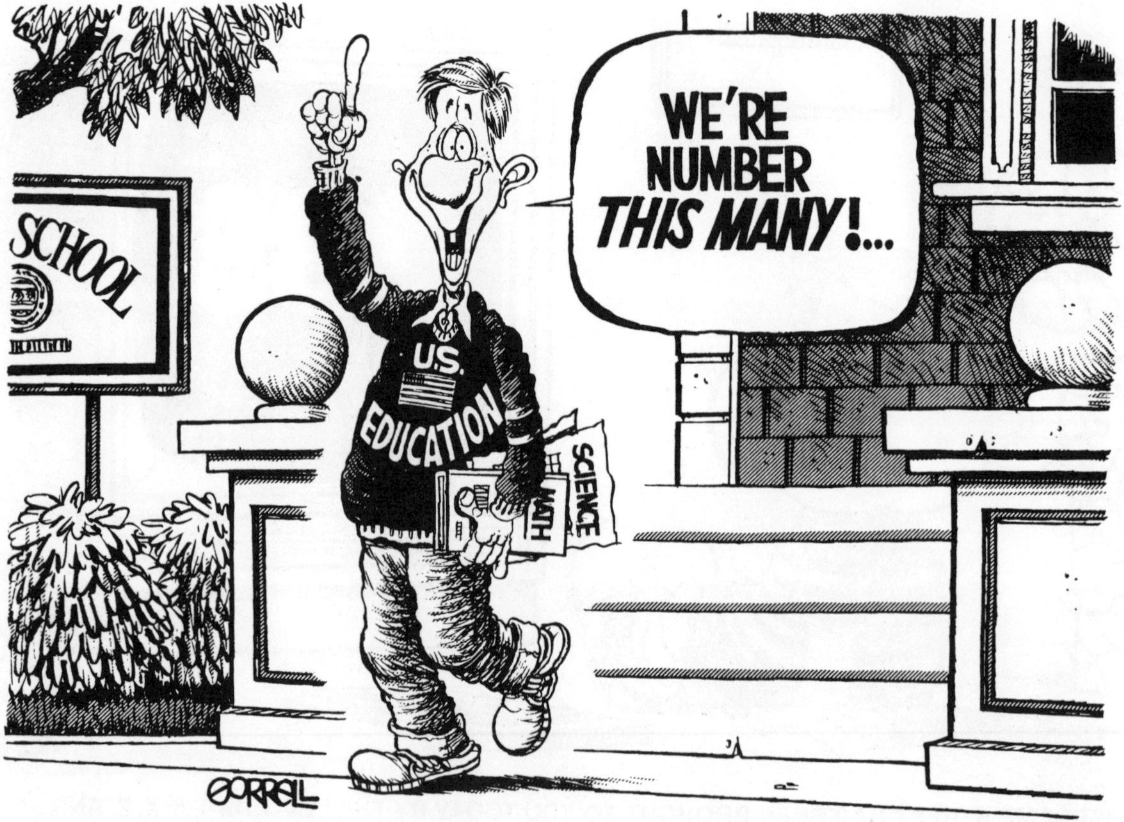
SCHOOL
U.S.
EDUCATION
MATH
SCIENCE
WE'RE NUMBER *THIS MANY*!...
GORRELL

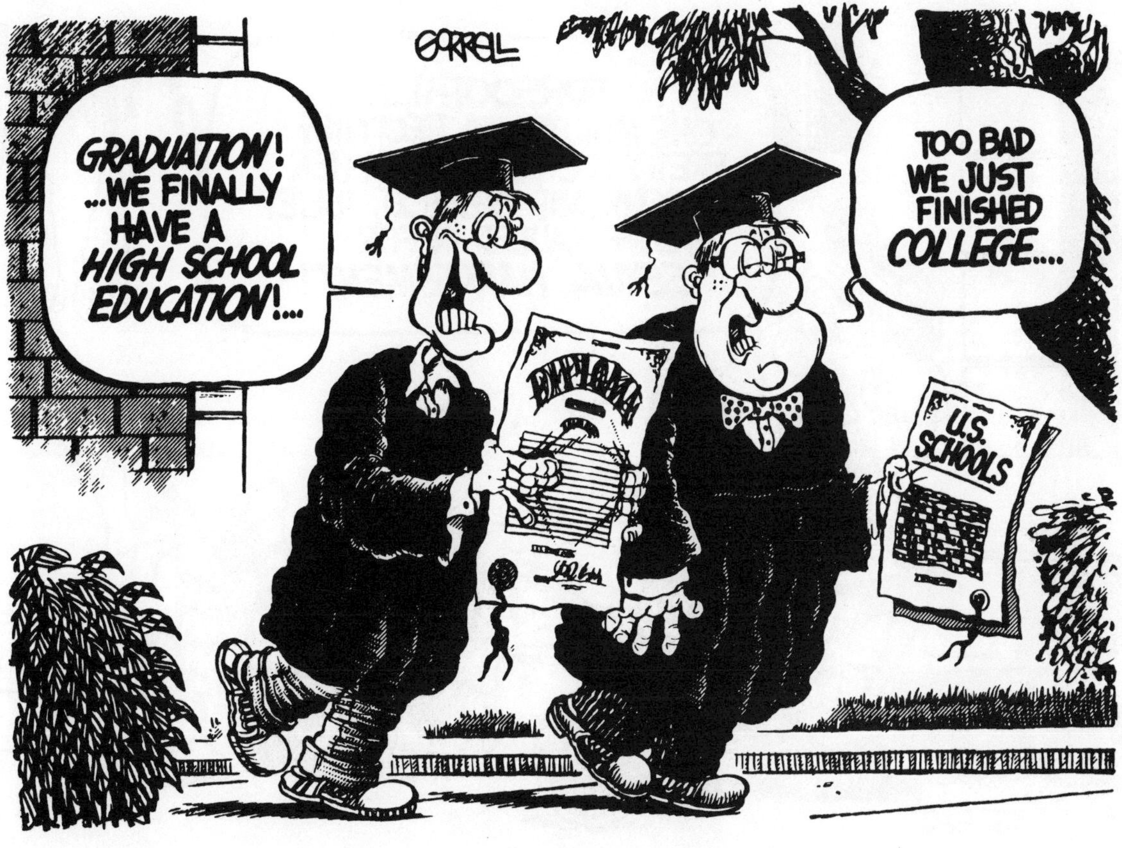
GORRELL
GRADUATION! ...WE FINALLY HAVE A HIGH SCHOOL EDUCATION!...
TOO BAD WE JUST FINISHED COLLEGE....
U.S. SCHOOLS

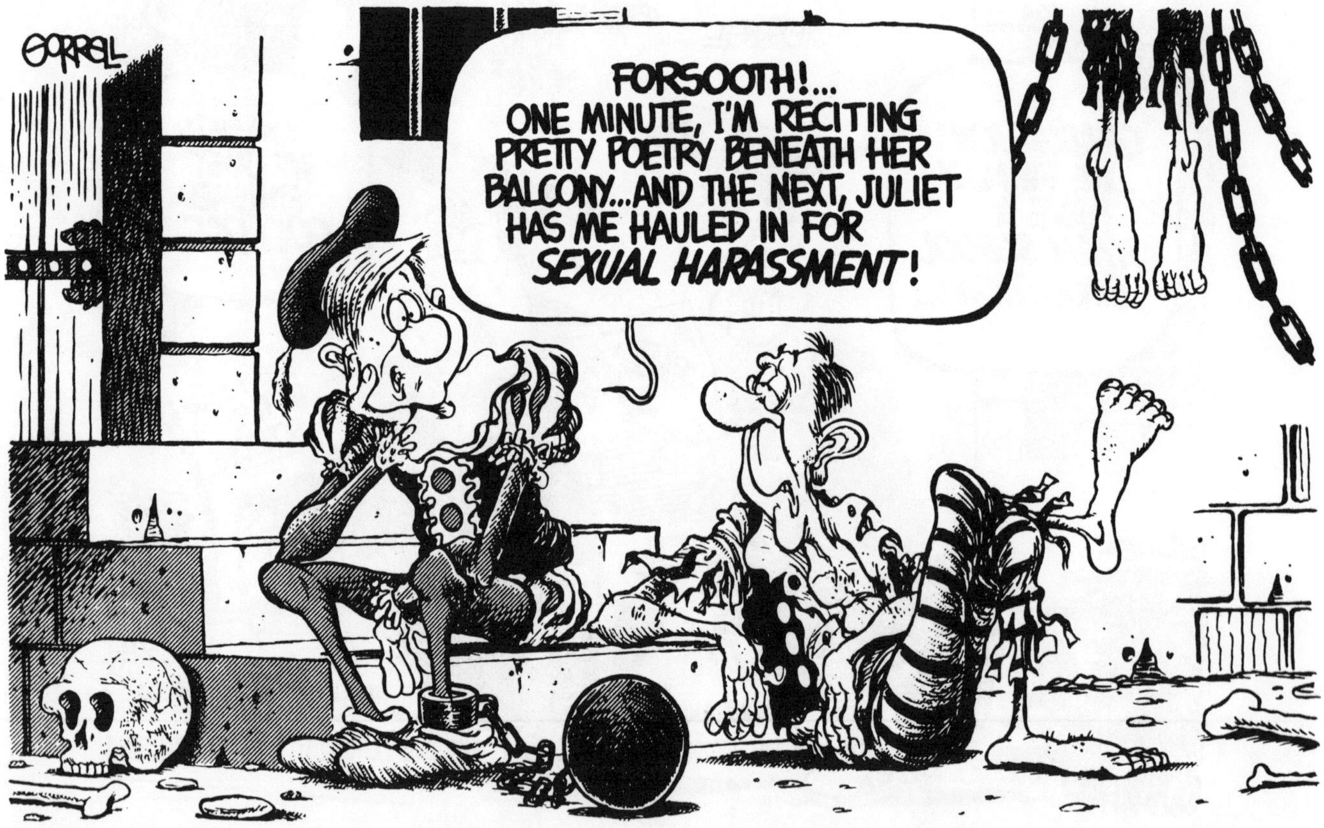
GORRELL
FORSOOTH!... ONE MINUTE, I'M RECITING PRETTY POETRY BENEATH HER BALCONY...AND THE NEXT, JULIET HAS ME HAULED IN FOR *SEXUAL HARASSMENT*!

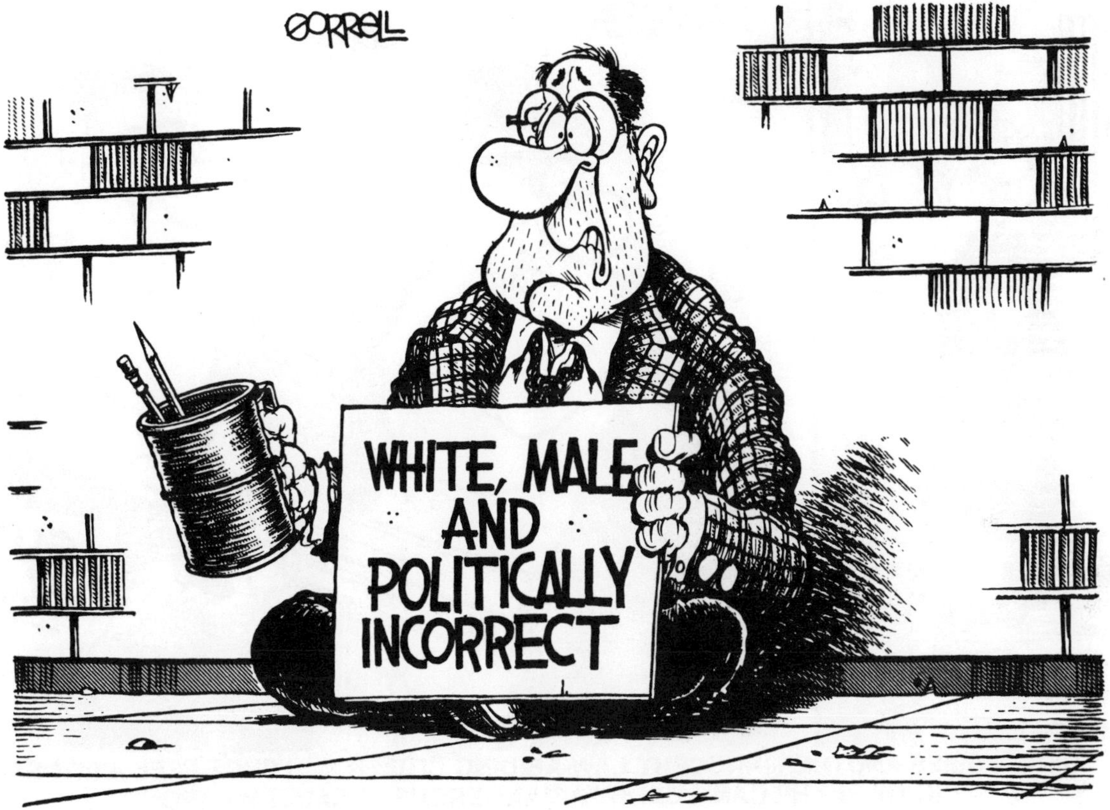
SORRELL
WHITE, MALE
AND
POLITICALLY
INCORRECT

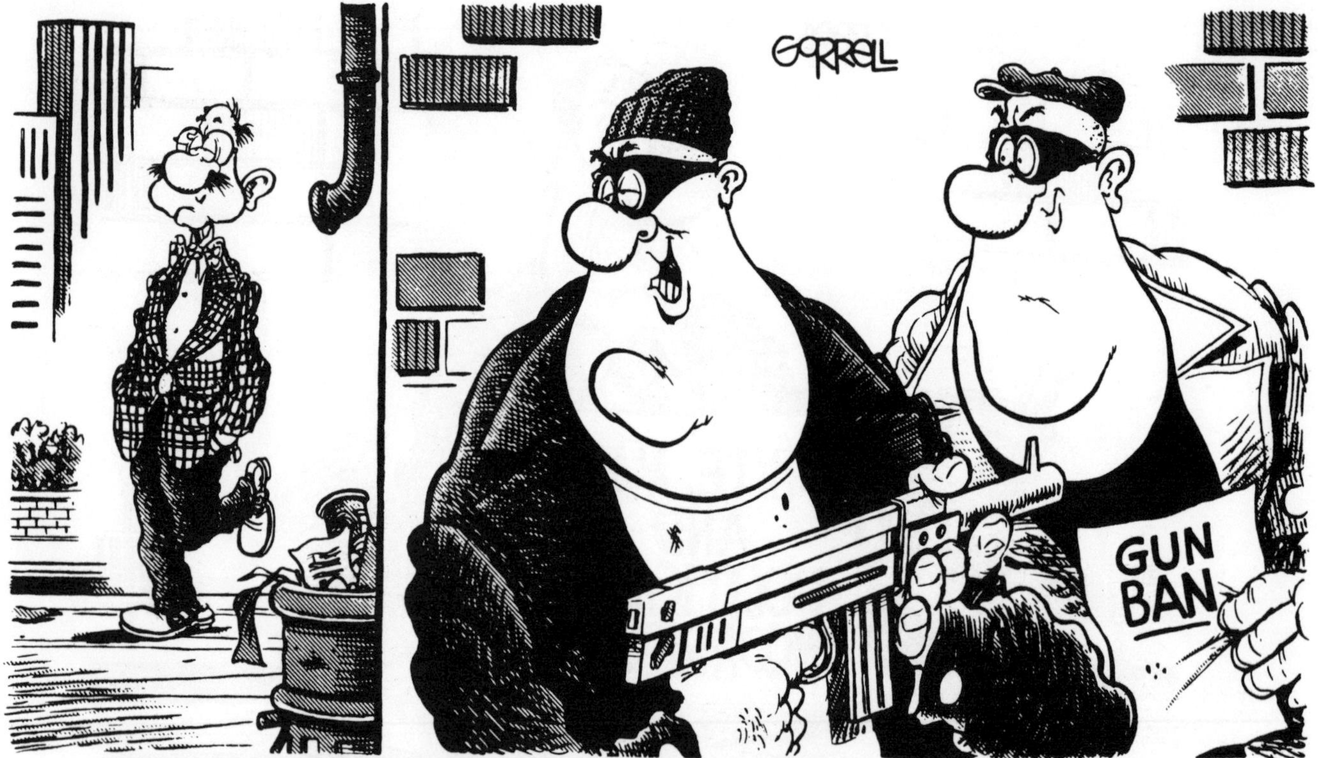
GORRELL
GUN
BAN

"HERE COMES ANOTHER INNOCENT, LAW-ABIDING CITIZEN . . . . I SURE FEEL A LOT SAFER KNOWING HE CAN'T CARRY A DANGEROUS ASSAULT WEAPON!"

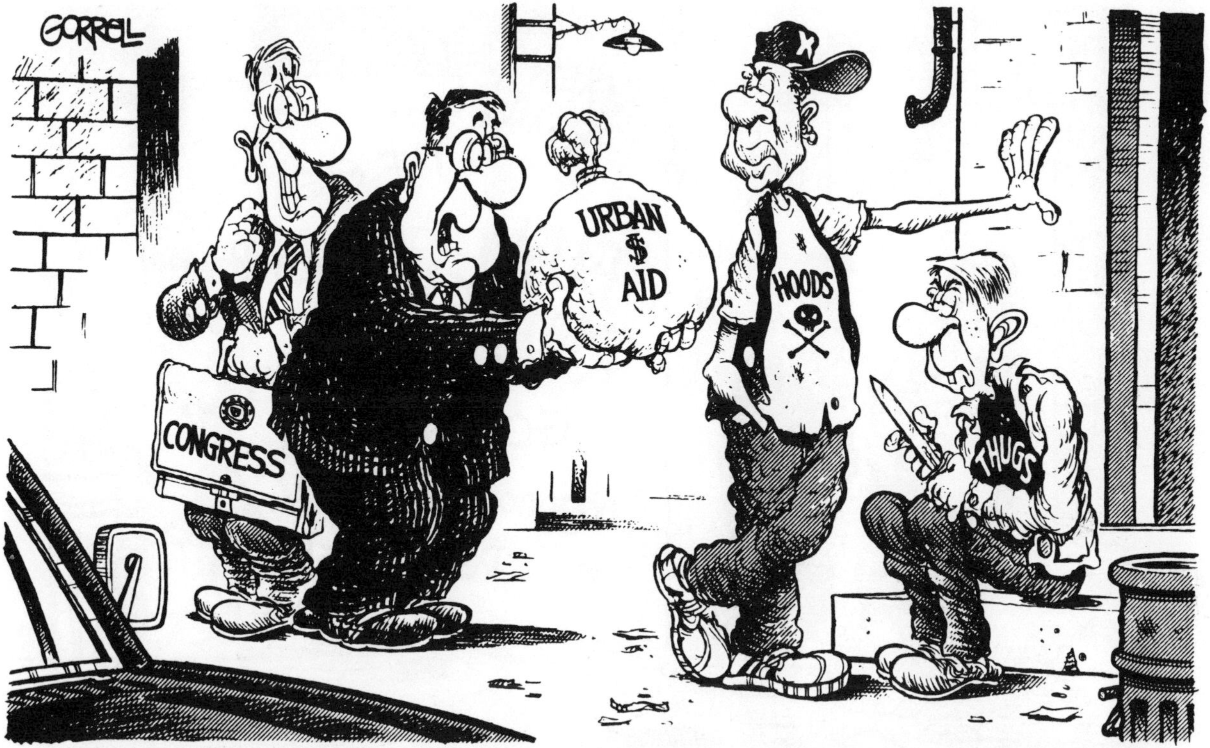
GORRELL
URBAN $ AID
CONGRESS
HOODS
THUGS

"HERE'S YOUR *PROTECTION MONEY*. . . WE MEAN YOUR *BRIBE*. . . WE MEAN YOUR *SUMMER JOBS PROGRAM*. . . . NOW, PROMISE NOT TO *BURN AND LOOT* OUR *CITIES*?!"

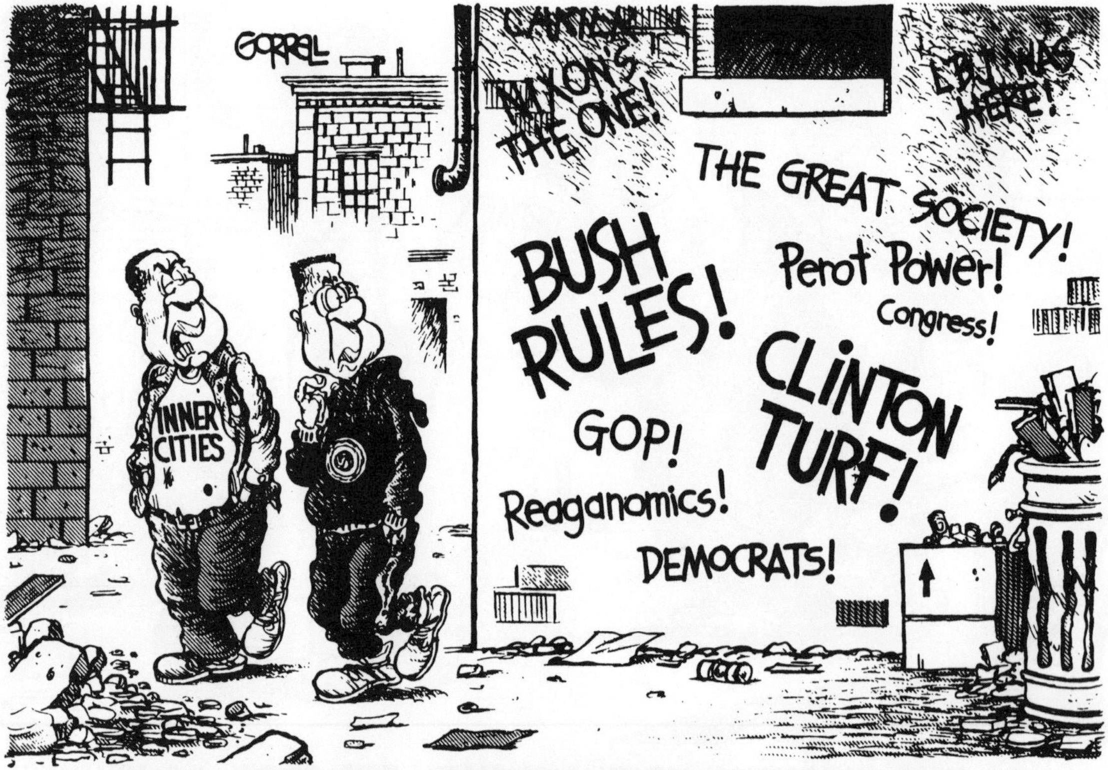
GORRELL
NIXON'S THE ONE!
LBJ WAS HERE!
THE GREAT SOCIETY!
BUSH RULES!
Perot Power!
Congress!
CLINTON TURF!
GOP!
Reaganomics!
DEMOCRATS!
INNER CITIES

"YEAH. . . . THIS MIGHT BE A DECENT NEIGHBORHOOD IF IT WEREN'T FOR ALL THE *GANG WARS!*"

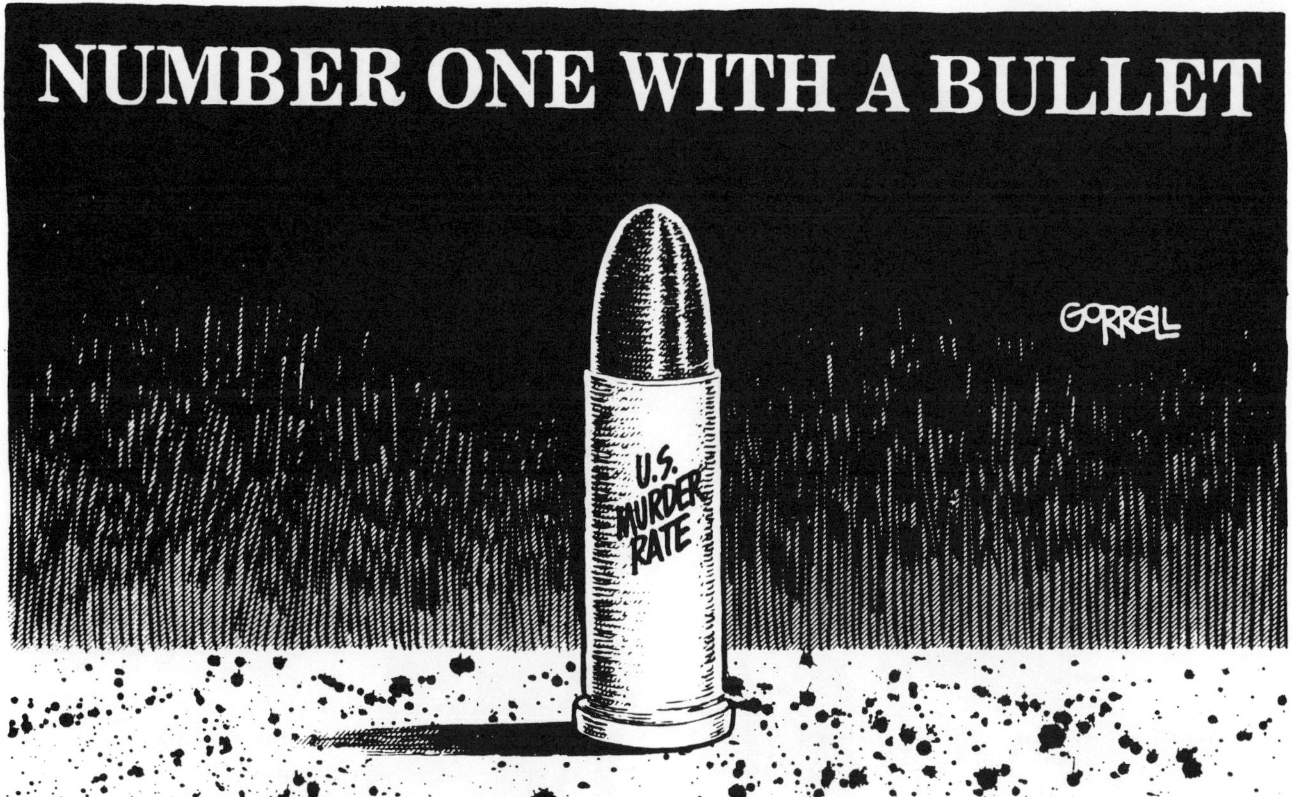
NUMBER ONE WITH A BULLET
U.S. MURDER RATE
GORRELL

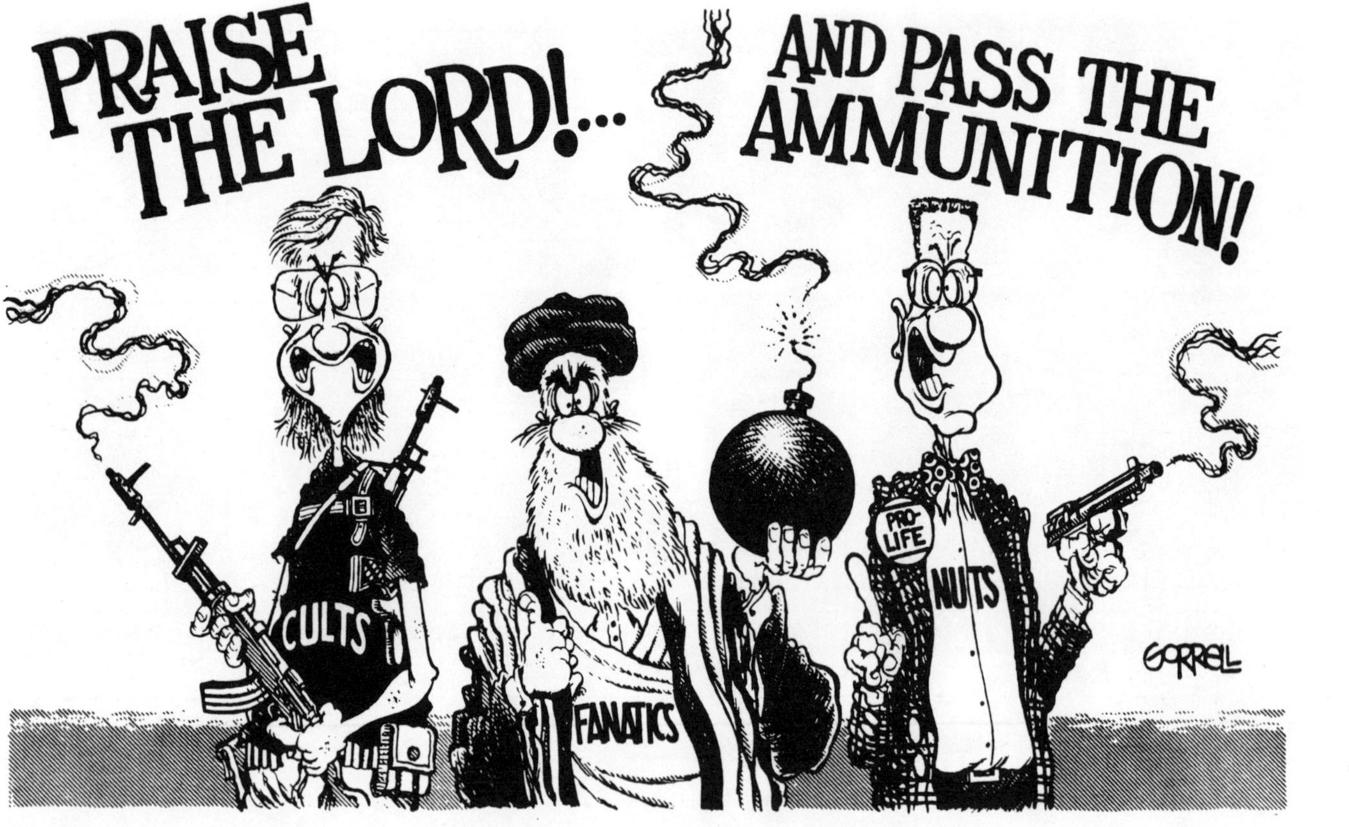
PRAISE THE LORD!...
AND PASS THE AMMUNITION!
CULTS
FANATICS
PRO-LIFE
NUTS
GORRELL

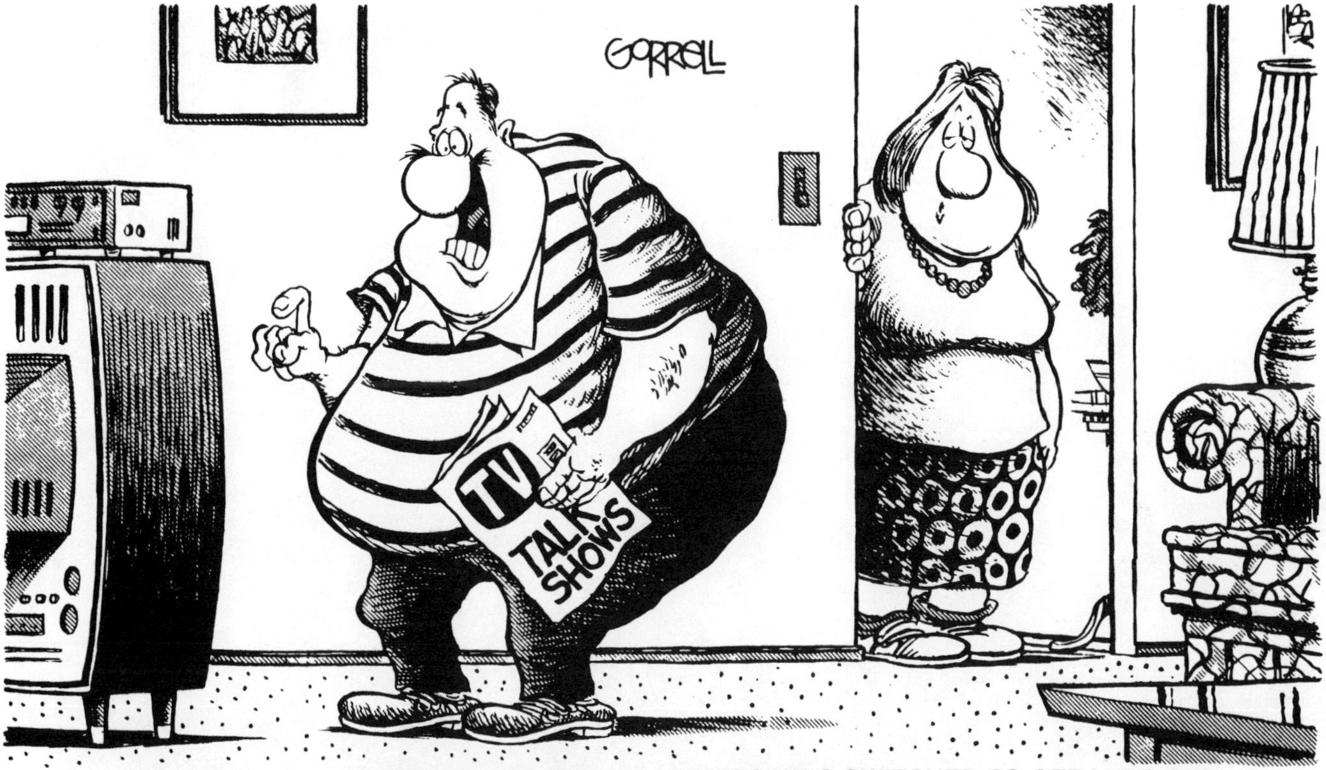
GORRELL
TV
TALK SHOWS

"HOT DOG! . . . DONAHUE HAS OPRAH ADDICTS WHO SWITCHED TO GERALDO AND DISCUSSED IT ON SALLY JESSY RAPHAEL!"

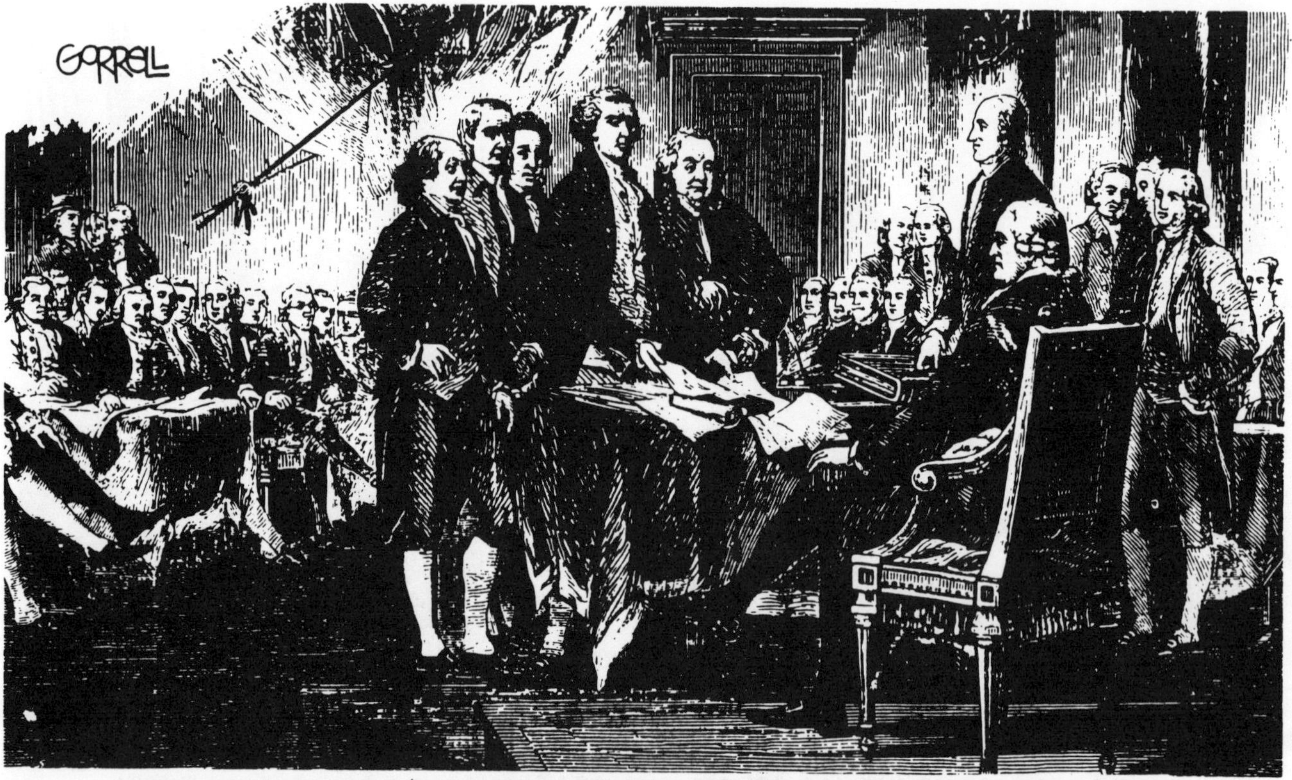
GORRELL

"ARE YOU SURE WE CAN DO THIS WITHOUT DEBATING IT FIRST ON LARRY KING?"

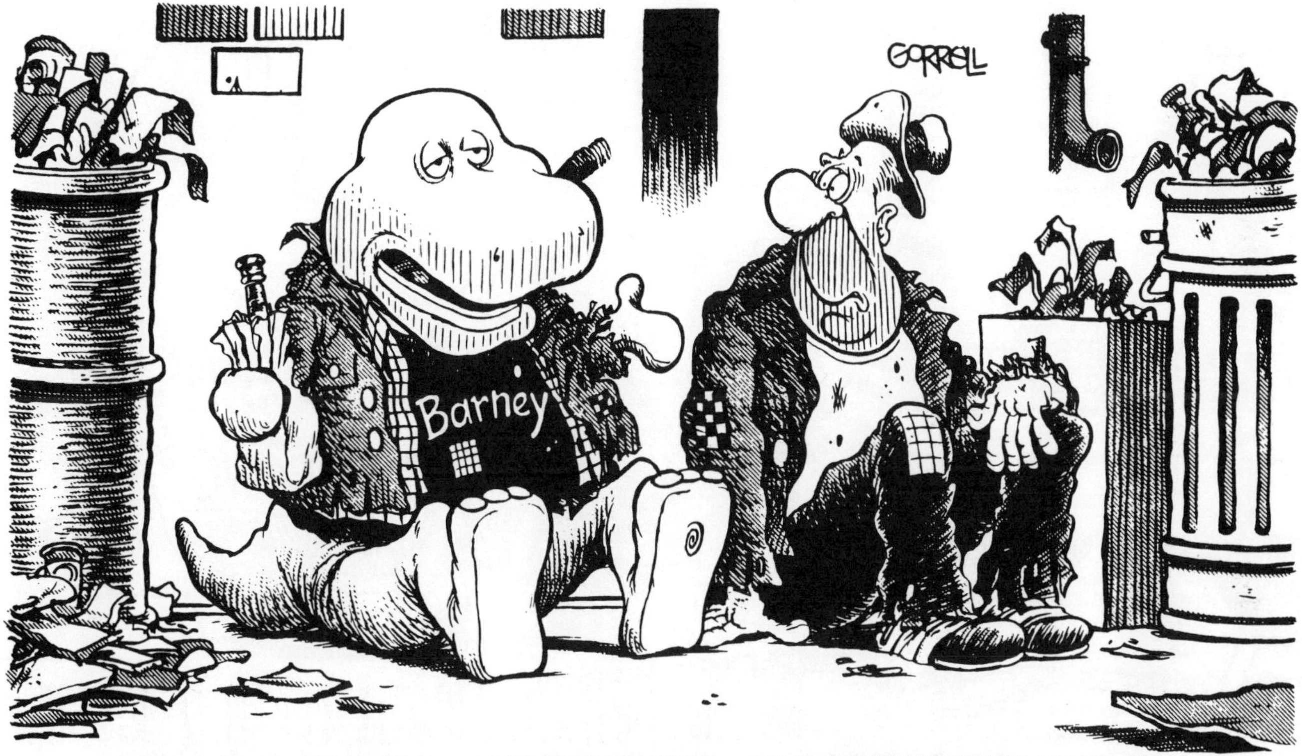
GORRELL
Barney

"I WAS AT THE TOP, ONCE . . . . MILLIONS OF FANS . . . I LOVED THEM, THEY LOVED ME . . .
THEN I FAILED MY AUDITION FOR *JURASSIC PARK* !"

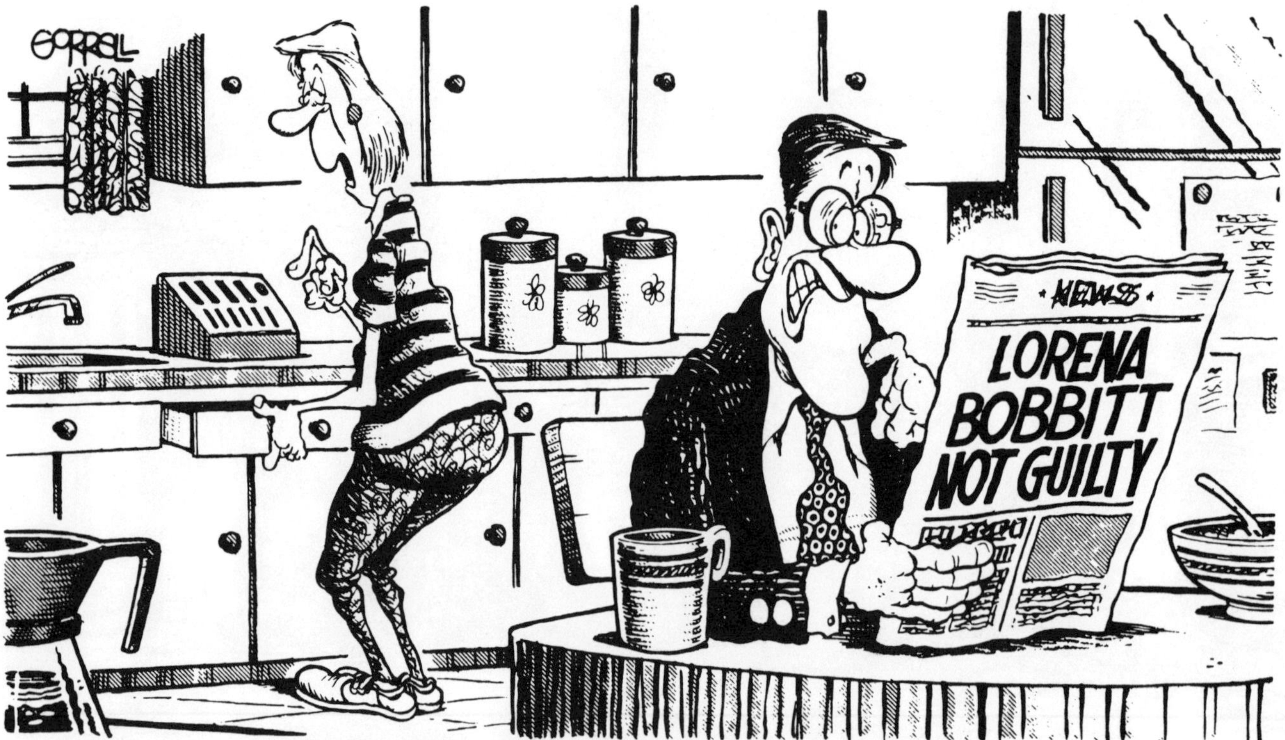
GORRELL
NEWS
LORENA BOBBITT NOT GUILTY
"THAT'S ODD . . . . WHAT IN THE WORLD HAPPENED TO ALL OUR KITCHEN KNIVES?!"

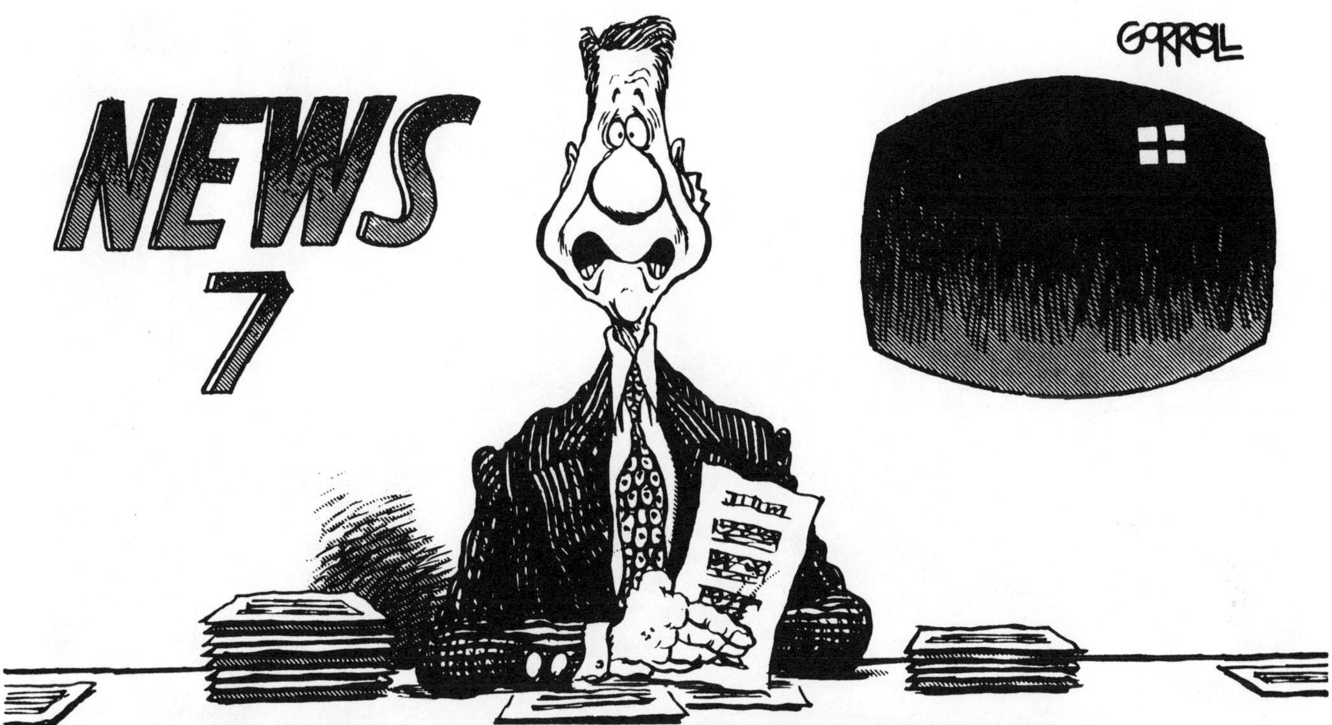
NEWS
7
GORRELL

"A NEWS UPDATE . . . . TONYA HARDING HAS ADMITTED TO CONSPIRING WITH THE MENENDEZ BROTHERS AND JOEY BUTTAFUOCO AFTER THE FACT TO WORK WITH LORENA BOBBITT IN EXTORTING A CASH SETTLEMENT FROM MICHAEL JACKSON!"

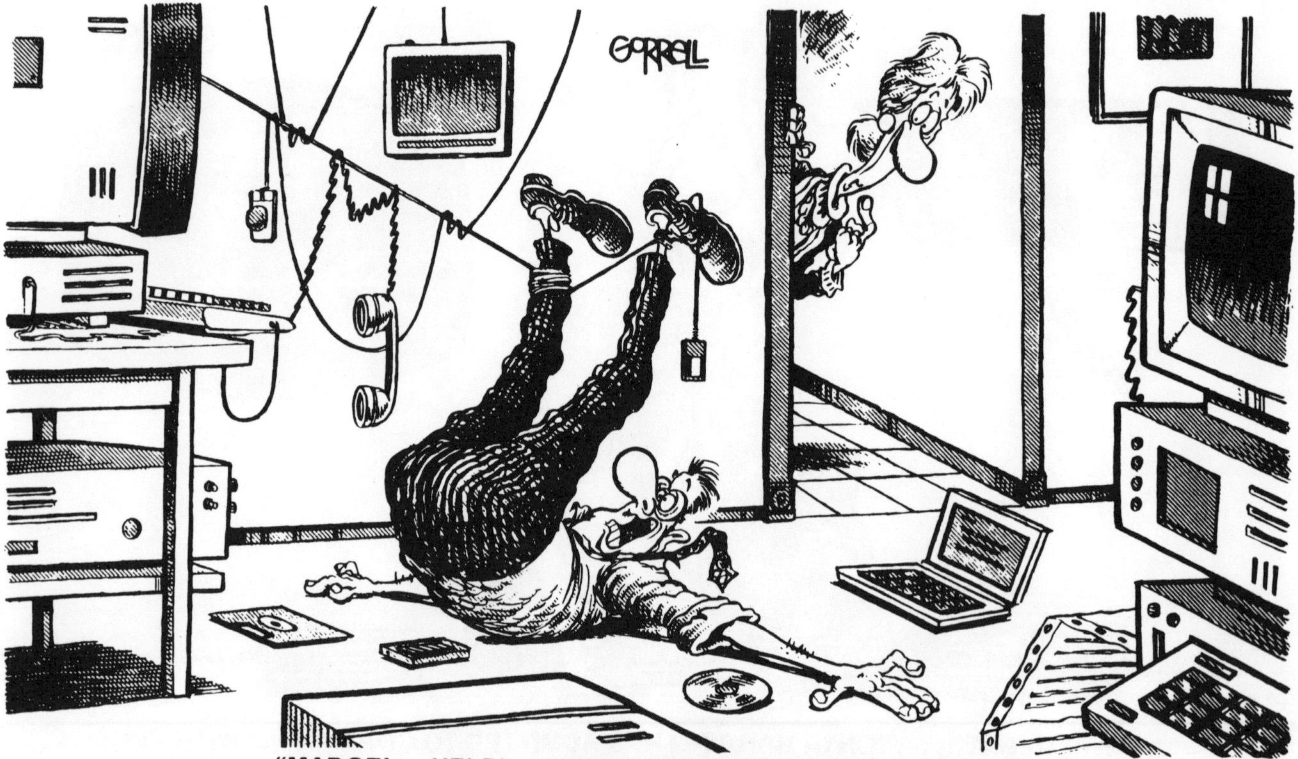
GORRELL

"MADGE! . . . HELP! . . . I HIT ANOTHER POTHOLE IN OUR NEW INFORMATION SUPERHIGHWAY!"

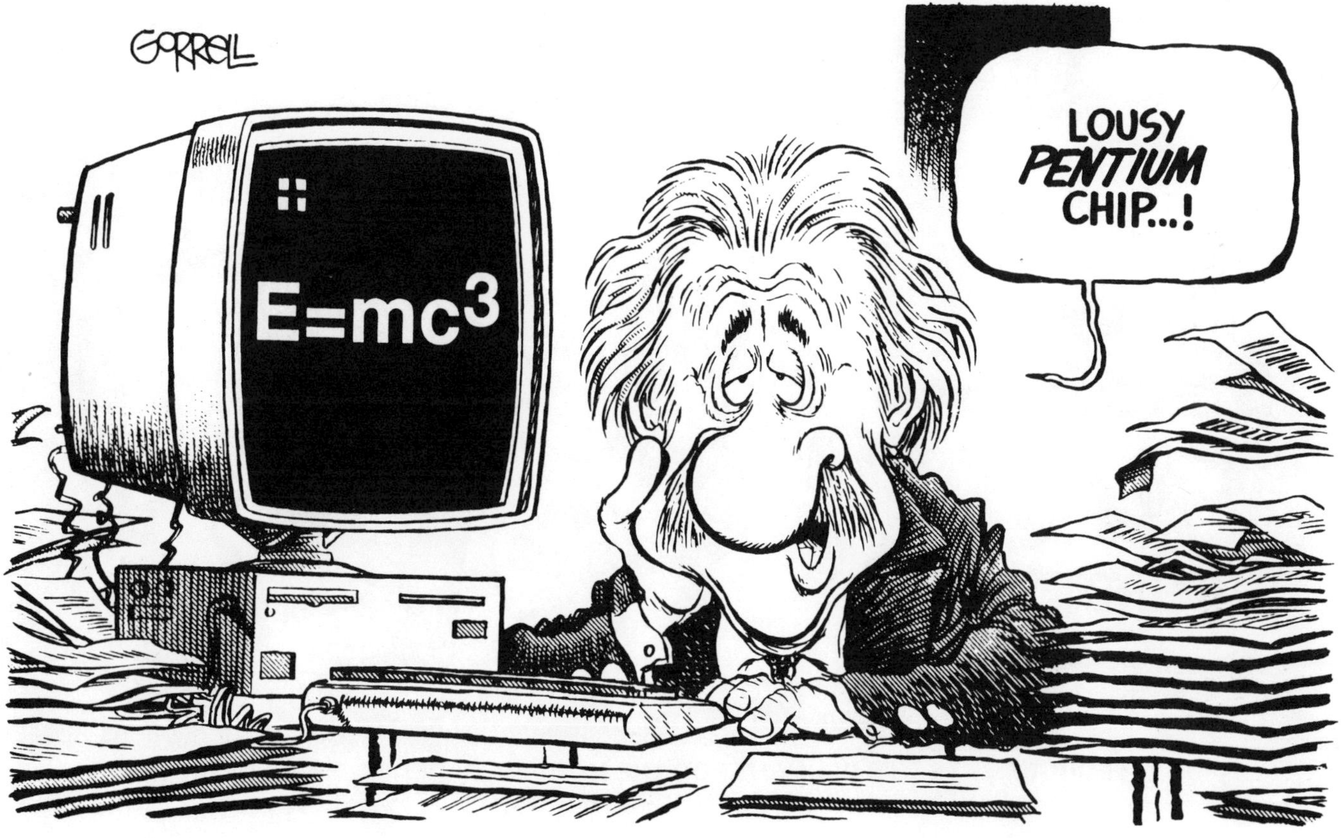
GORRELL
E=mc3
LOUSY PENTIUM CHIP...!

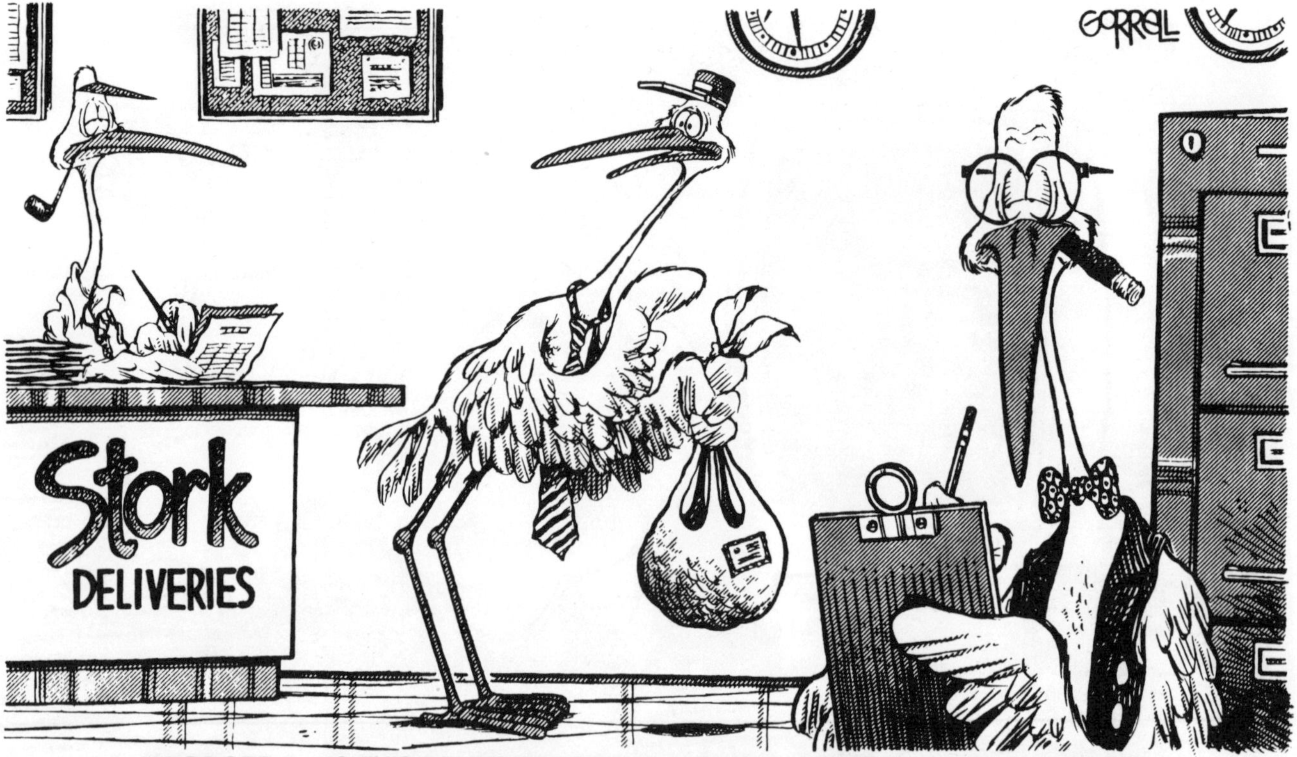
GORRELL
Stork
DELIVERIES

"I FORGET . . . . IS THIS DELIVERY FOR THE NATURAL PARENTS, THE SURROGATE PARENTS, THE ADOPTIVE PARENTS, OR THE ATTORNEYS?!"

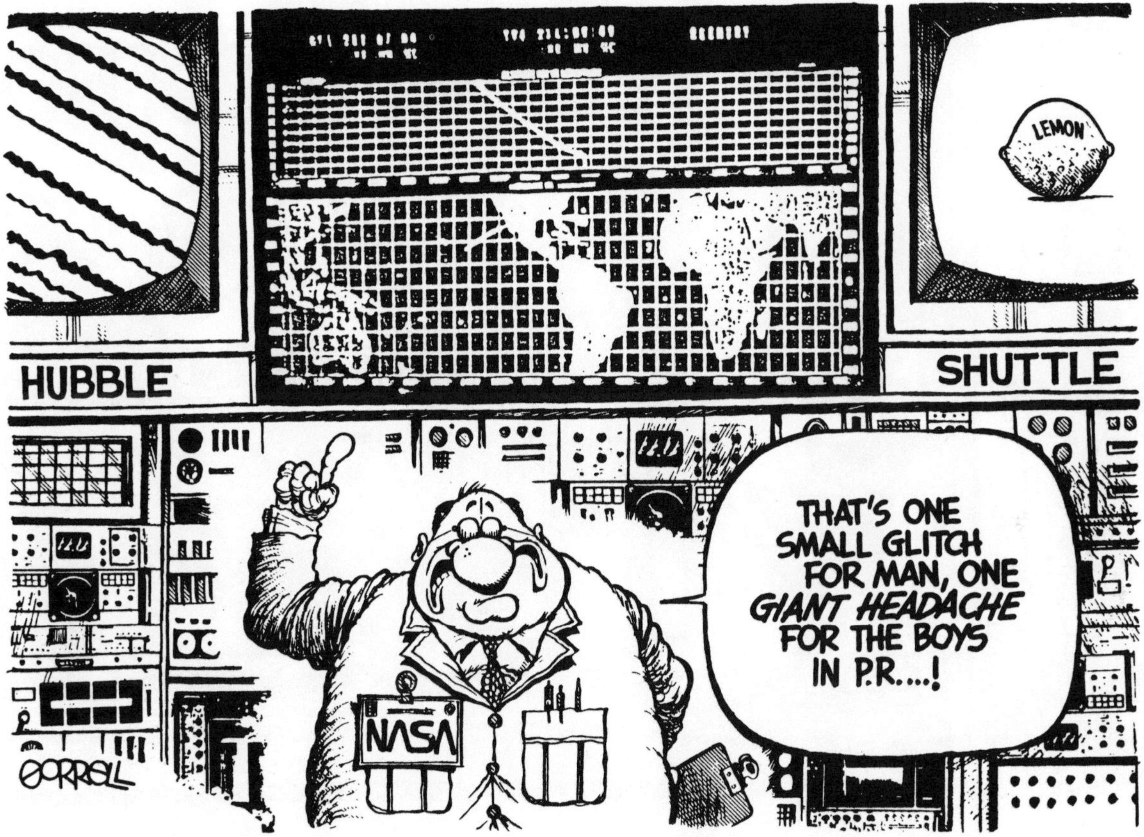

HUBBLE
SHUTTLE
LEMON
NASA
THAT'S ONE SMALL GLITCH FOR MAN, ONE *GIANT HEADACHE* FOR THE BOYS IN P.R....!
GORRELL

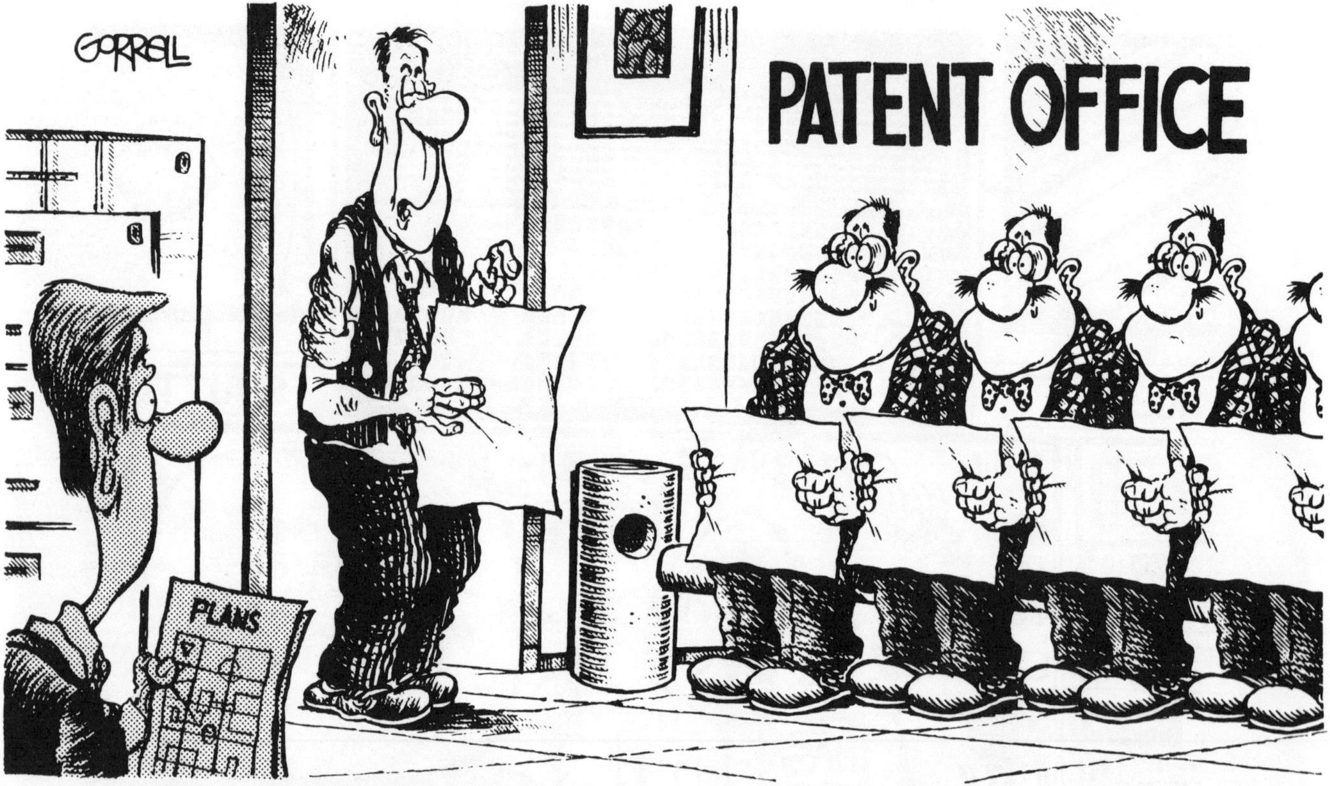
GORRELL
PATENT OFFICE
PLANS

"OKAY . . . . WHO'S THE WISE GUY CLAIMING A NEW BREAKTHROUGH IN HUMAN CLONING?!"

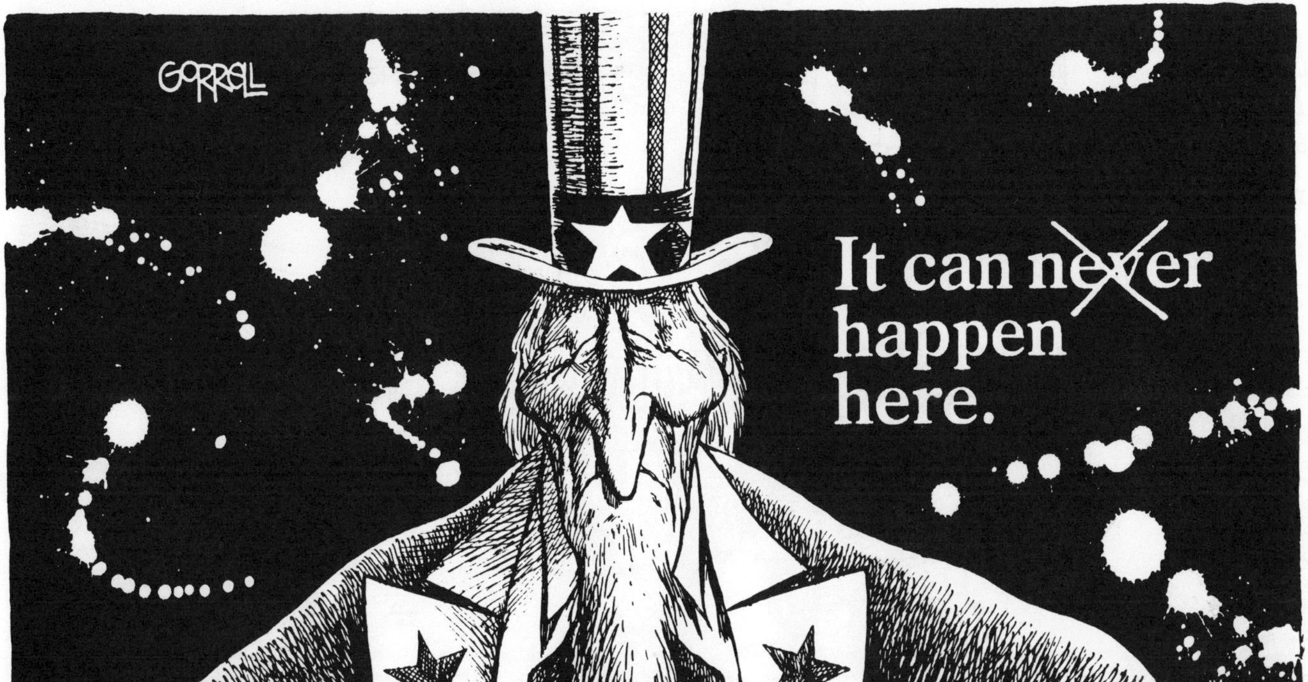
GORRELL
It can never
happen
here.

OKLAHOMA CITY - APRIL 19, 1995

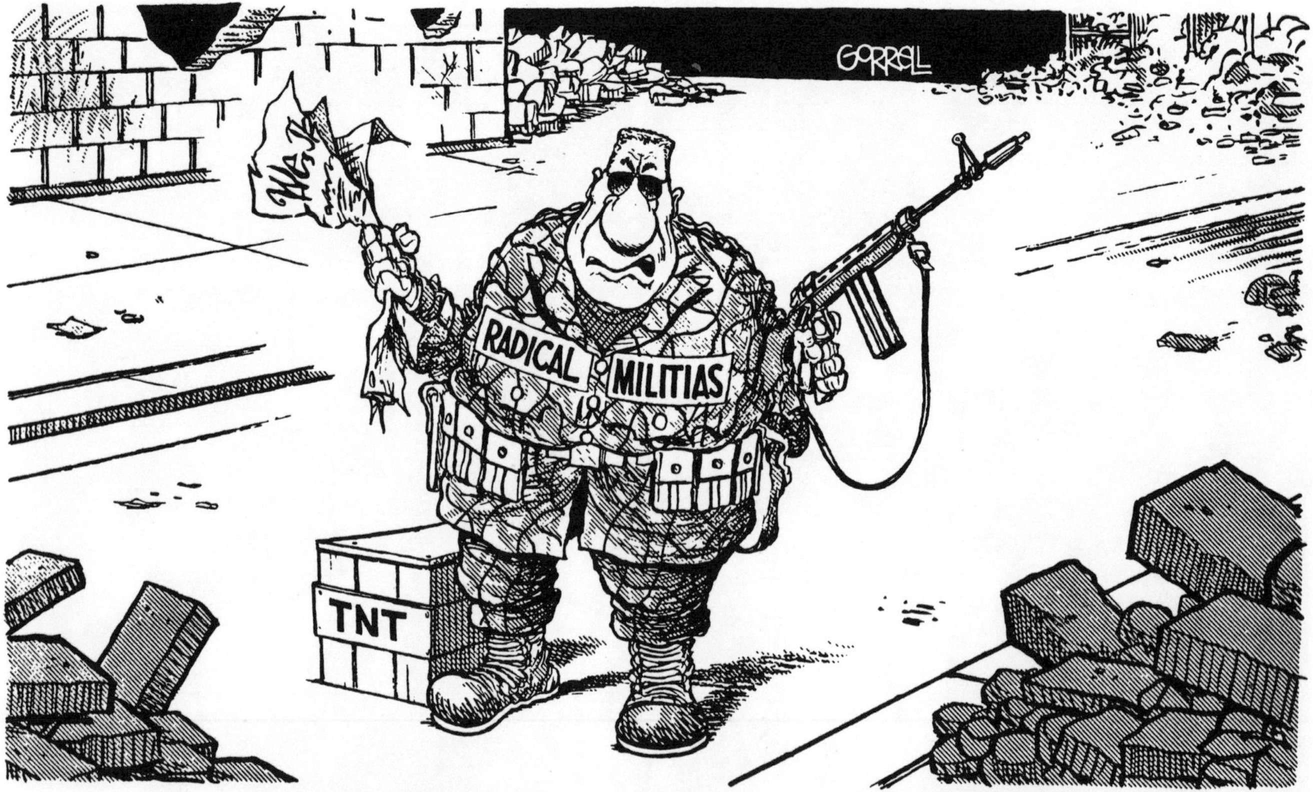
GORRELL
We
RADICAL
MILITIAS
TNT

"WE HAD TO DESTROY THE CONSTITUTION IN ORDER TO SAVE IT!"

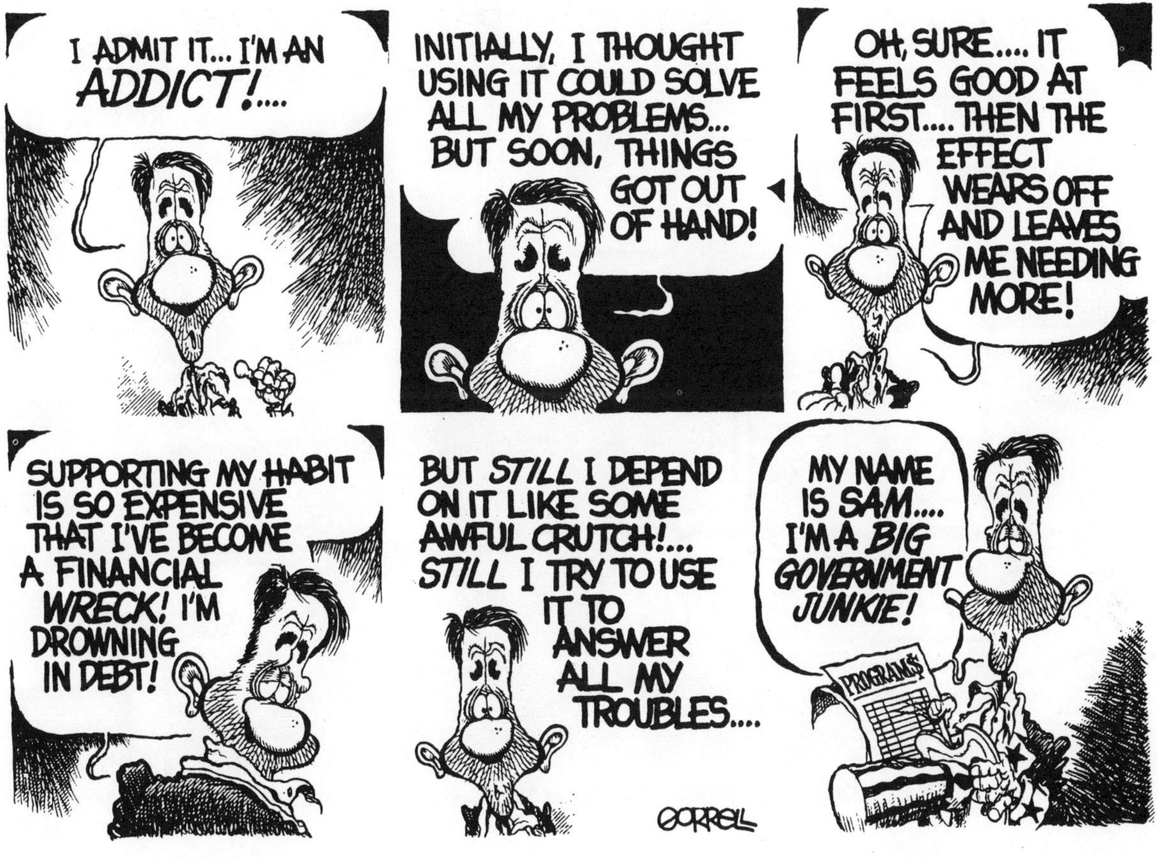
I ADMIT IT... I'M AN ADDICT!....
INITIALLY, I THOUGHT USING IT COULD SOLVE ALL MY PROBLEMS... BUT SOON, THINGS GOT OUT OF HAND!
OH, SURE.... IT FEELS GOOD AT FIRST.... THEN THE EFFECT WEARS OFF AND LEAVES ME NEEDING MORE!
SUPPORTING MY HABIT IS SO EXPENSIVE THAT I'VE BECOME A FINANCIAL WRECK! I'M DROWNING IN DEBT!
BUT STILL I DEPEND ON IT LIKE SOME AWFUL CRUTCH!... STILL I TRY TO USE IT TO ANSWER ALL MY TROUBLES....
MY NAME IS SAM.... I'M A BIG GOVERNMENT JUNKIE!
PROGRAM$
GORRELL

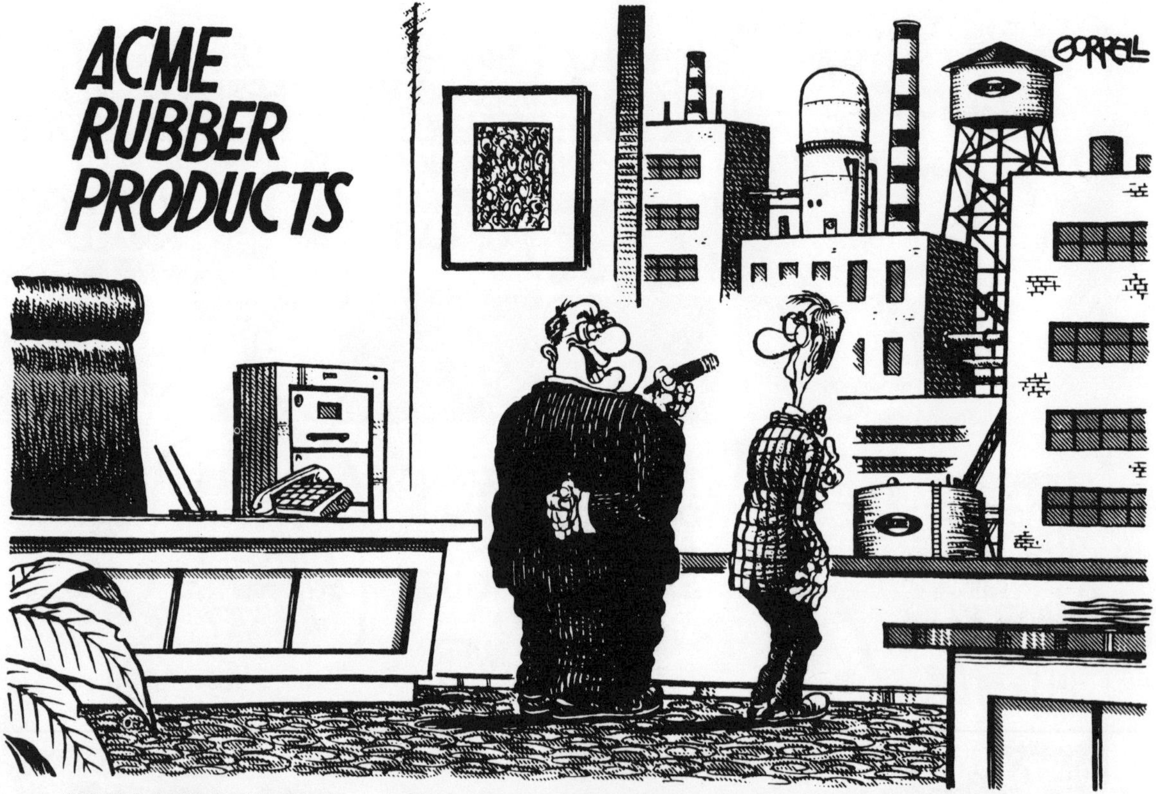
ACME
RUBBER
PRODUCTS
GORRELL

"TIRES AND CONDOMS? . . . HECK NO! WE MAKE *CHECKBOOKS FOR CONGRESSMEN!*"

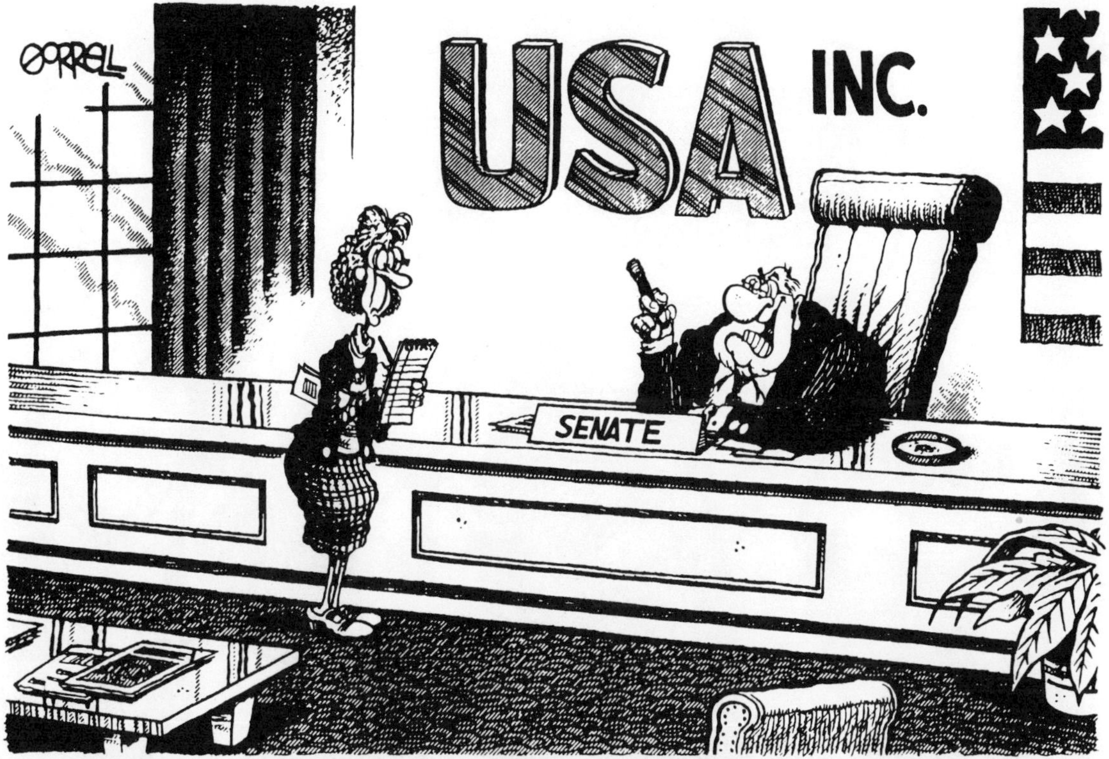
SORRELL
USA INC.
SENATE

"REVISE THOSE DEFICIT FIGURES UPWARD, REDUCE OUR REVENUE PROJECTIONS, FILE FOR BANKRUPTCY, AND — OH, YEAH — PROCESS THAT *PAY-RAISE* I VOTED MYSELF . . . !"

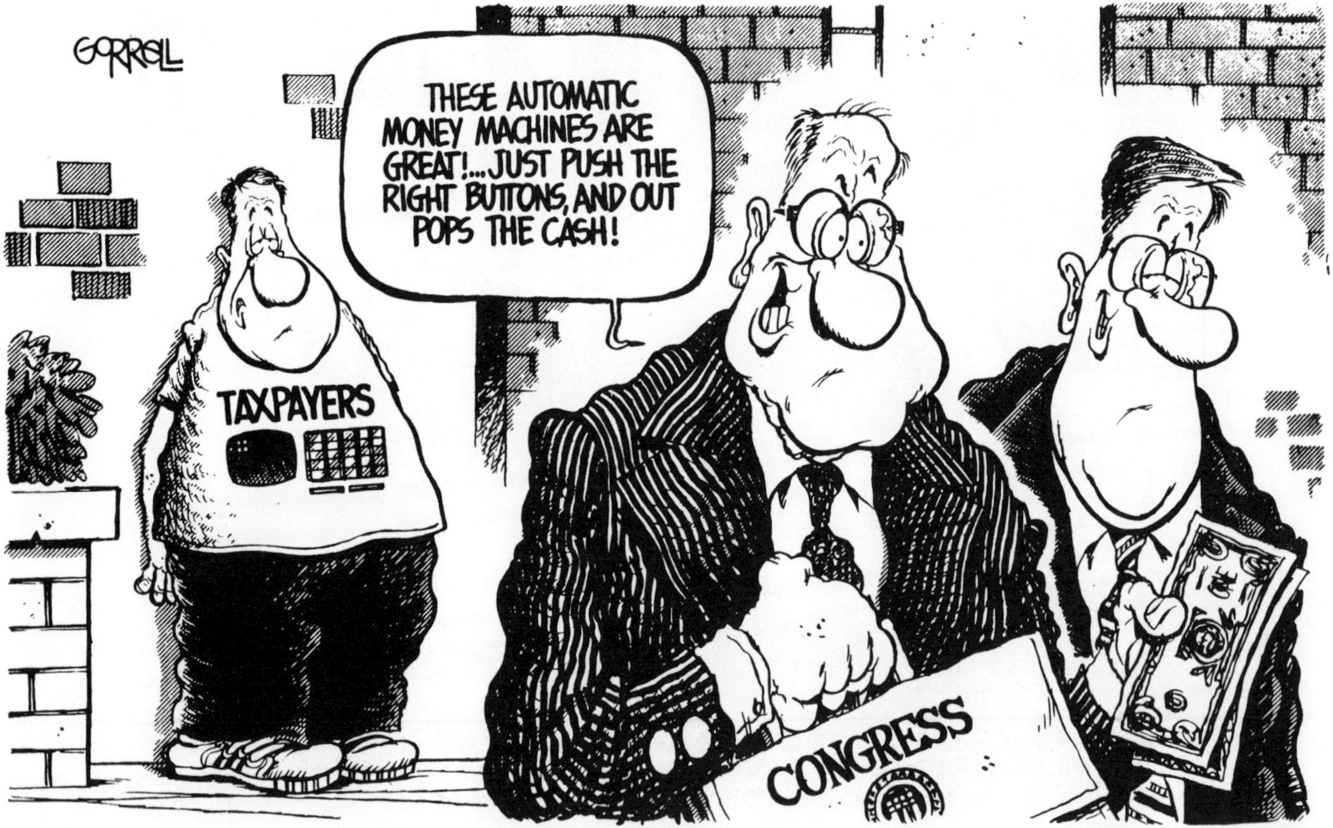
GORRELL
THESE AUTOMATIC MONEY MACHINES ARE GREAT!...JUST PUSH THE RIGHT BUTTONS, AND OUT POPS THE CASH!
TAXPAYERS
CONGRESS

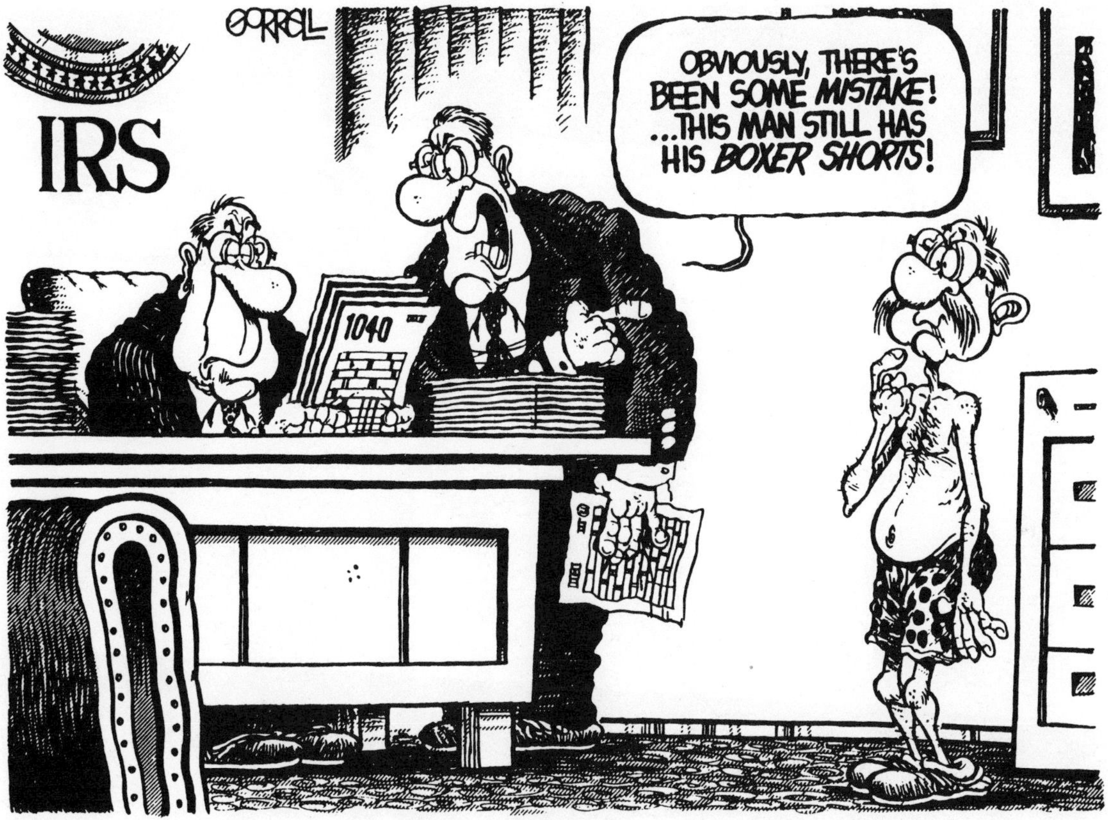
GORRELL
IRS
OBVIOUSLY, THERE'S BEEN SOME *MISTAKE*! ...THIS MAN STILL HAS HIS *BOXER SHORTS*!
1040

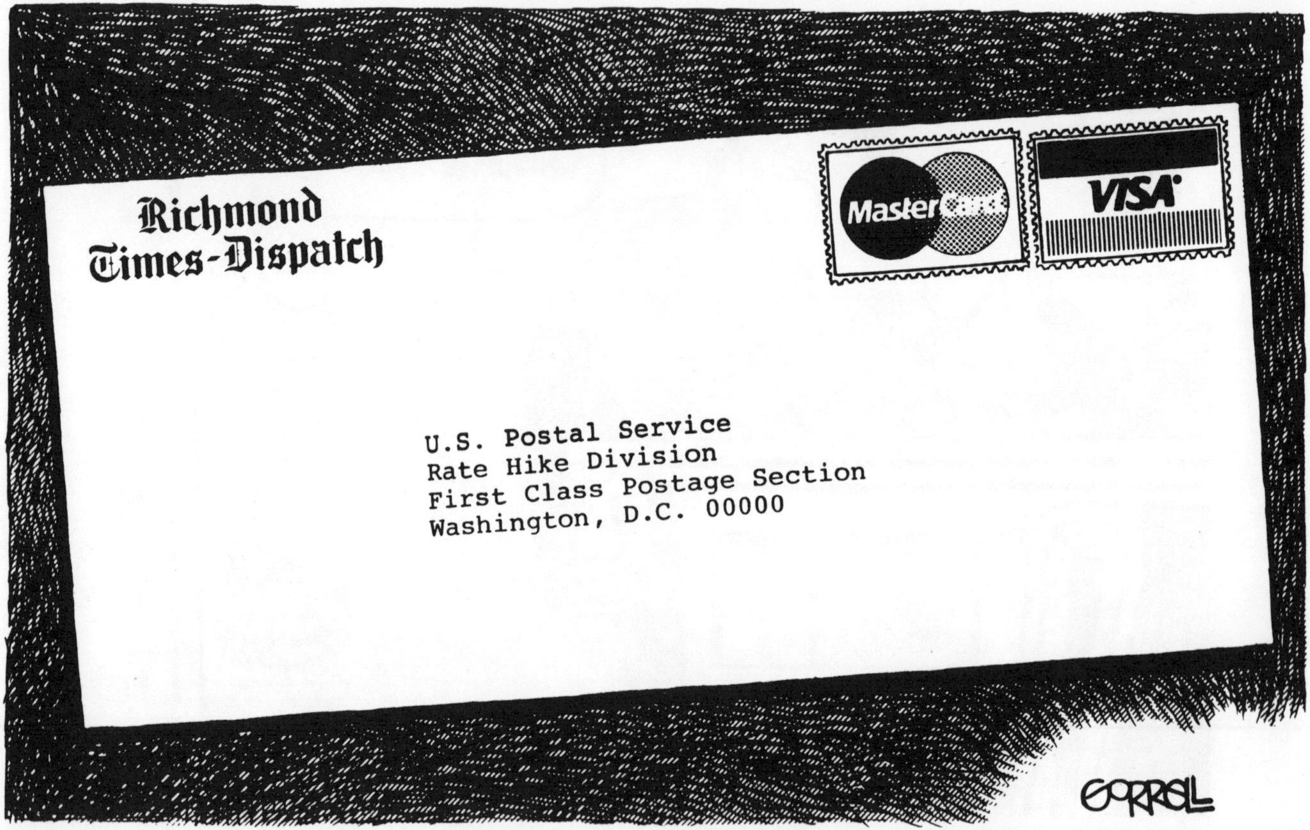
Richmond Times-Dispatch
MasterCard
VISA
U.S. Postal Service
Rate Hike Division
First Class Postage Section
Washington, D.C. 00000
GORRELL

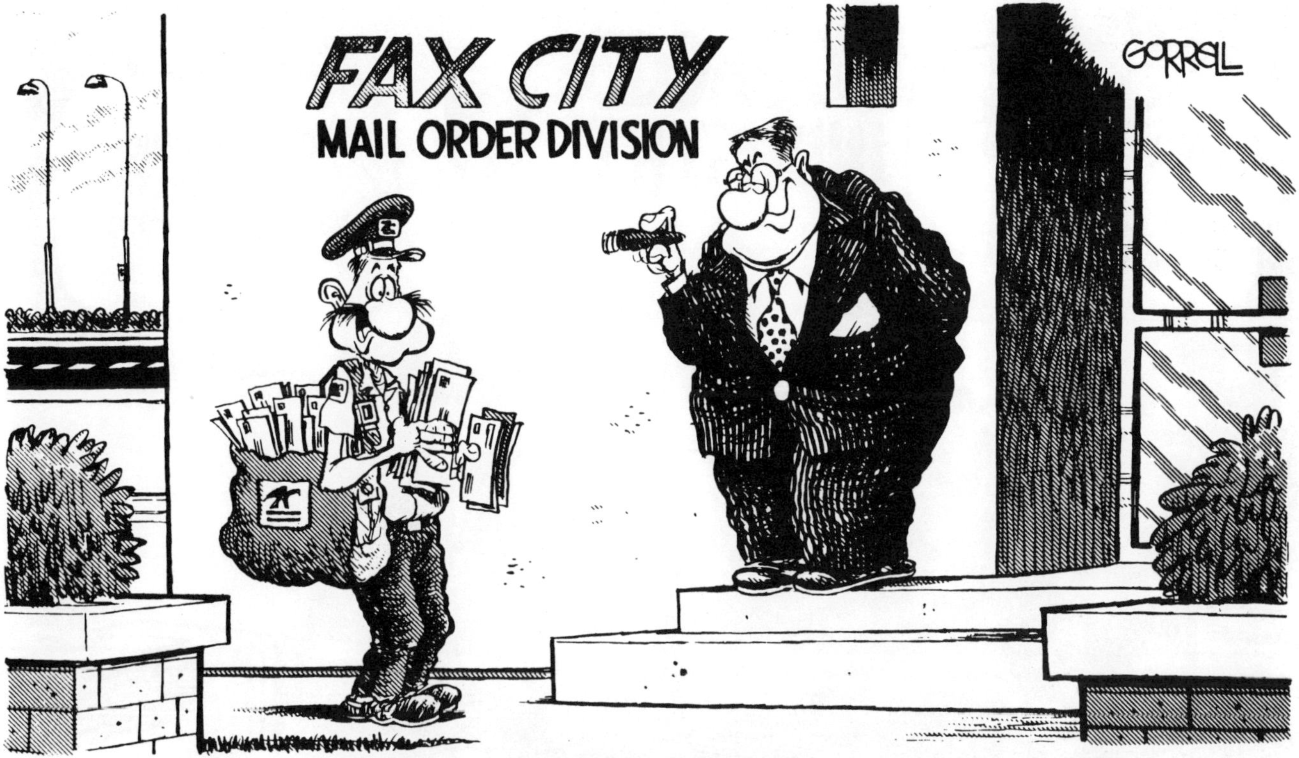
FAX CITY
MAIL ORDER DIVISION
GORRELL

"STRANGE . . . . EVER SINCE WE INCREASED POSTAGE RATES AGAIN, THIS ADDRESS SURE GETS A LOT MORE MAIL!"

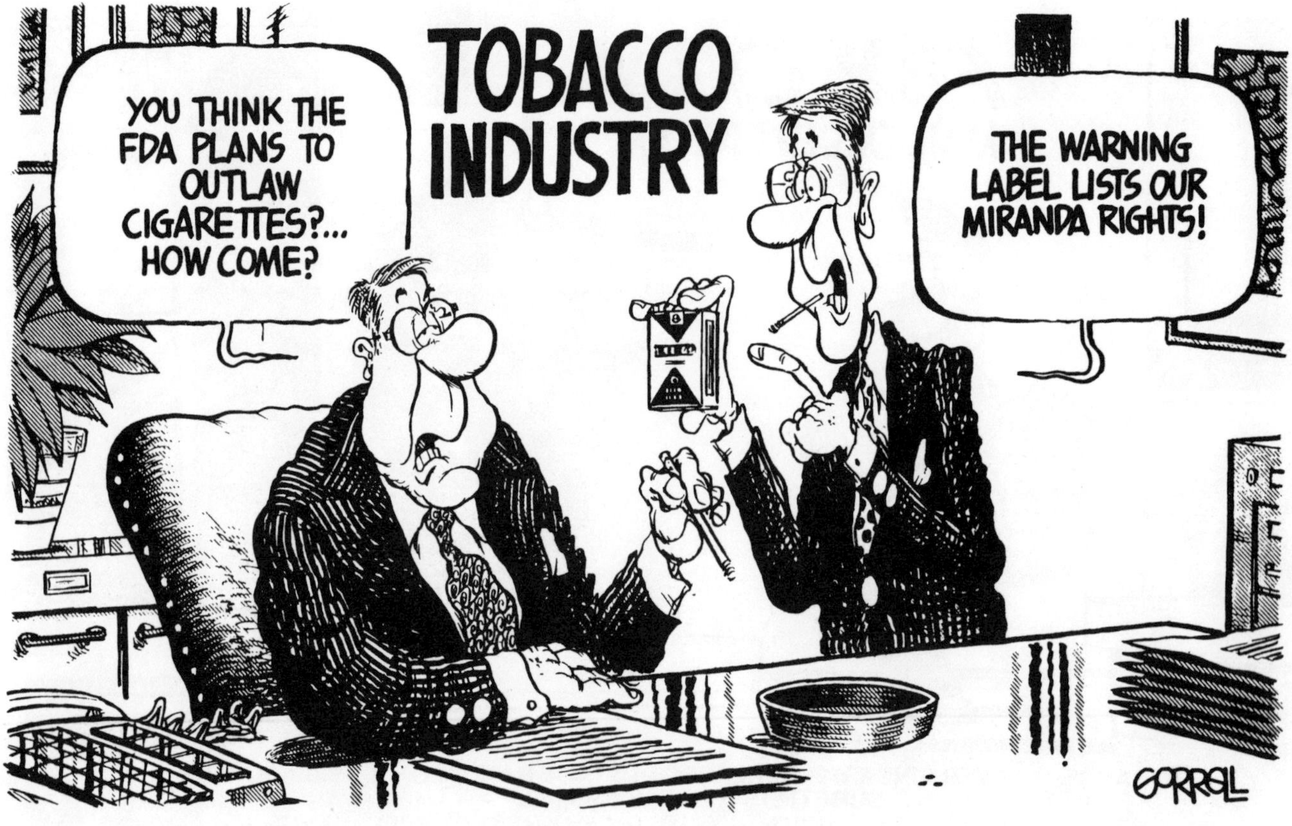
TOBACCO INDUSTRY
YOU THINK THE FDA PLANS TO OUTLAW CIGARETTES?... HOW COME?
THE WARNING LABEL LISTS OUR MIRANDA RIGHTS!
GORRELL

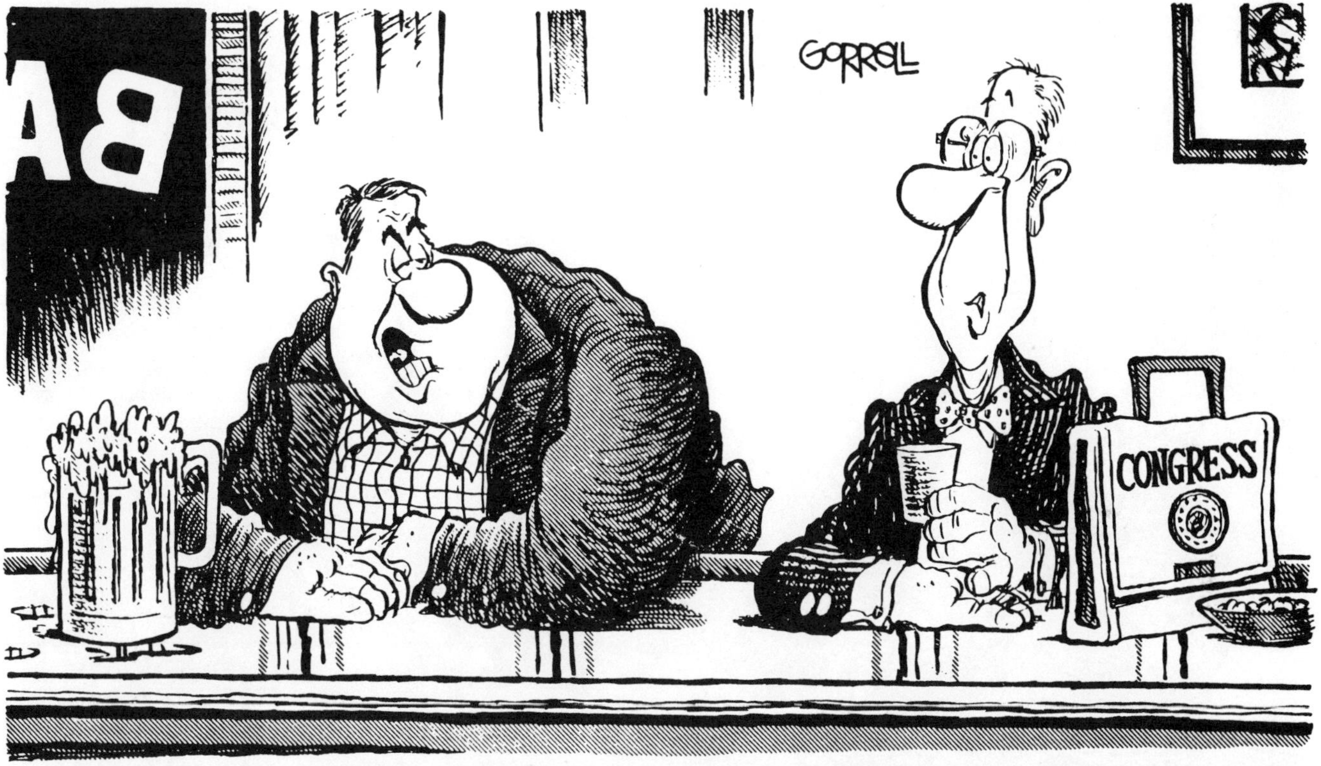
GORRELL
CONGRESS

"YOU WANNA TALK UNFUNDED MANDATES? . . . A SECOND MORTGAGE, TWO CAR PAYMENTS, AND THREE KIDS WITH BRACES. . . . NOW *THOSE* ARE UNFUNDED MANDATES!"

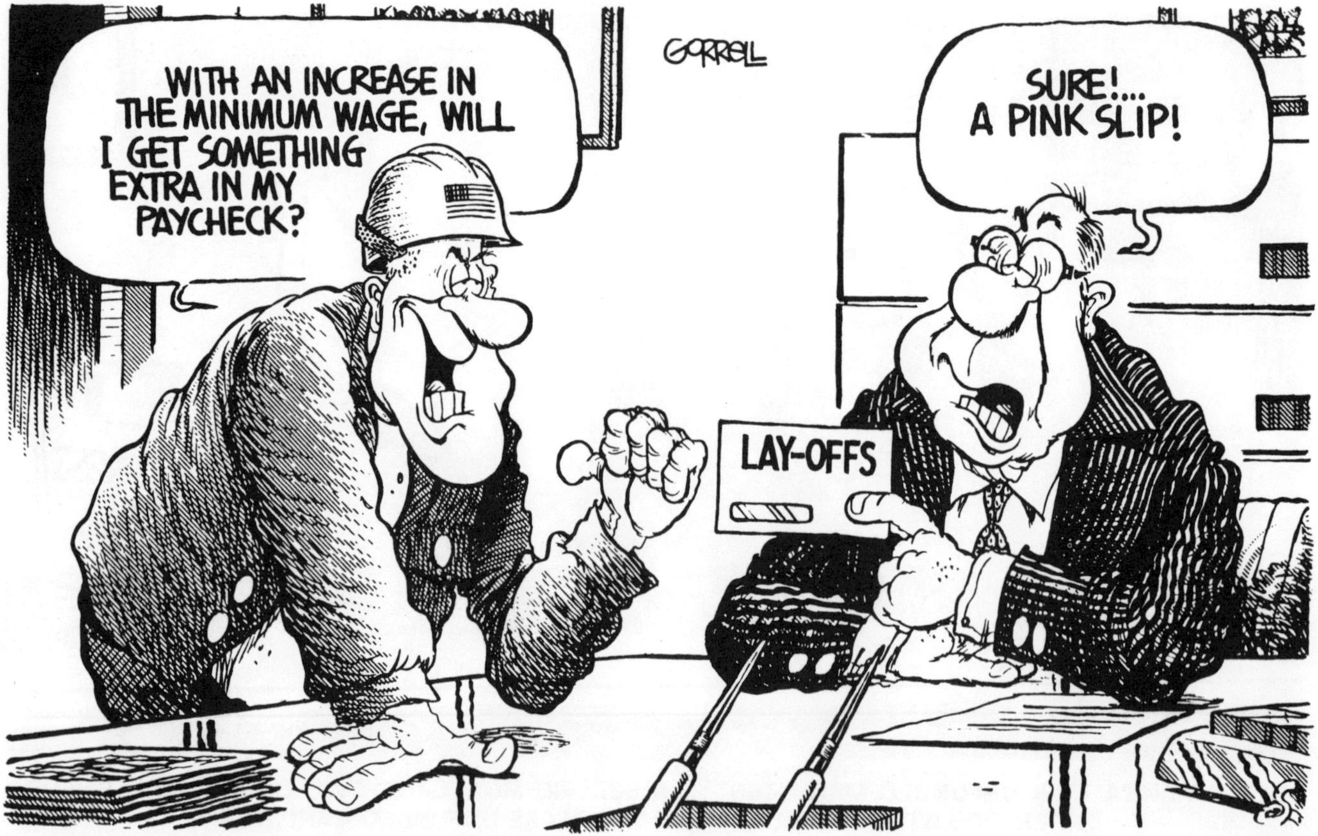
GORRELL
WITH AN INCREASE IN THE MINIMUM WAGE, WILL I GET SOMETHING EXTRA IN MY PAYCHECK?
SURE!... A PINK SLIP!
LAY-OFFS

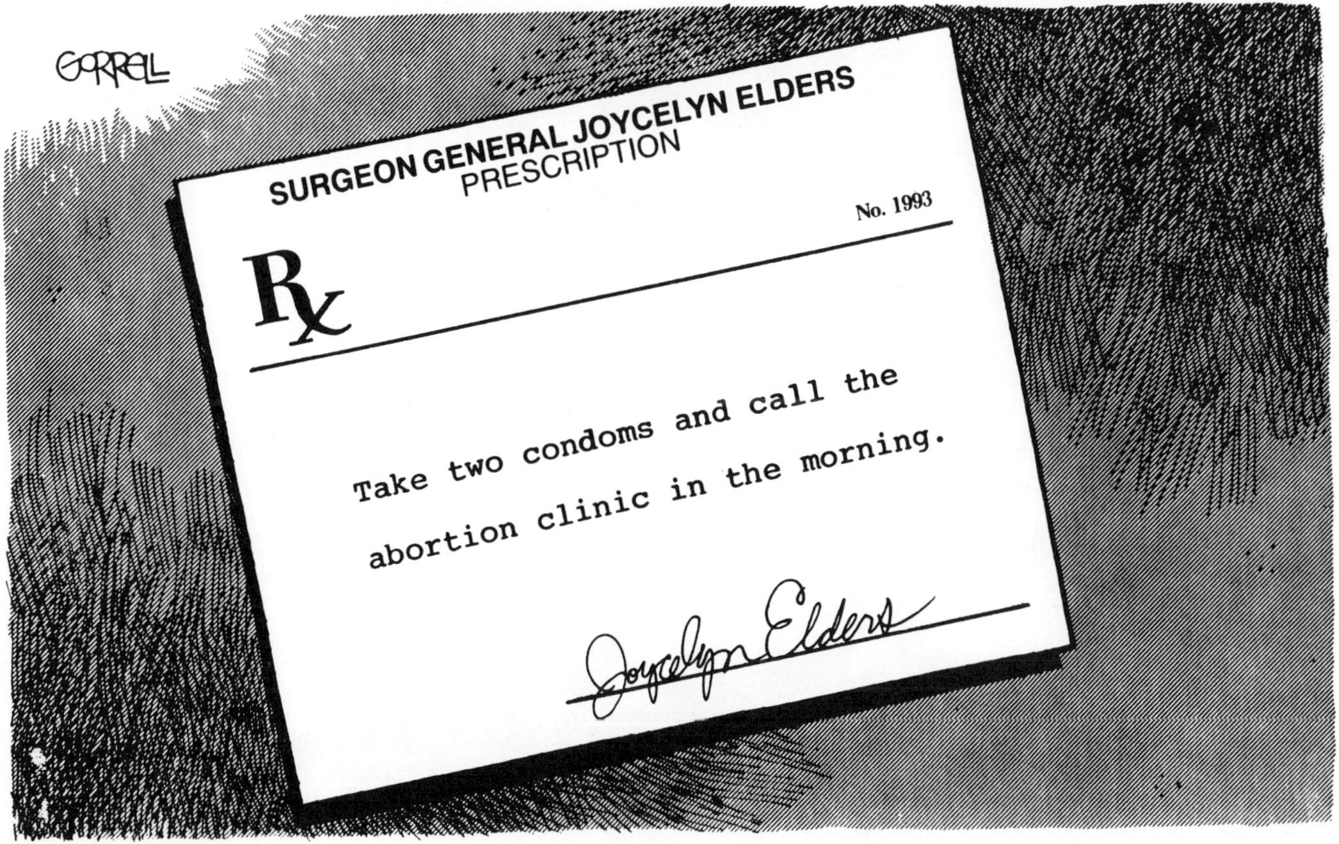
GORRELL
SURGEON GENERAL JOYCELYN ELDERS
PRESCRIPTION
No. 1993
Rx
Take two condoms and call the
abortion clinic in the morning.
Joycelyn Elders

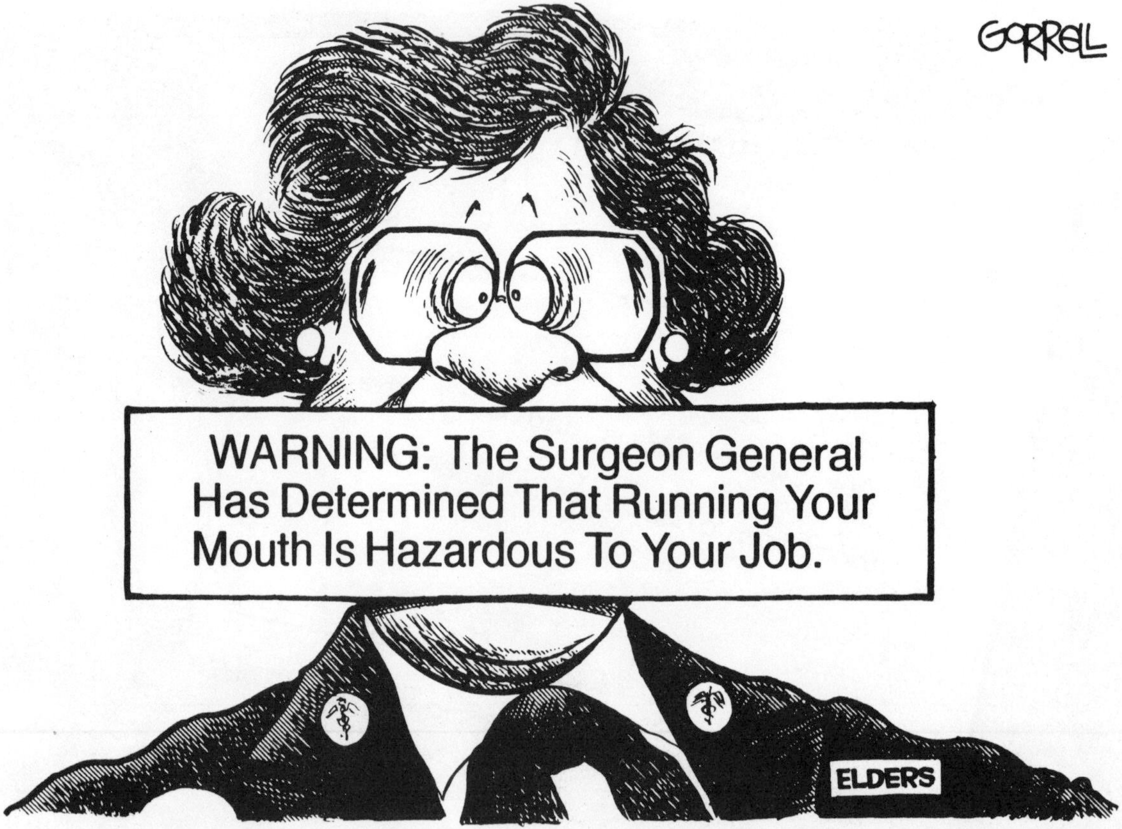
GORRELL
WARNING: The Surgeon General Has Determined That Running Your Mouth Is Hazardous To Your Job.
ELDERS

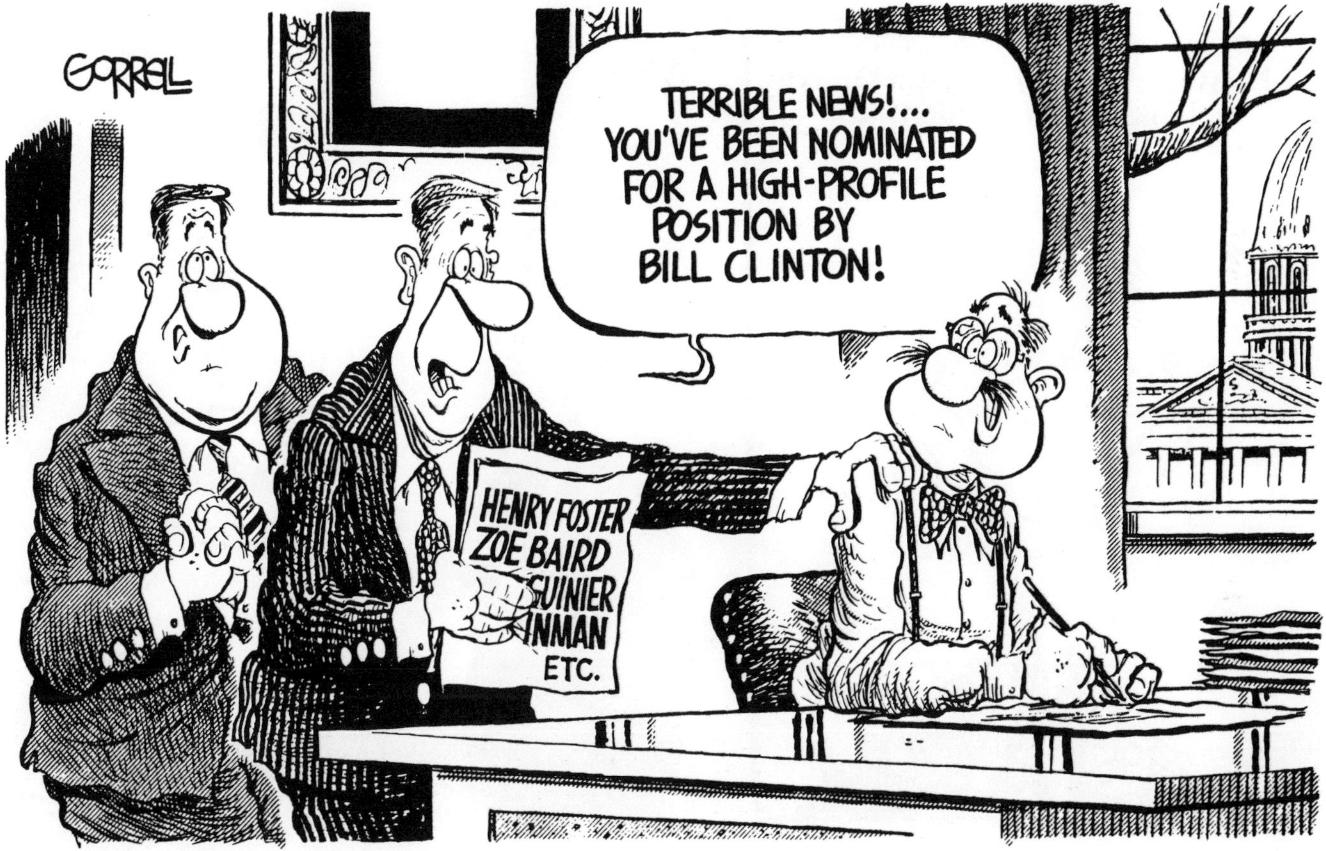
GORRELL
TERRIBLE NEWS!... YOU'VE BEEN NOMINATED FOR A HIGH-PROFILE POSITION BY BILL CLINTON!
HENRY FOSTER
ZOE BAIRD
GUINIER
INMAN
ETC.

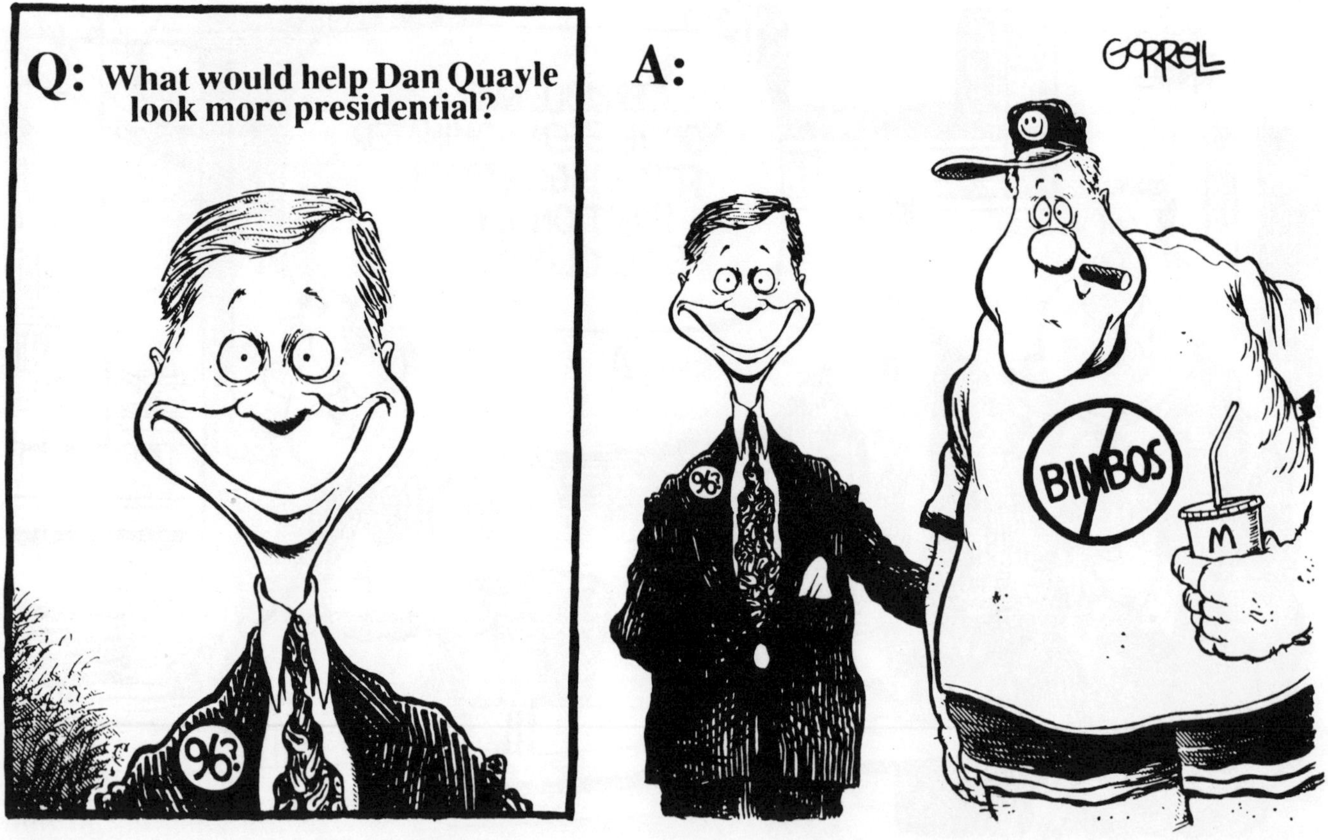
Q: What would help Dan Quayle look more presidential?
A:
GORRELL
96?
BIMBOS
M

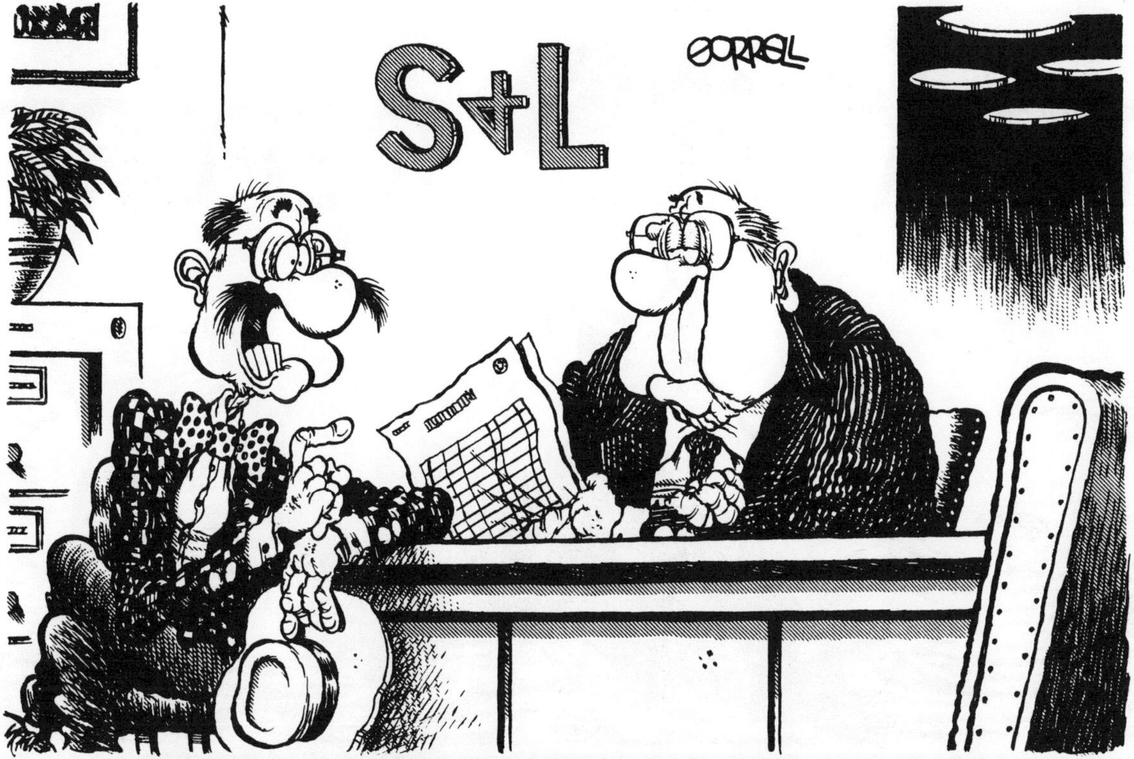
S+L
SORRELL

"I NEED TO BORROW SOME MONEY TO BAIL OUT MY BANK SO I CAN CASH A CHECK TO BAIL OUT YOUR SAVINGS AND LOAN . . . !"

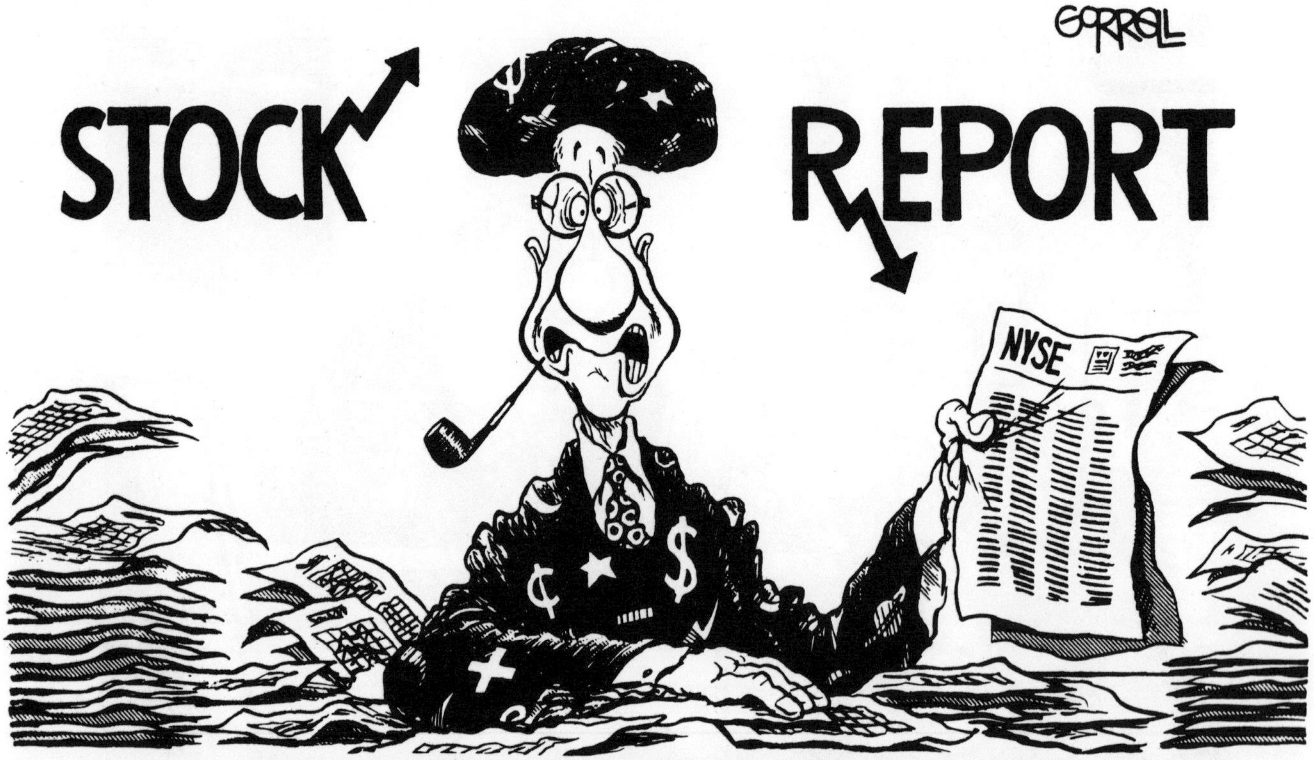
GORRELL
STOCK
REPORT
NYSE

"THE OUIJA BOARD INDICATES A BEAR MARKET, WHILE TEA LEAVES POINT TO A RECORD HIGH DOW AND TAROT CARDS SHOW HEAVY VOLUME IN MIXED TRADING . . . !"

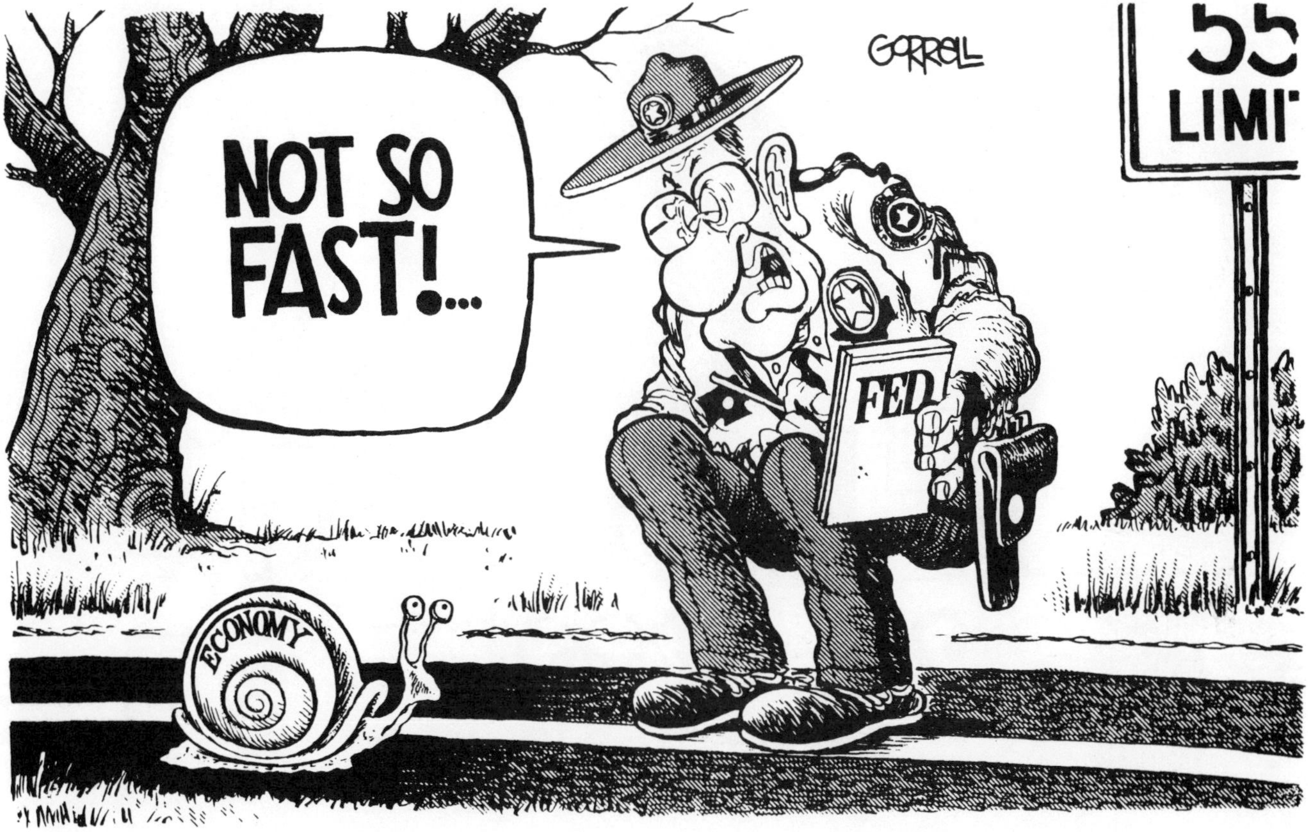
GORRELL
NOT SO FAST!...
55
LIMI
FED
ECONOMY

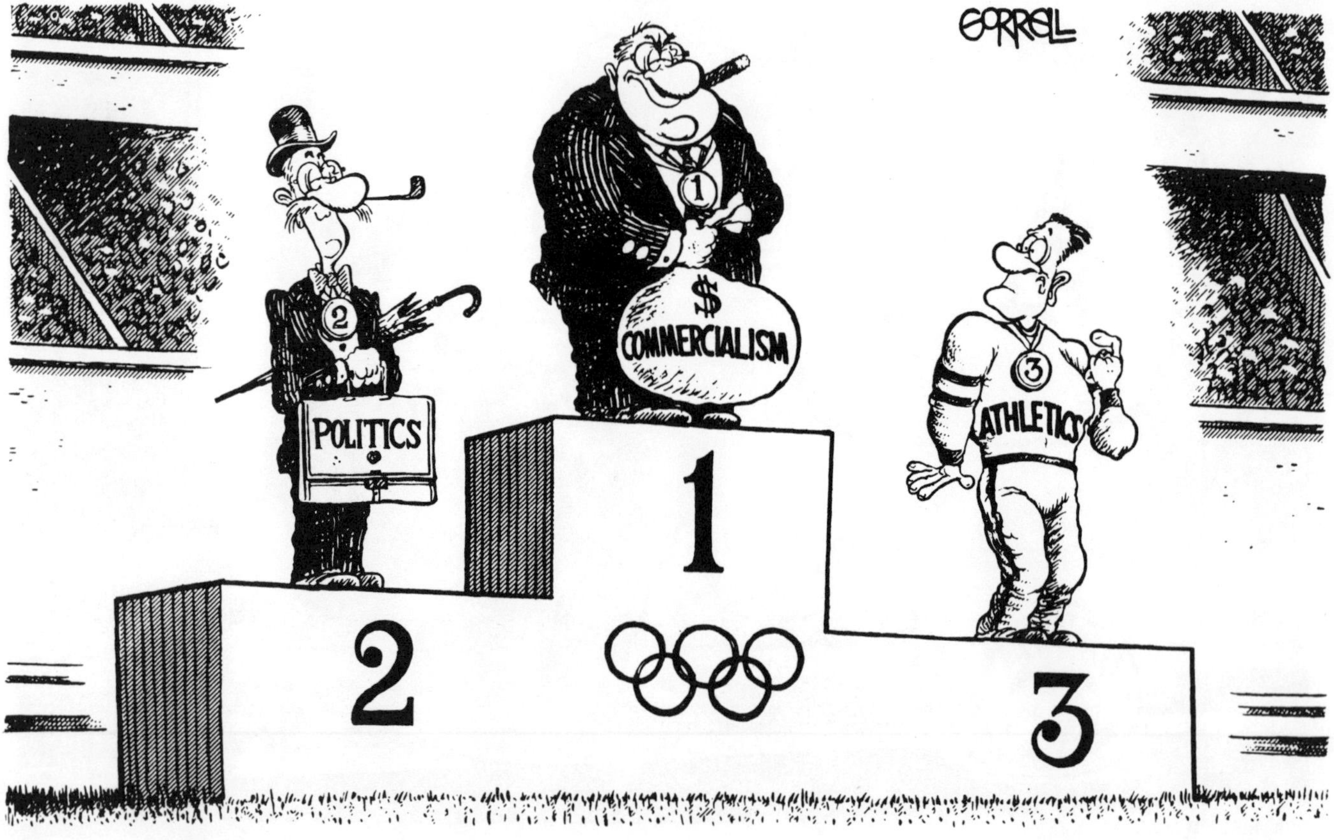
GORRELL
POLITICS
2
$
COMMERCIALISM
1
ATHLETICS
3
1
2
3

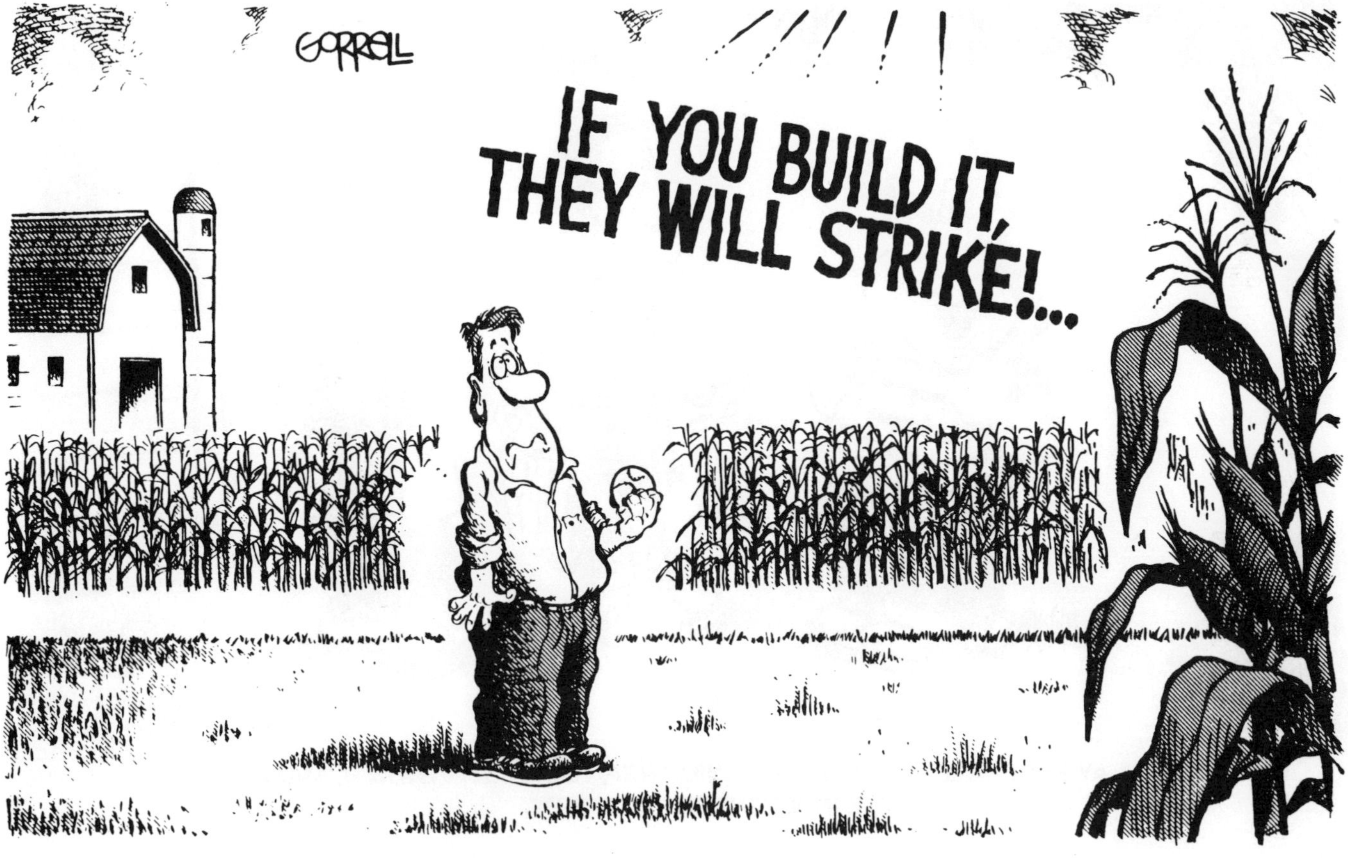
GORRELL
IF YOU BUILD IT, THEY WILL STRIKE!...

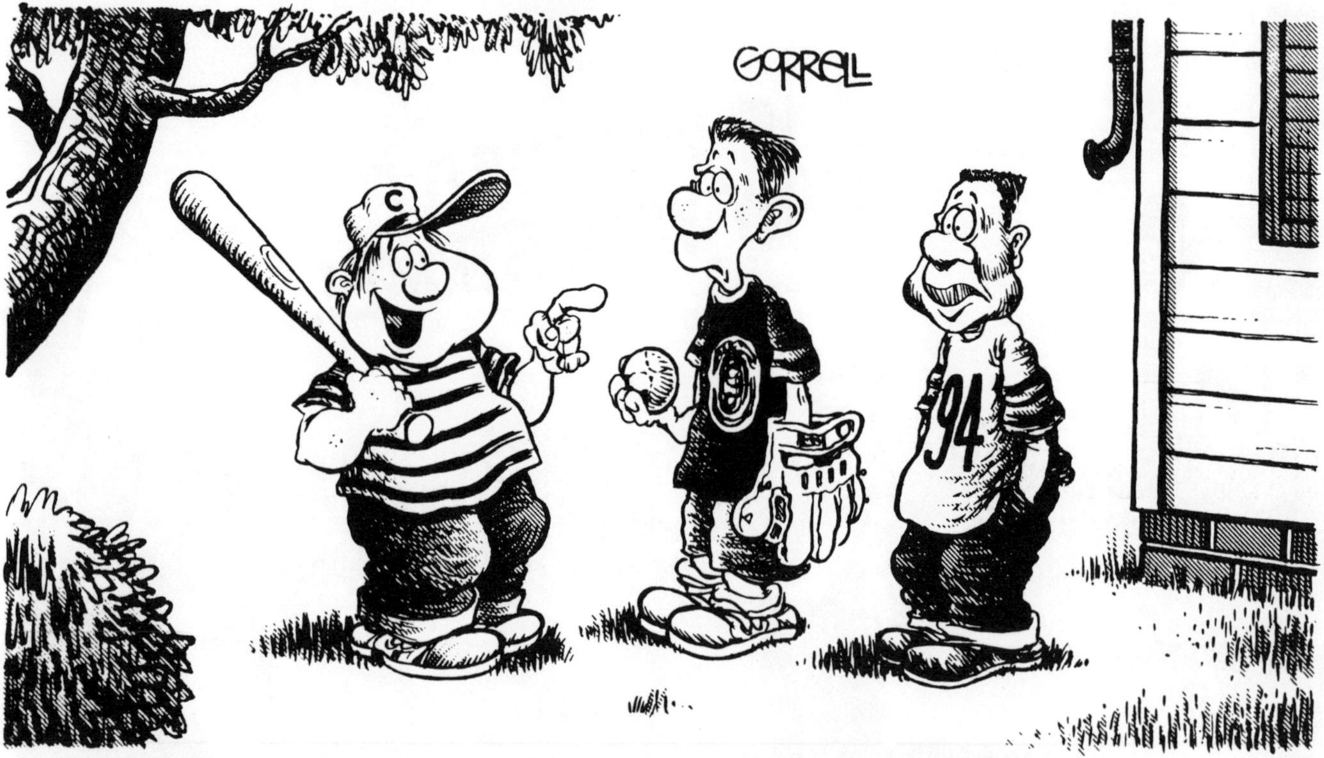
GORRELL
C
94

"LET'S PLAY BASEBALL!... I'LL BE THE UNION REP, YOU BE THE OWNER, AND BILLY IS THE INDEPENDENT ARBITER!"

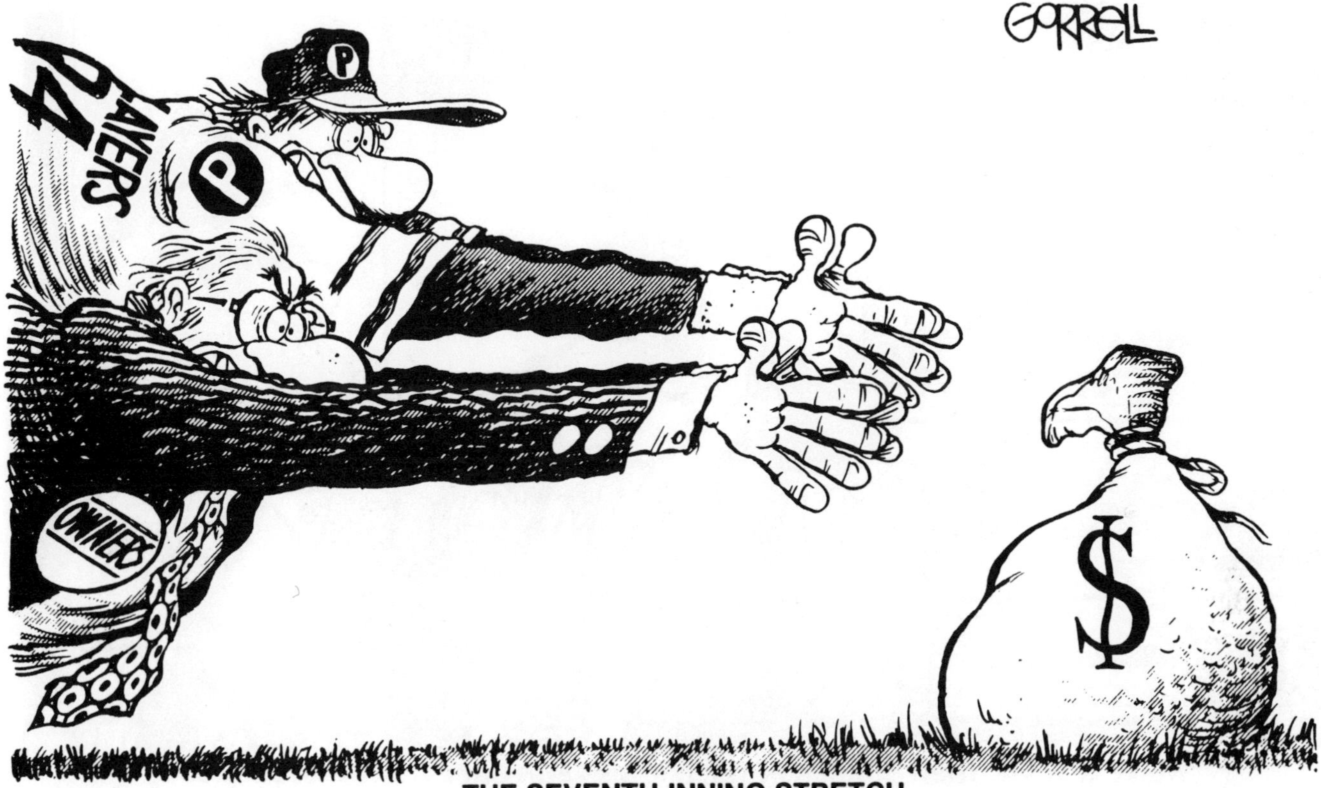
GORRELL
24
PLAYERS
P
P
OWNERS
$

THE SEVENTH-INNING STRETCH

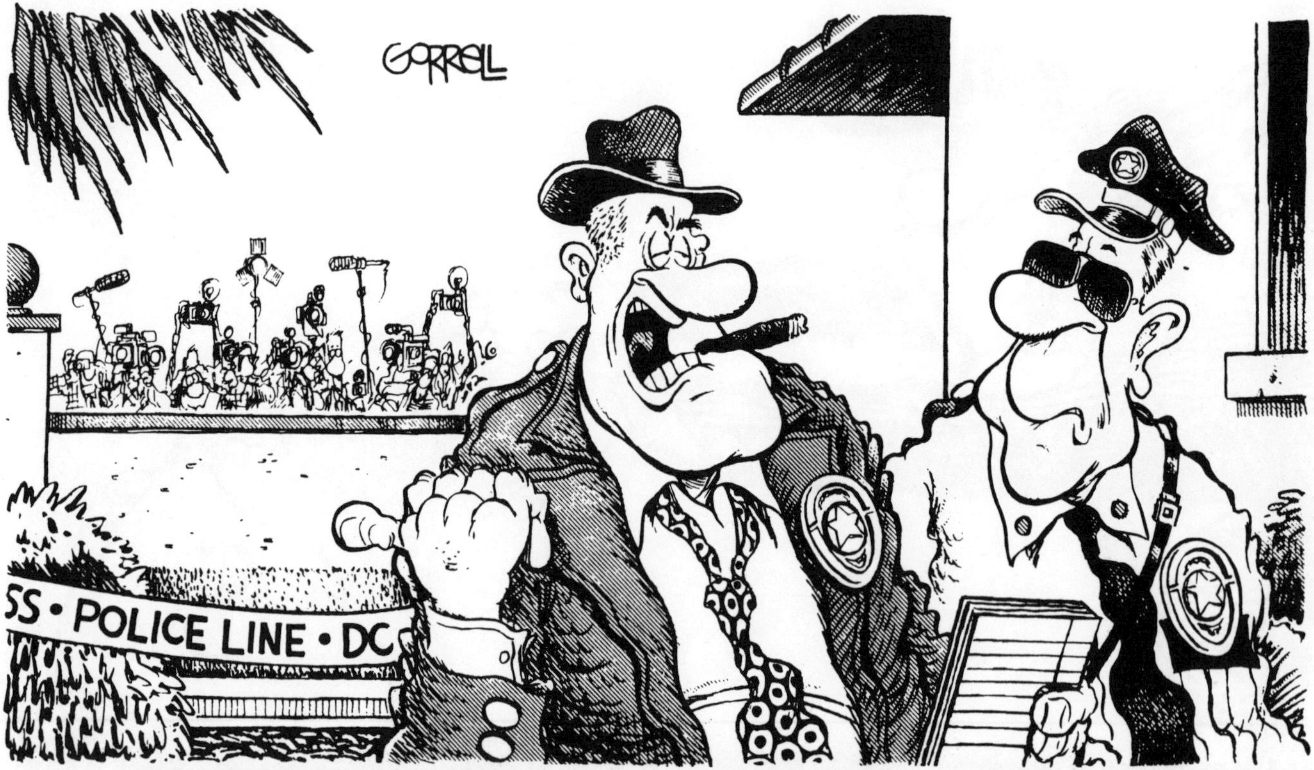
GORRELL
SS • POLICE LINE • DC

"WE'VE GOT ANOTHER MURDER IN THE O.J. SIMPSON CASE.... THE MEDIA'S JUST BEATEN THIS STORY TO DEATH!"

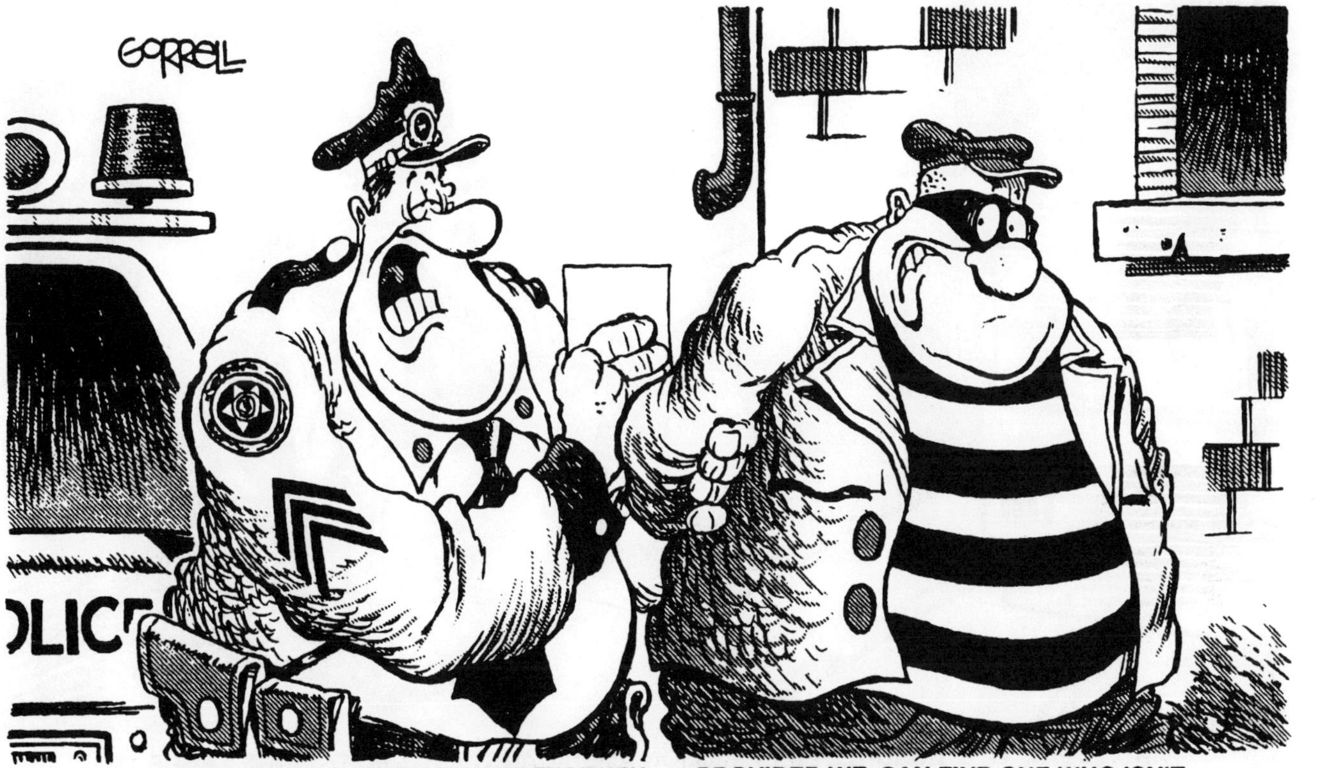
GORRELL
OLICE

"YOU HAVE THE RIGHT TO AN ATTORNEY . . . . PROVIDED WE CAN FIND ONE WHO ISN'T BUSY ON THE O.J. SIMPSON DEFENSE TEAM!"

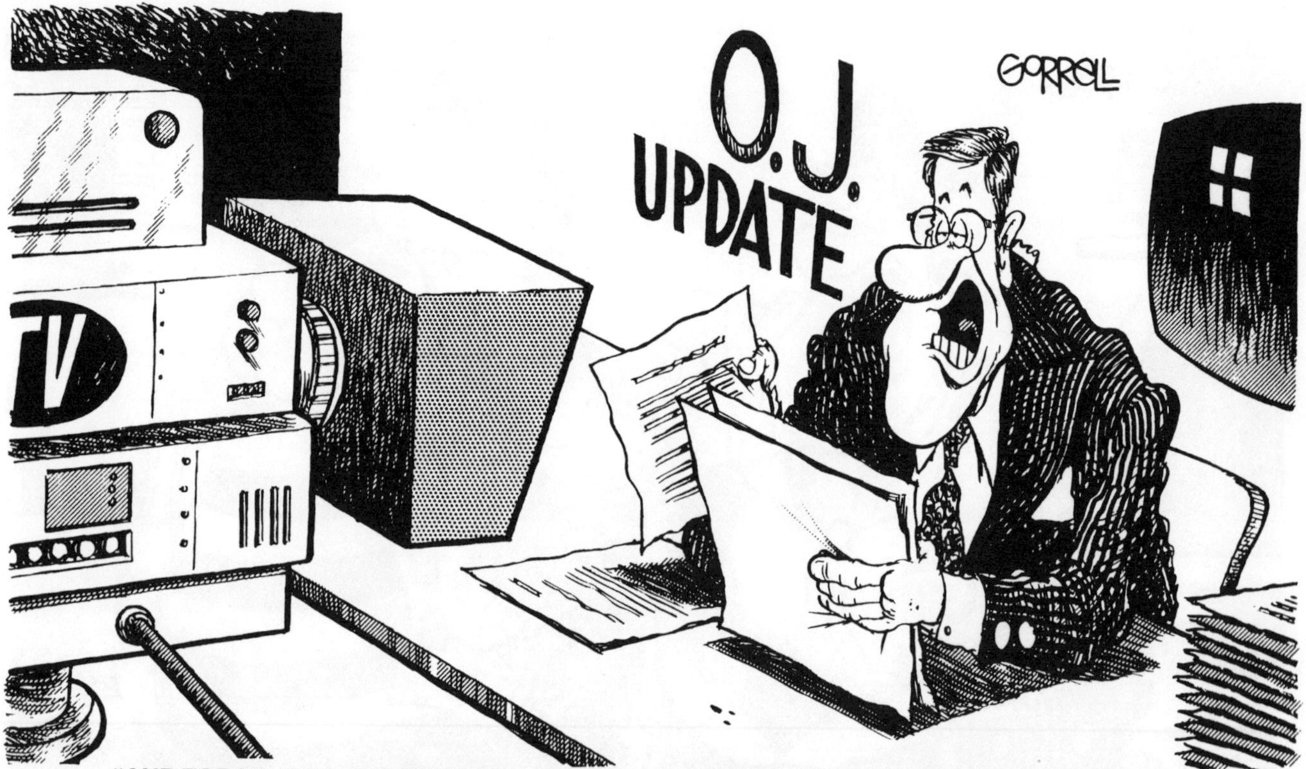
O.J.
UPDATE
GORRELL
TV

"AND TODAY, TWO HUNDRED FIFTY MILLION AMERICANS PETITIONED JUDGE LANCE ITO TO SEQUESTER THEM FROM ANY FURTHER EXPOSURE TO THE O.J. SIMPSON TRIAL!"

Foreign Matters

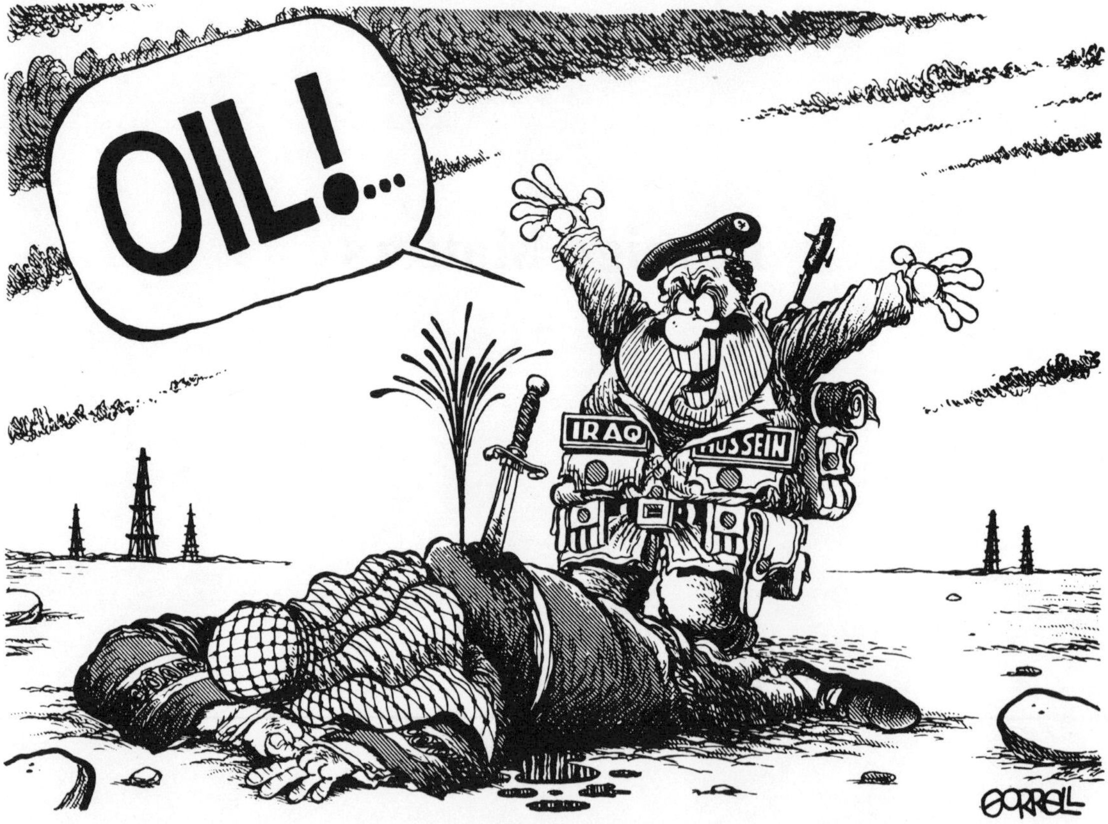
OIL!...
IRAQ
HUSSEIN
GORRELL

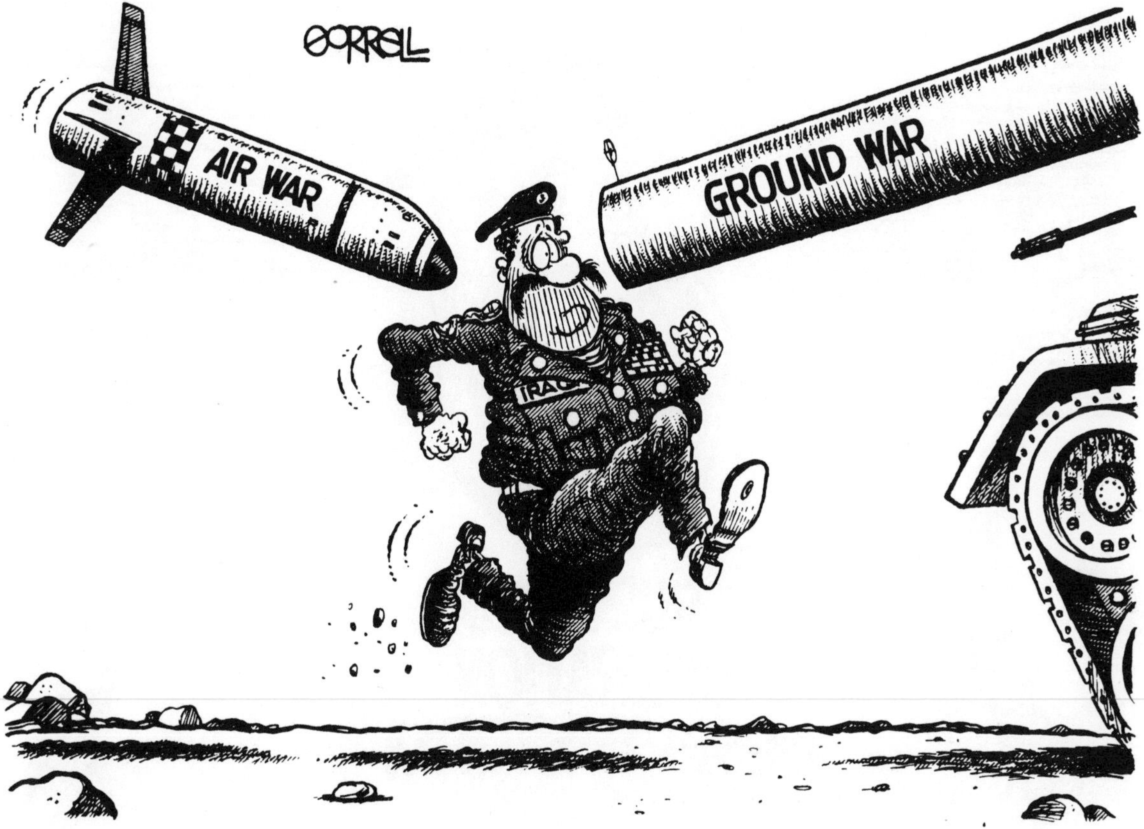
GORRELL
AIR WAR
GROUND WAR
IRAQ

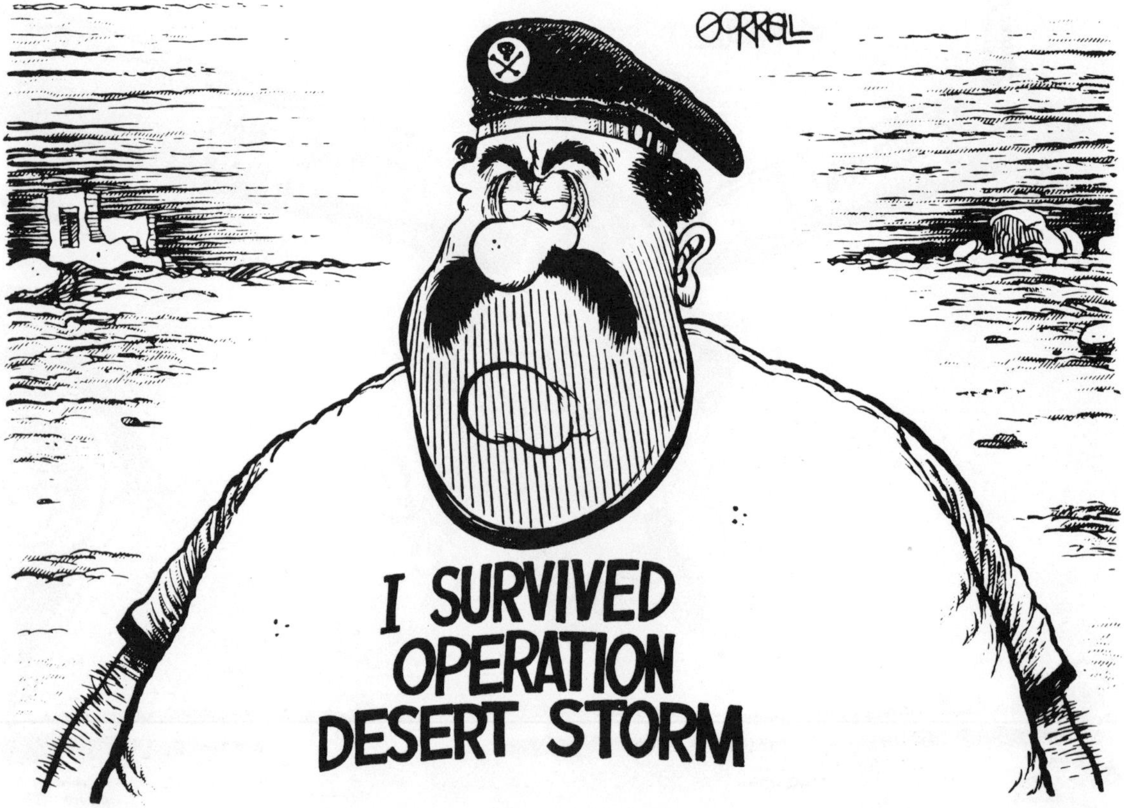
GORRELL
I SURVIVED OPERATION DESERT STORM

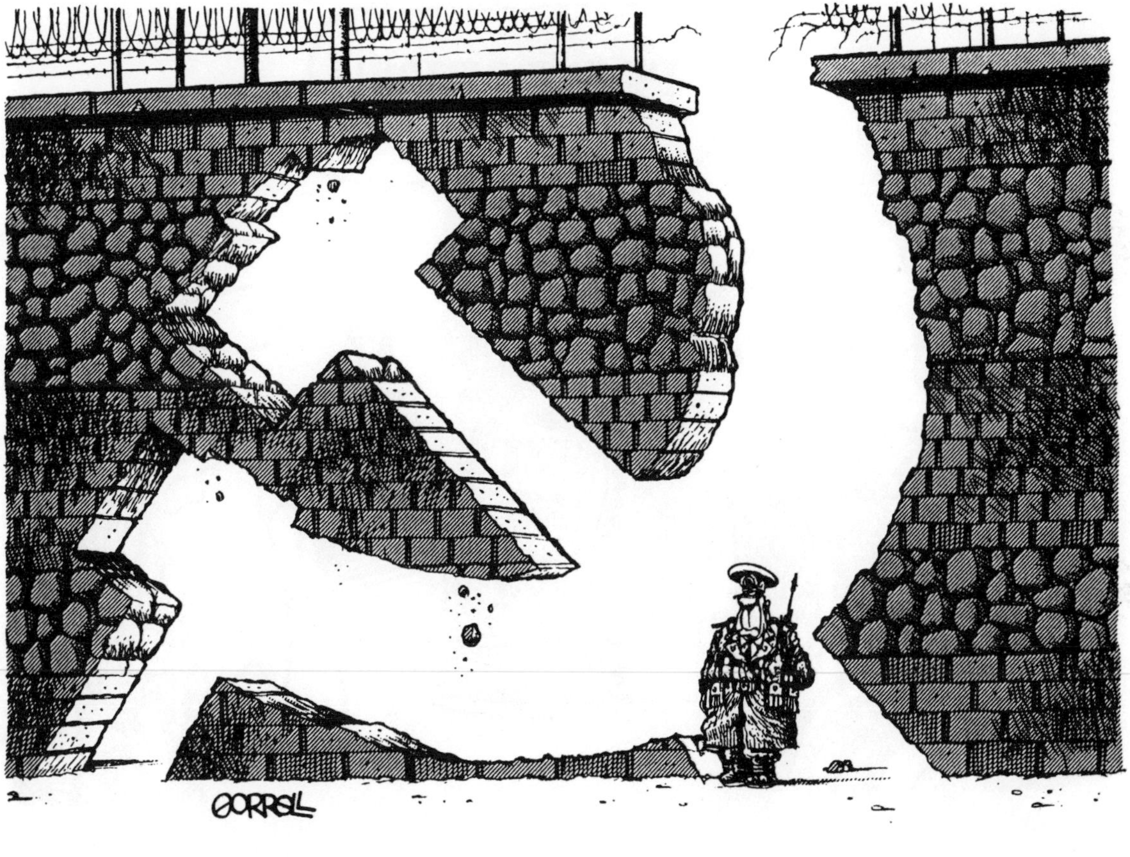
GORRELL

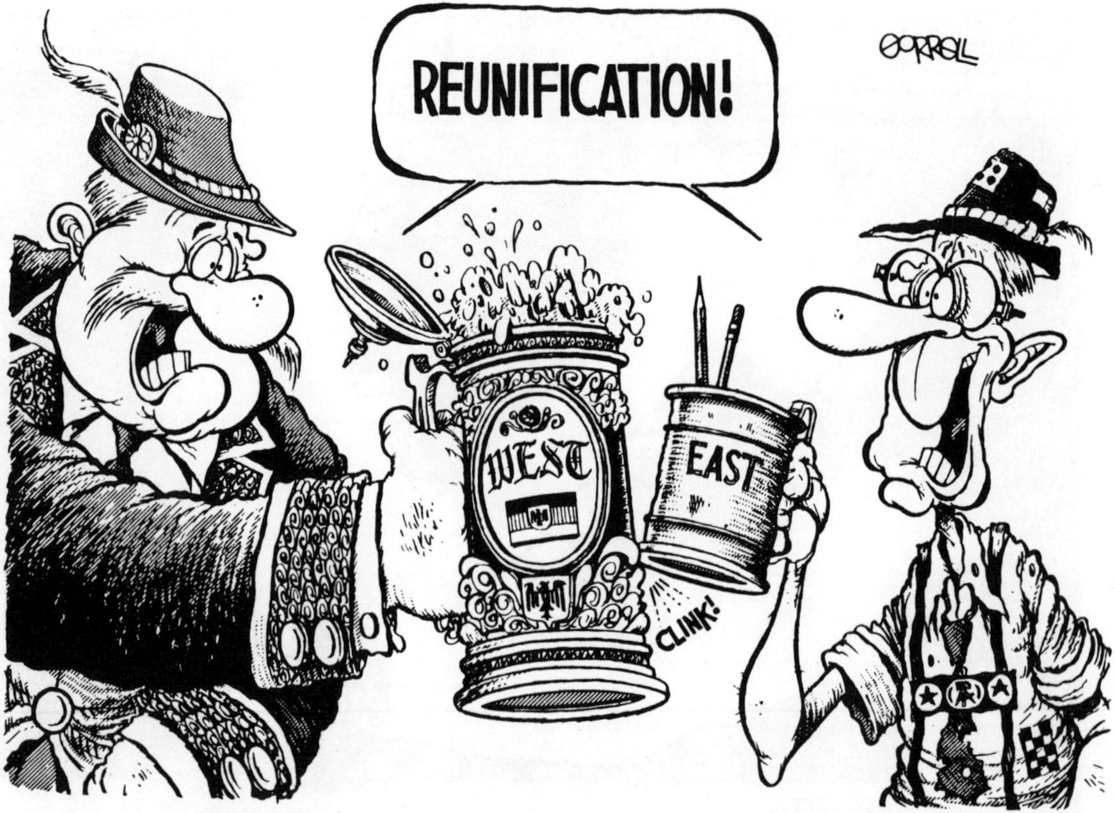

REUNIFICATION!
GORRELL
WEST
EAST
CLINK!

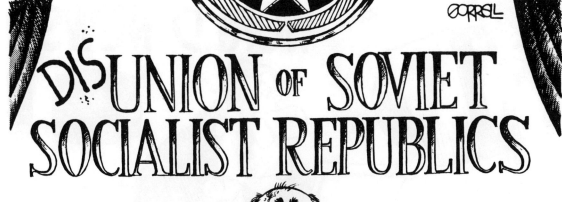

DISUNION OF SOVIET SOCIALIST REPUBLICS

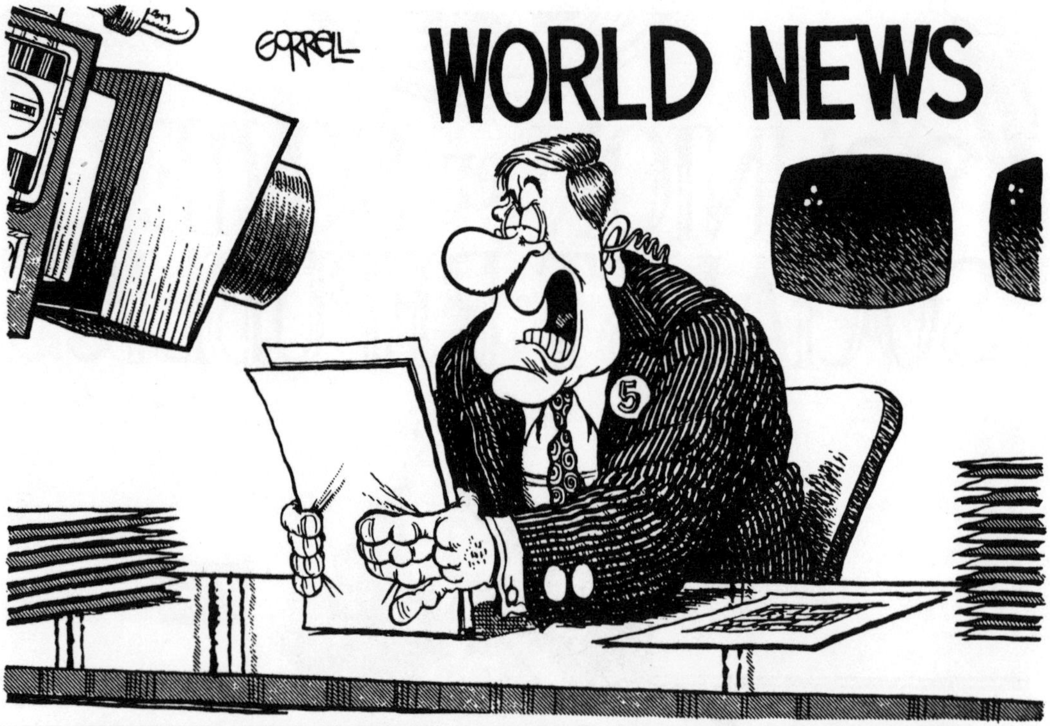
GORRELL
WORLD NEWS
5

"AND IN WHAT USED TO BE THE SOVIET UNION, THERE WAS ANOTHER MEETING BETWEEN A BUNCH OF LEADERS I NEVER *HEARD OF* FROM A LOT OF NEW COUNTRIES I CAN'T *PRONOUNCE . . . !*"

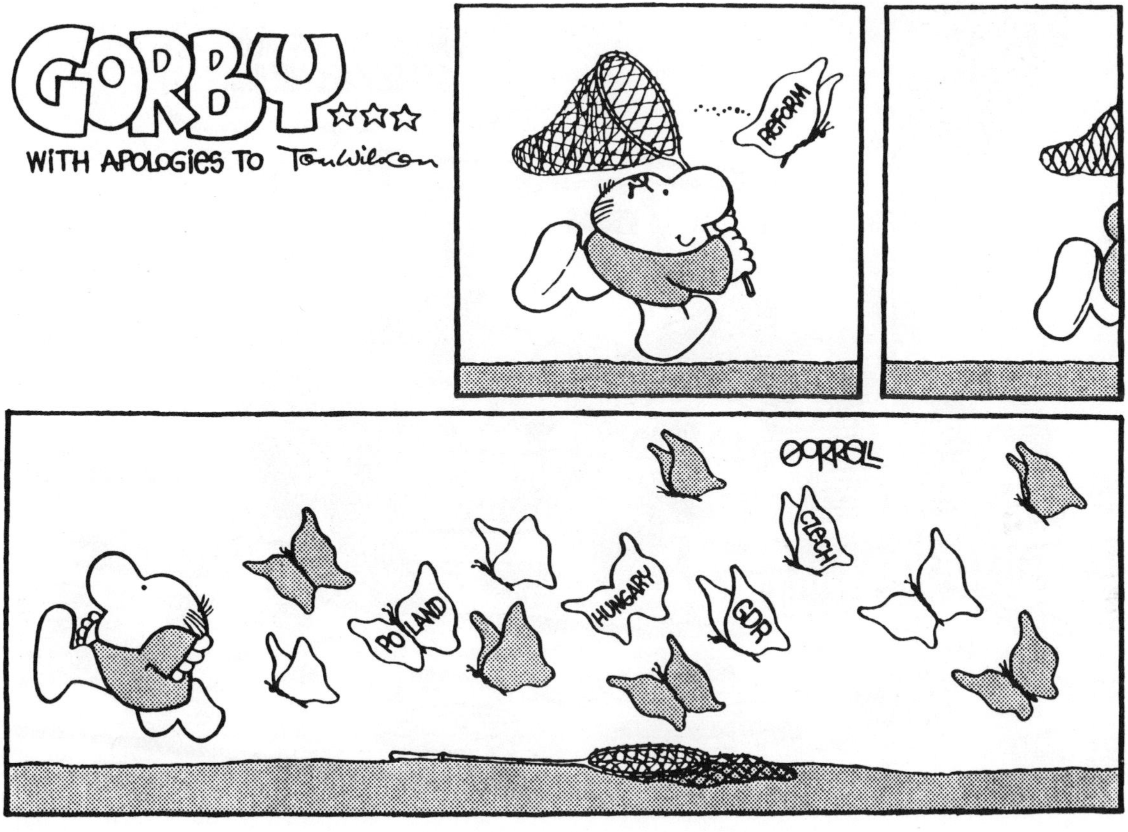
GORBY
WITH APOLOGIES TO Tom Wilson
REFORM
GORRELL
CZECH
POLAND
HUNGARY
GDR

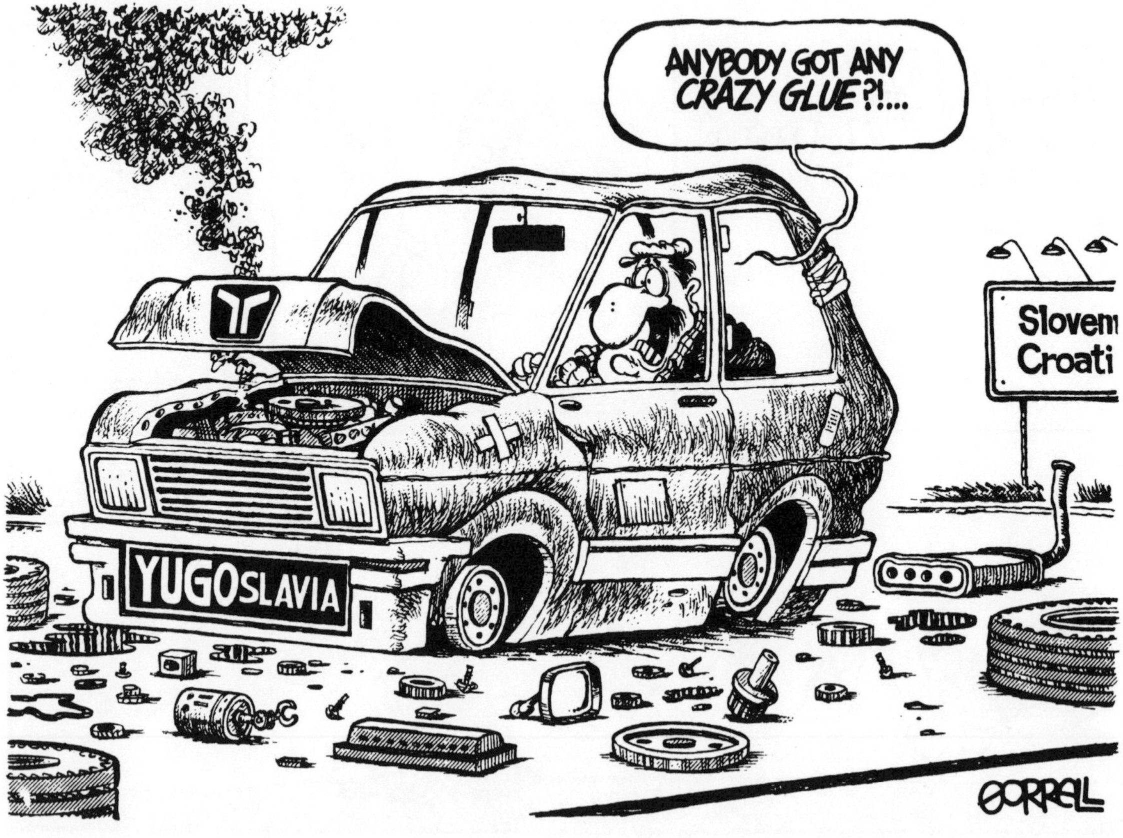
ANYBODY GOT ANY CRAZY GLUE?!....
Sloven
Croati
YUGOSLAVIA
GORRELL

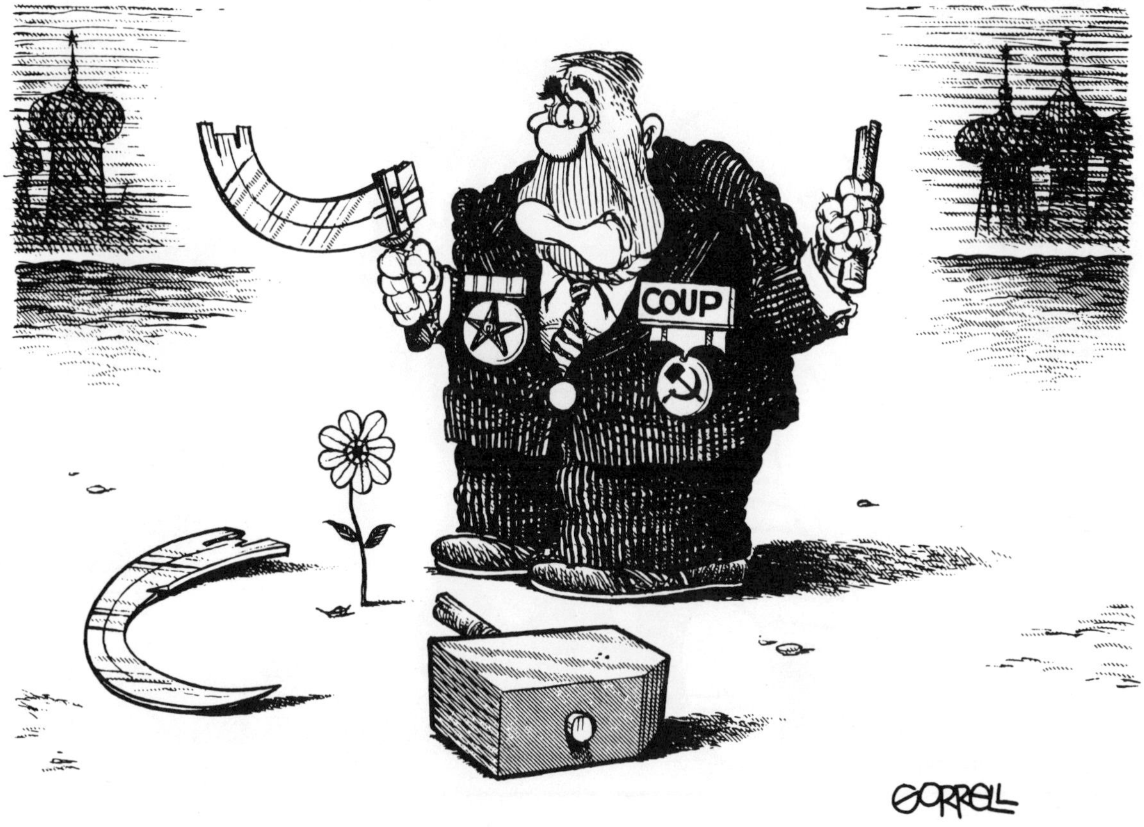
COUP
GORRELL

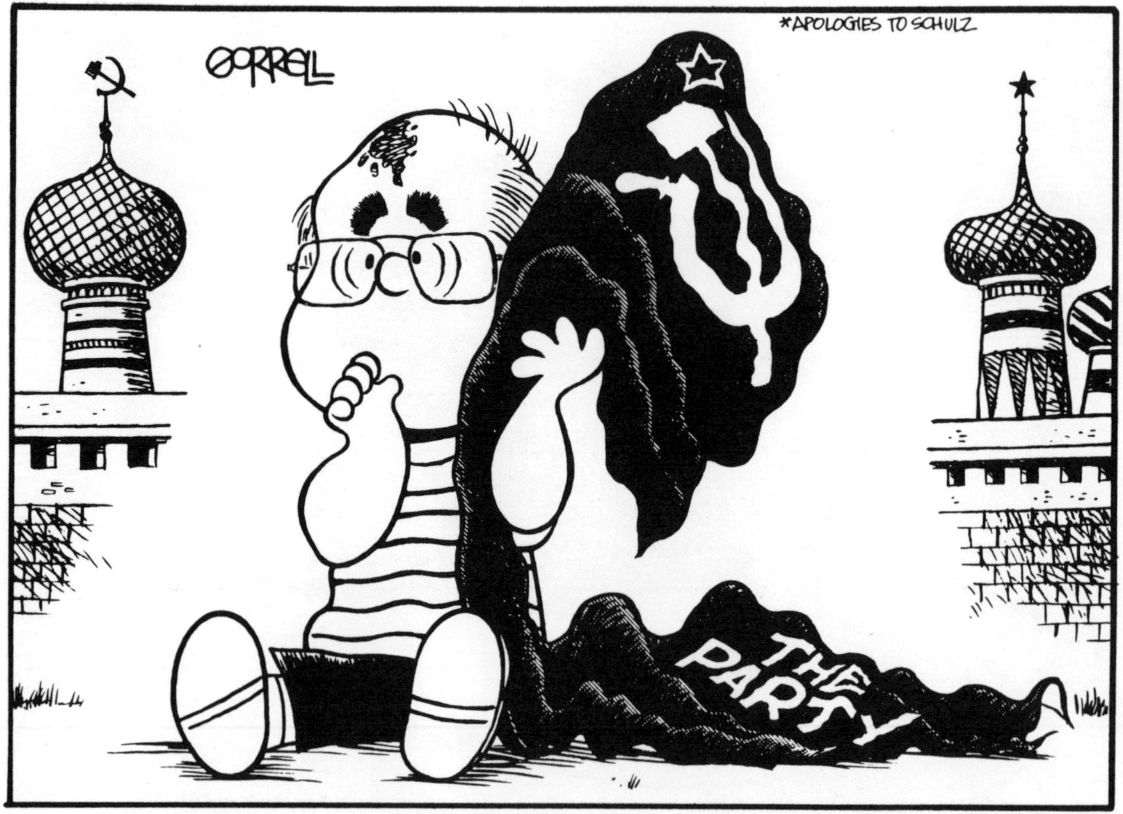
*APOLOGIES TO SCHULZ
GORRELL
THE PARTY

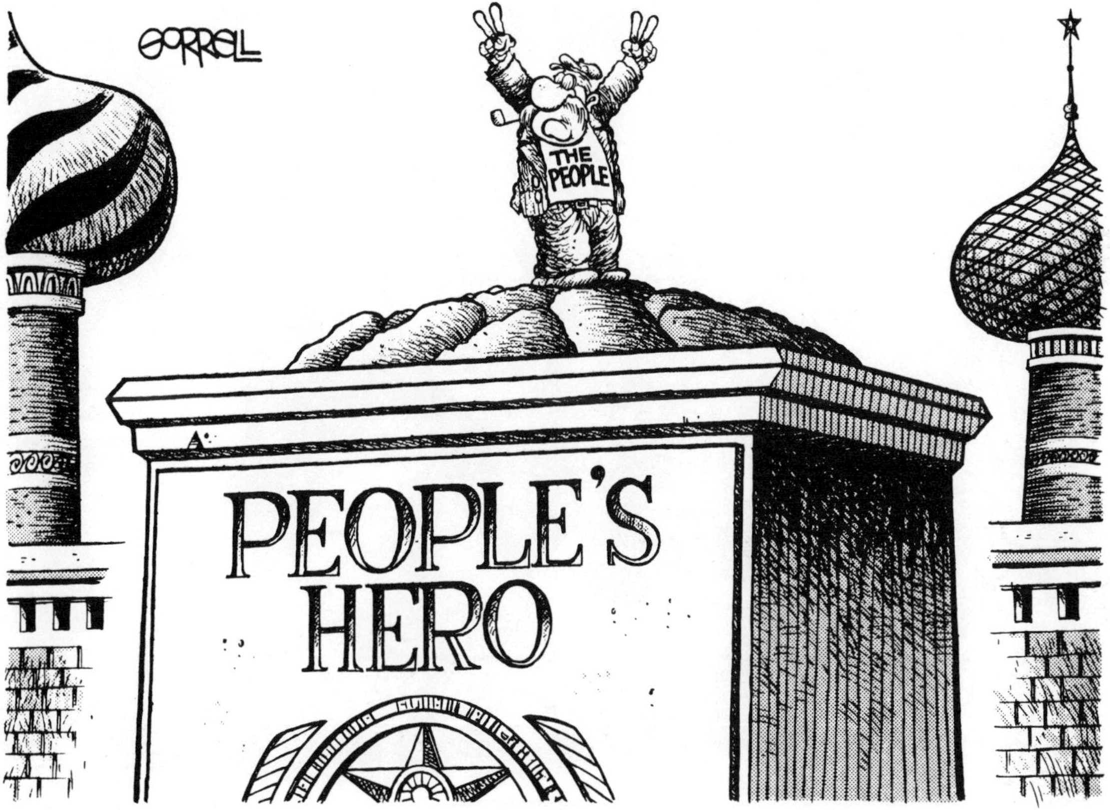
GORRELL
THE PEOPLE
PEOPLE'S HERO

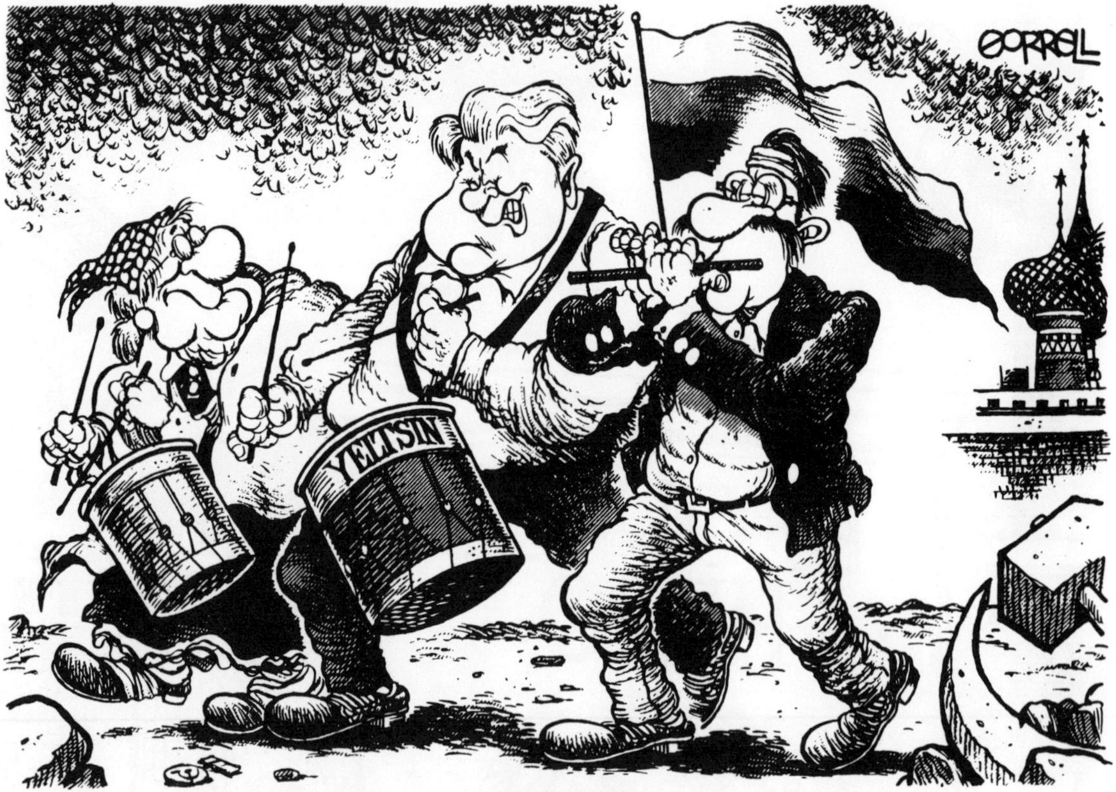
GORRELL
YELTSIN

SPIRIT OF '91

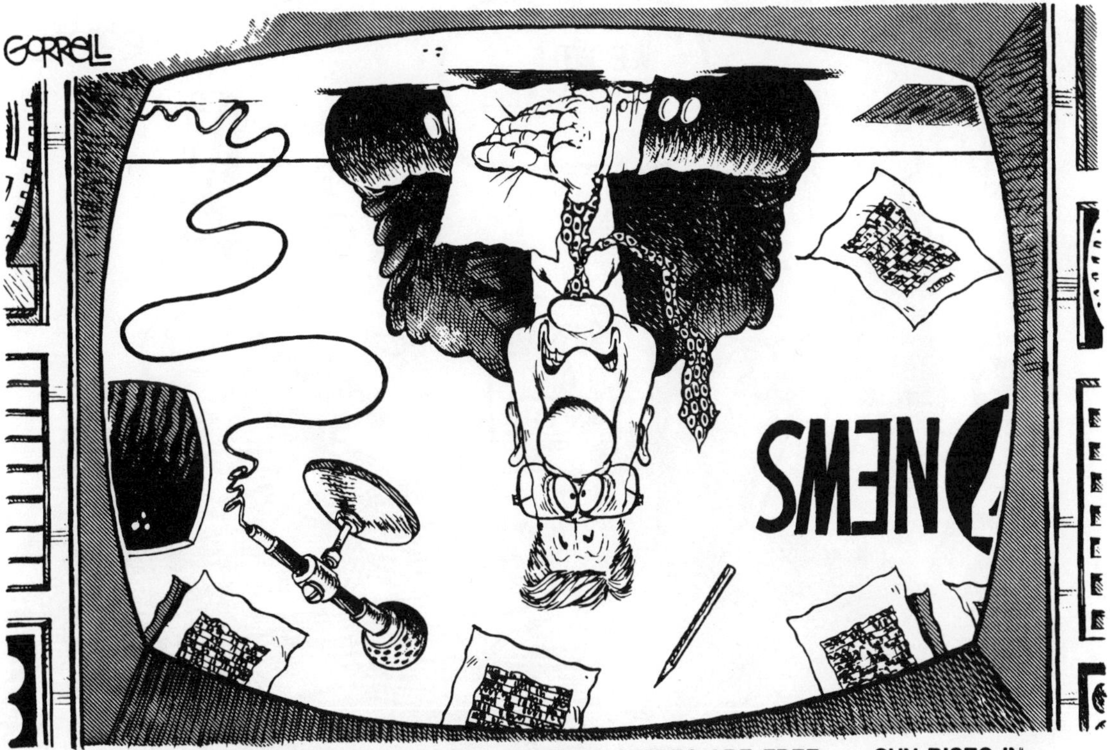
GORRELL
NEWS

"SOVIET COMMUNISM COLLAPSES. . . . BALTIC STATES ARE FREE. . . . SUN RISES IN THE WEST. . . . MORE NEWS AFTER THESE MESSAGES. . .!"

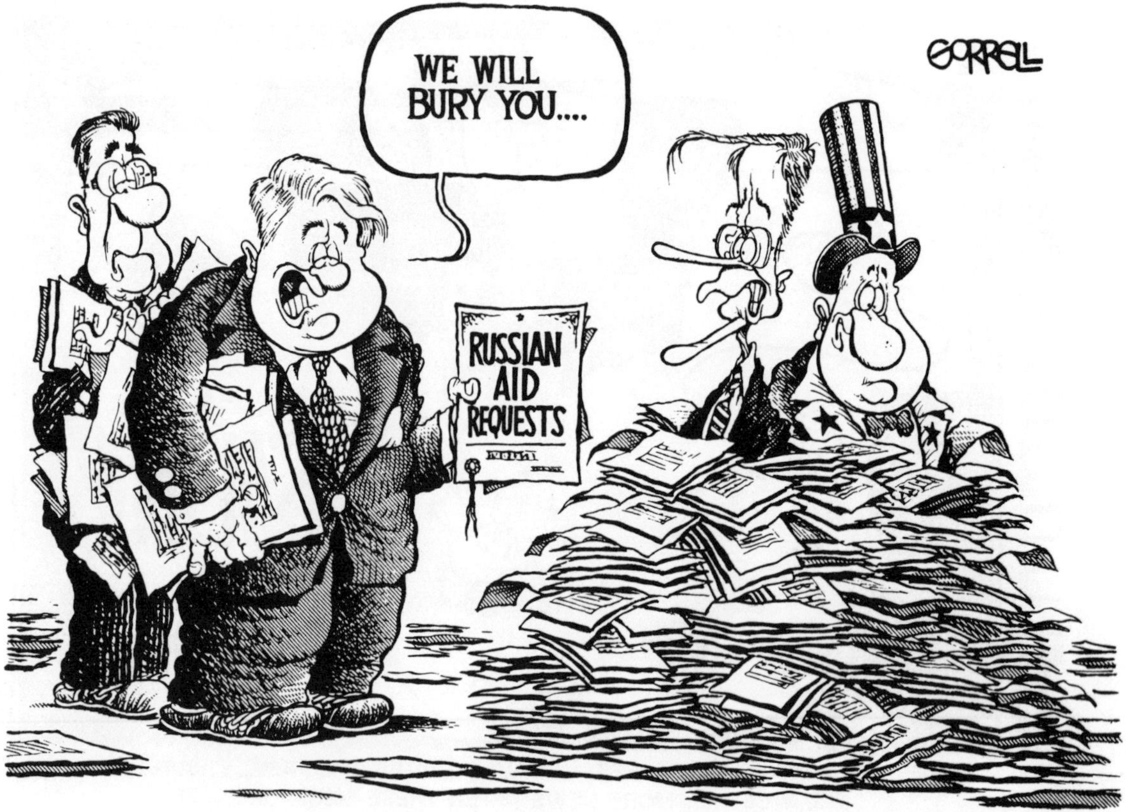
WE WILL BURY YOU....
RUSSIAN AID REQUESTS
GORRELL

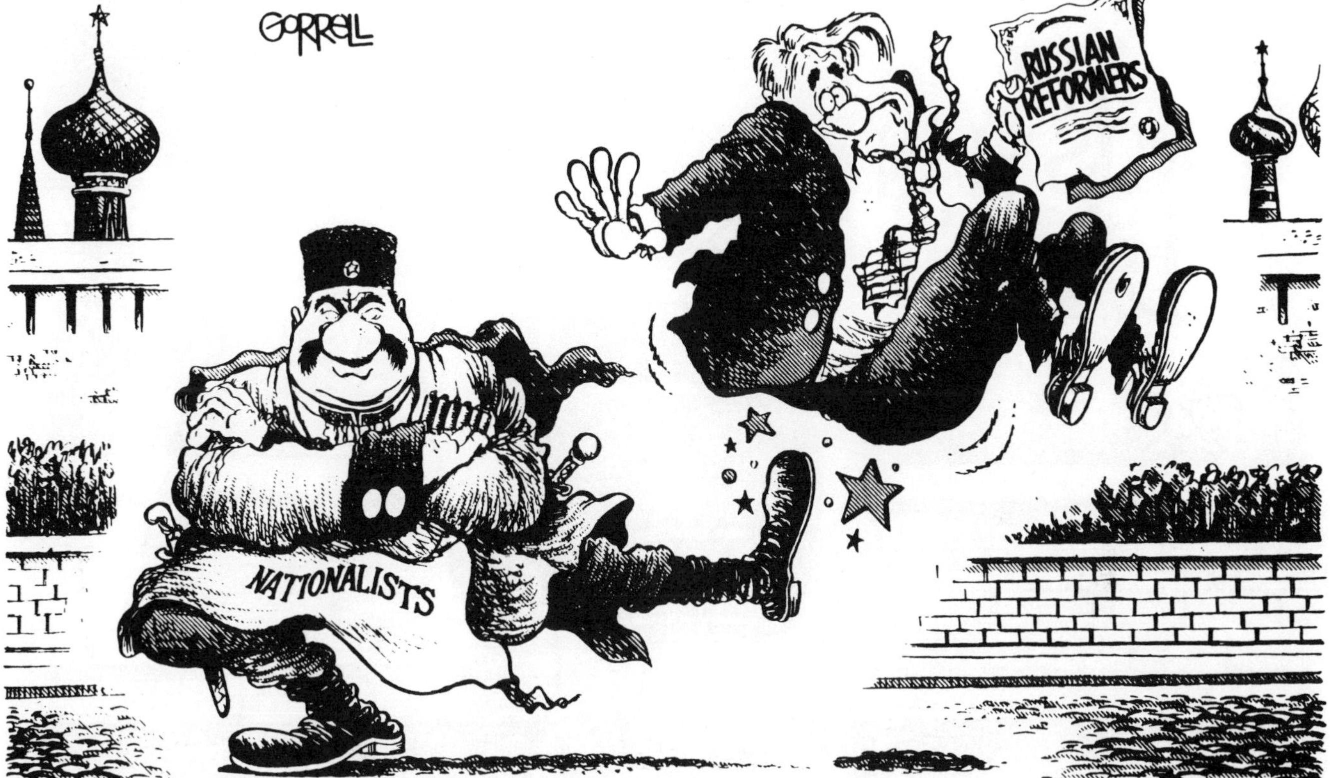
GORRELL
RUSSIAN REFORMERS
NATIONALISTS

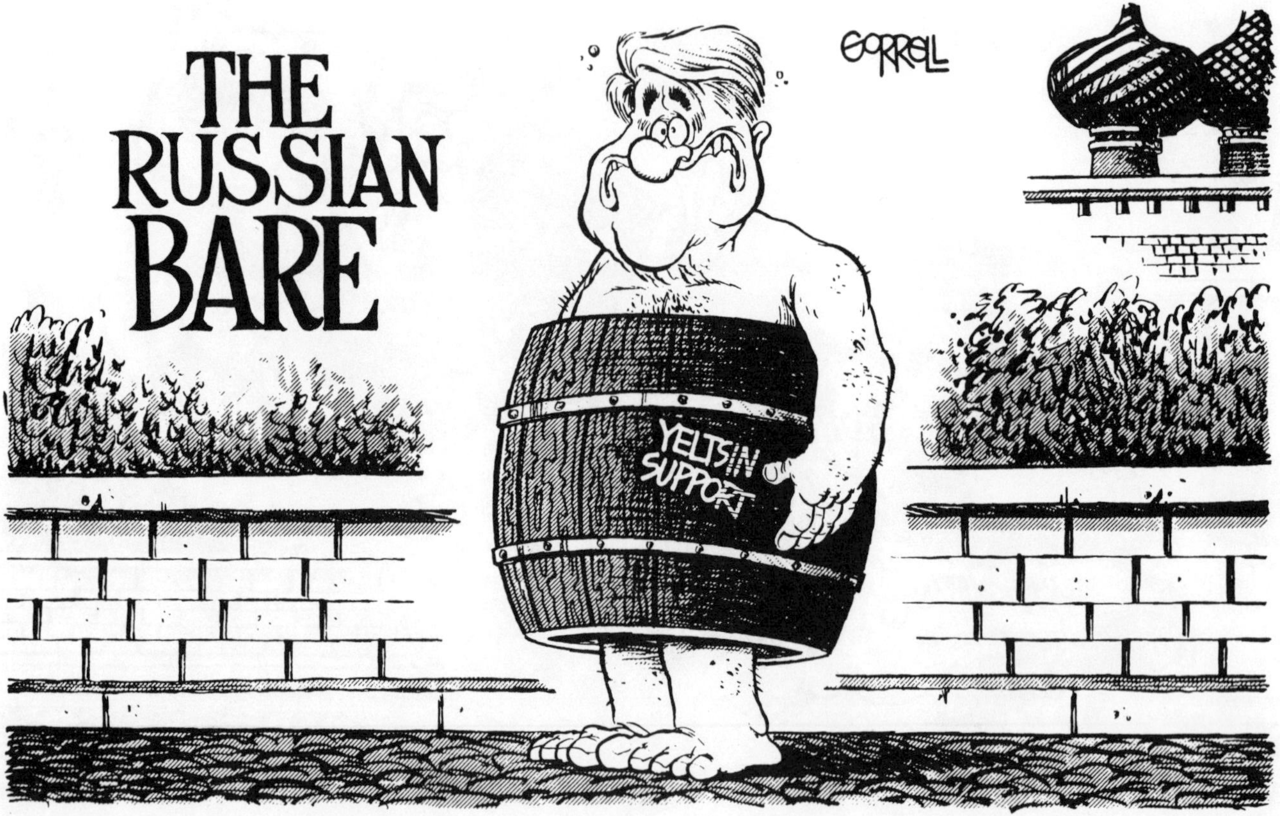
THE RUSSIAN BARE
GORRELL
YELTSIN SUPPORT

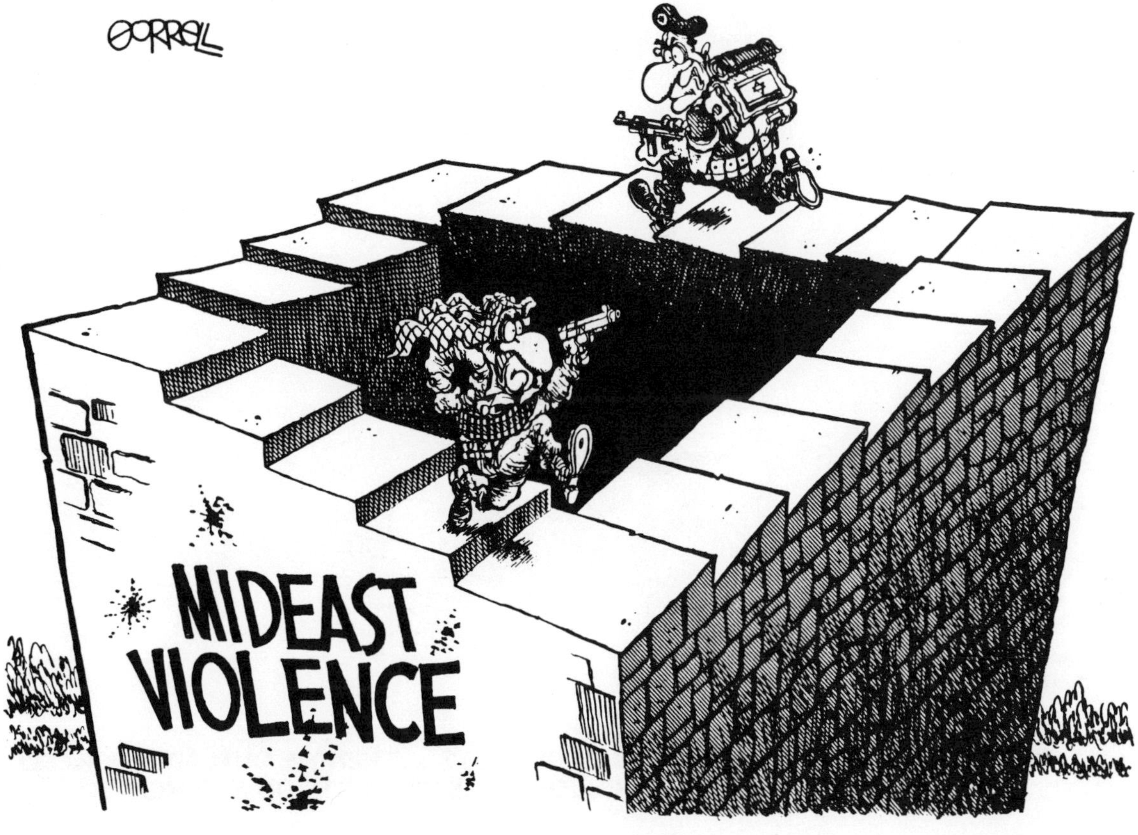
GORRELL
MIDEAST
VIOLENCE

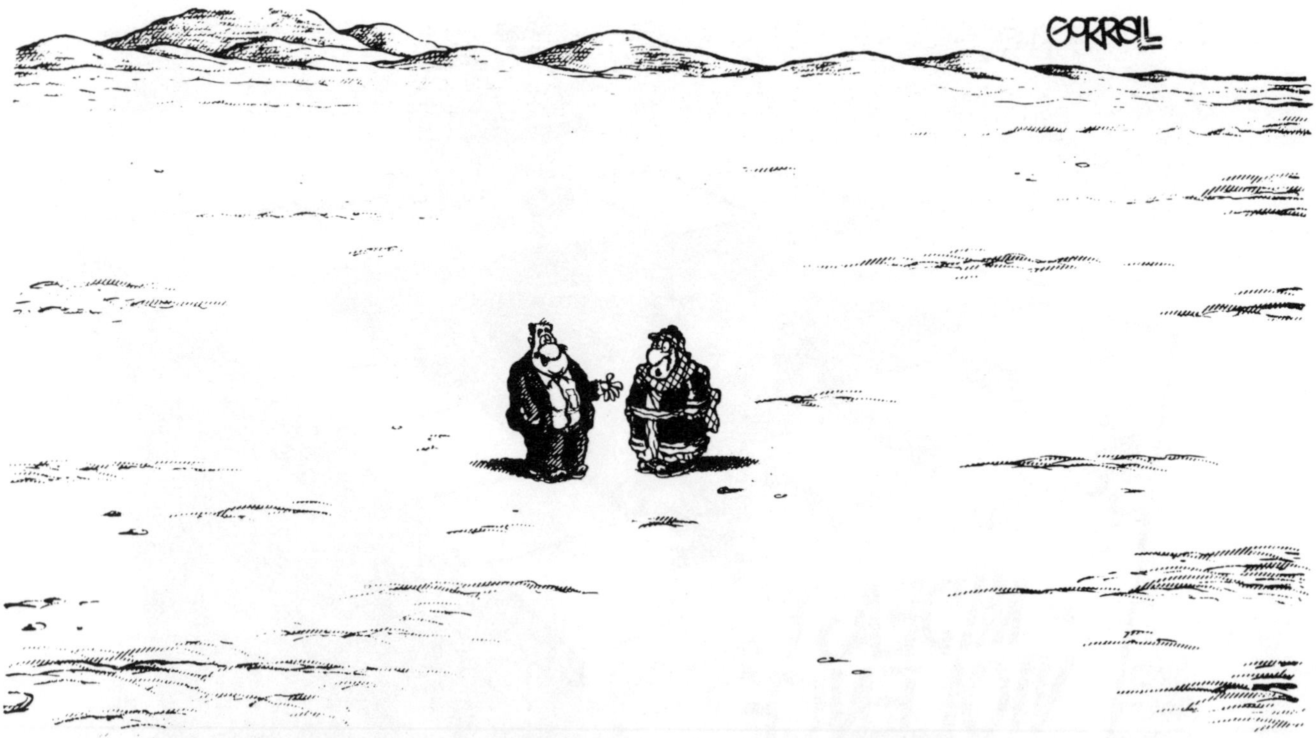
GORRELL

"WELL, FIRST WE OUTLAWED ARAB EXTREMISTS . . . THEN WE OUTLAWED ISRAELI EXTREMISTS . . . AND NOW IT LOOKS LIKE IT'S JUST YOU AND ME!"

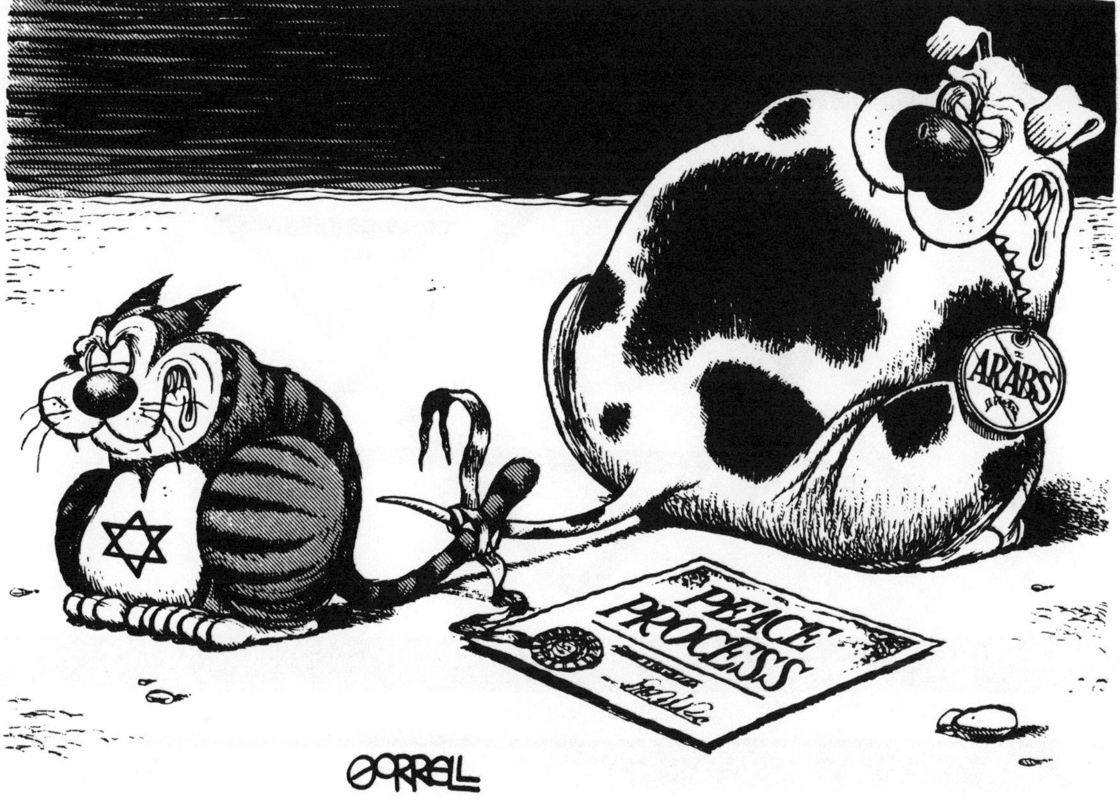
ARABS
PEACE PROCESS
GORRELL

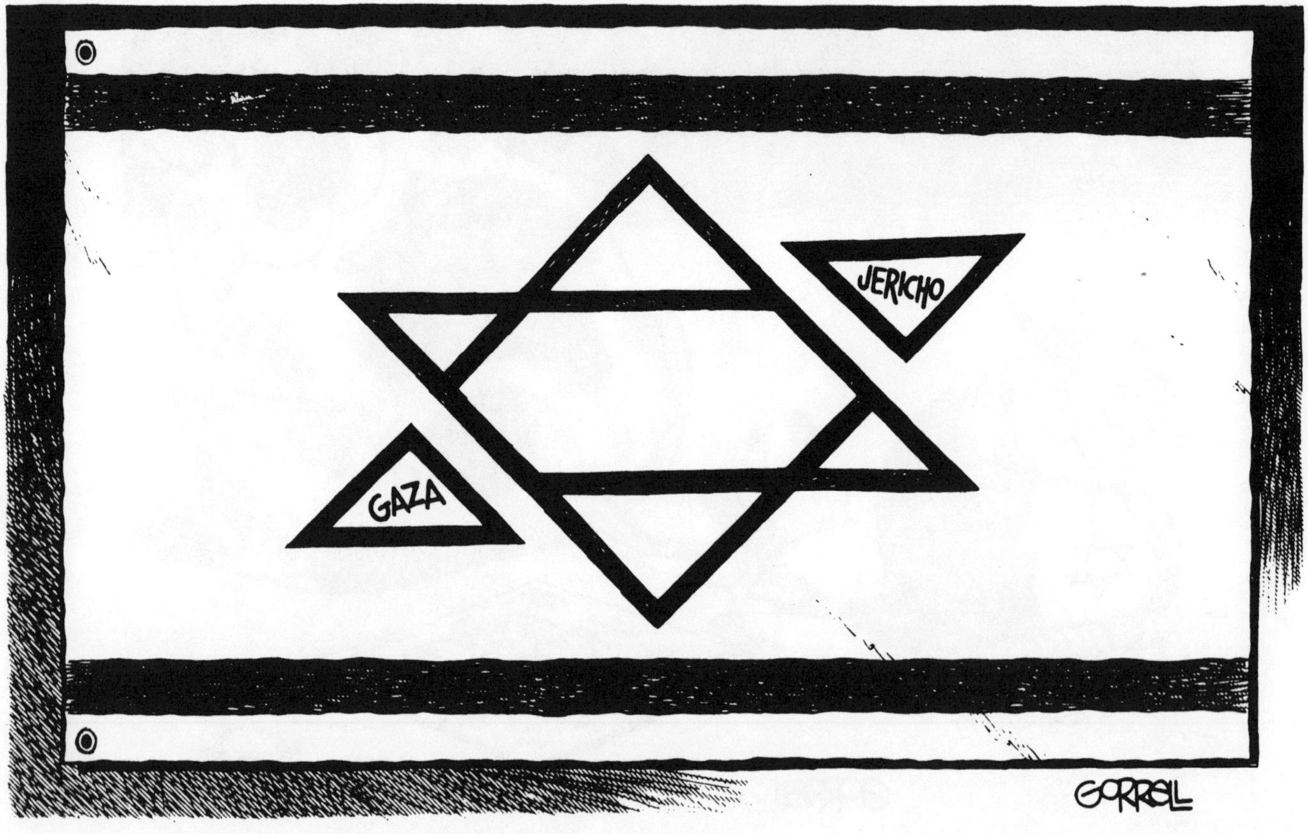
JERICHO
GAZA
GORRELL

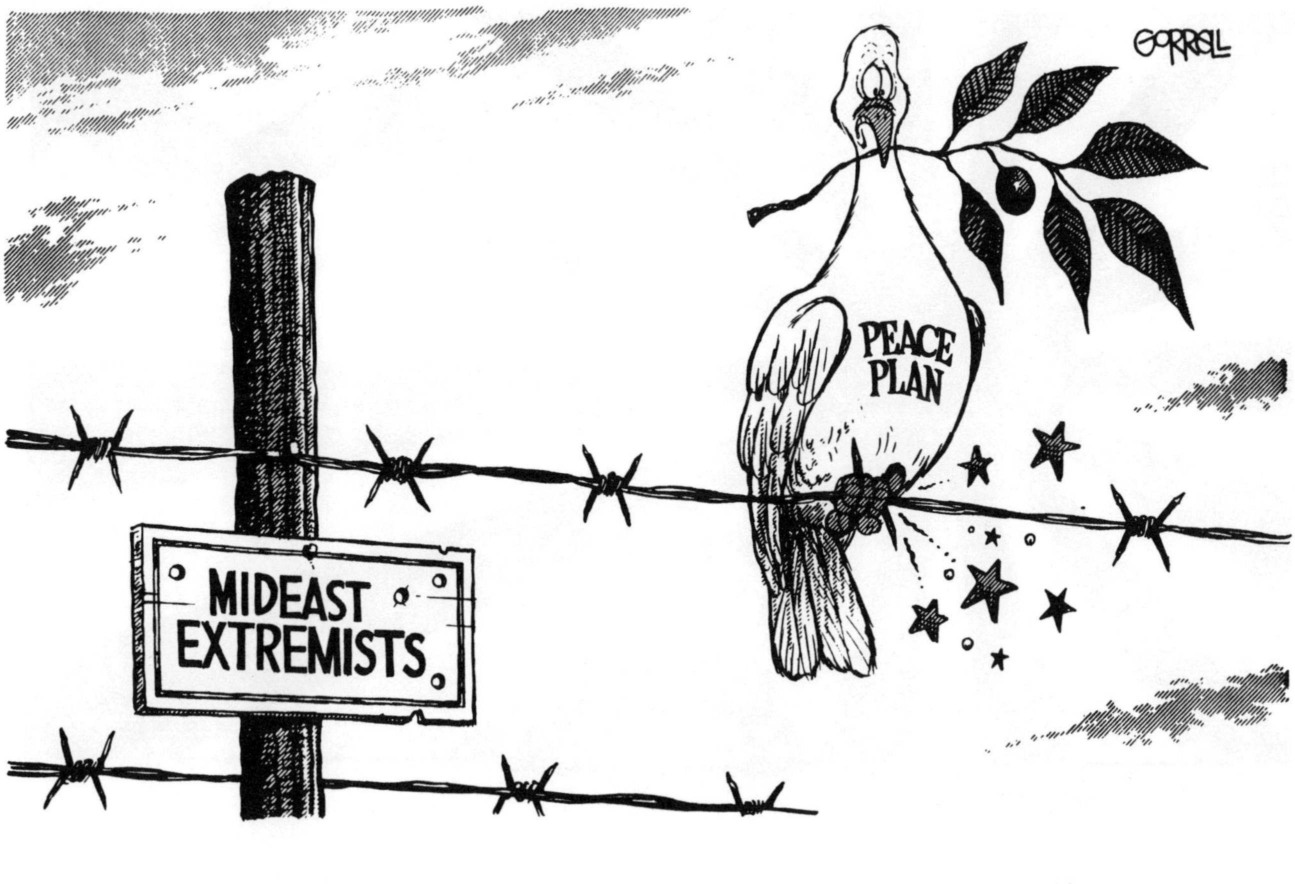
GORRELL
PEACE PLAN
MIDEAST EXTREMISTS

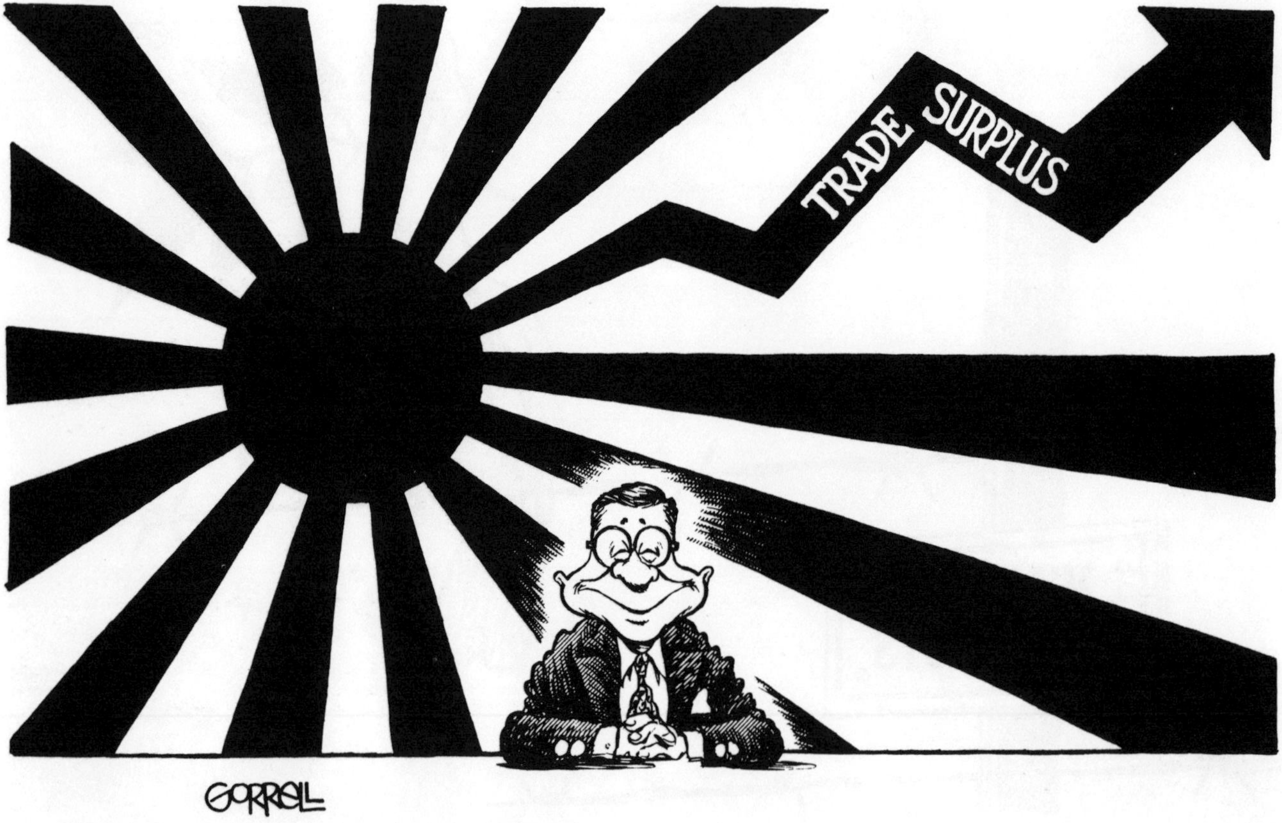
TRADE SURPLUS
GORRELL

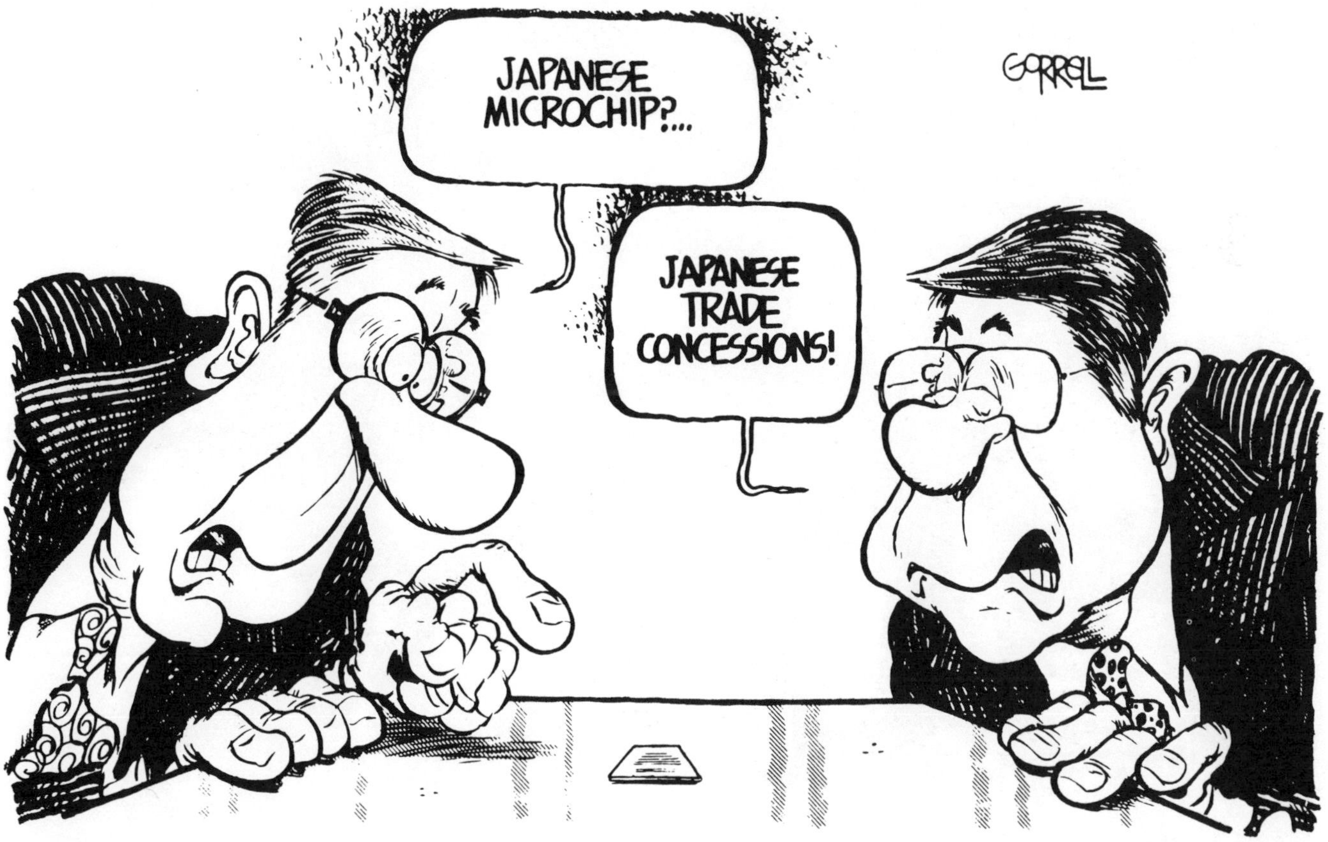
JAPANESE MICROCHIP?...
JAPANESE TRADE CONCESSIONS!
GORRELL

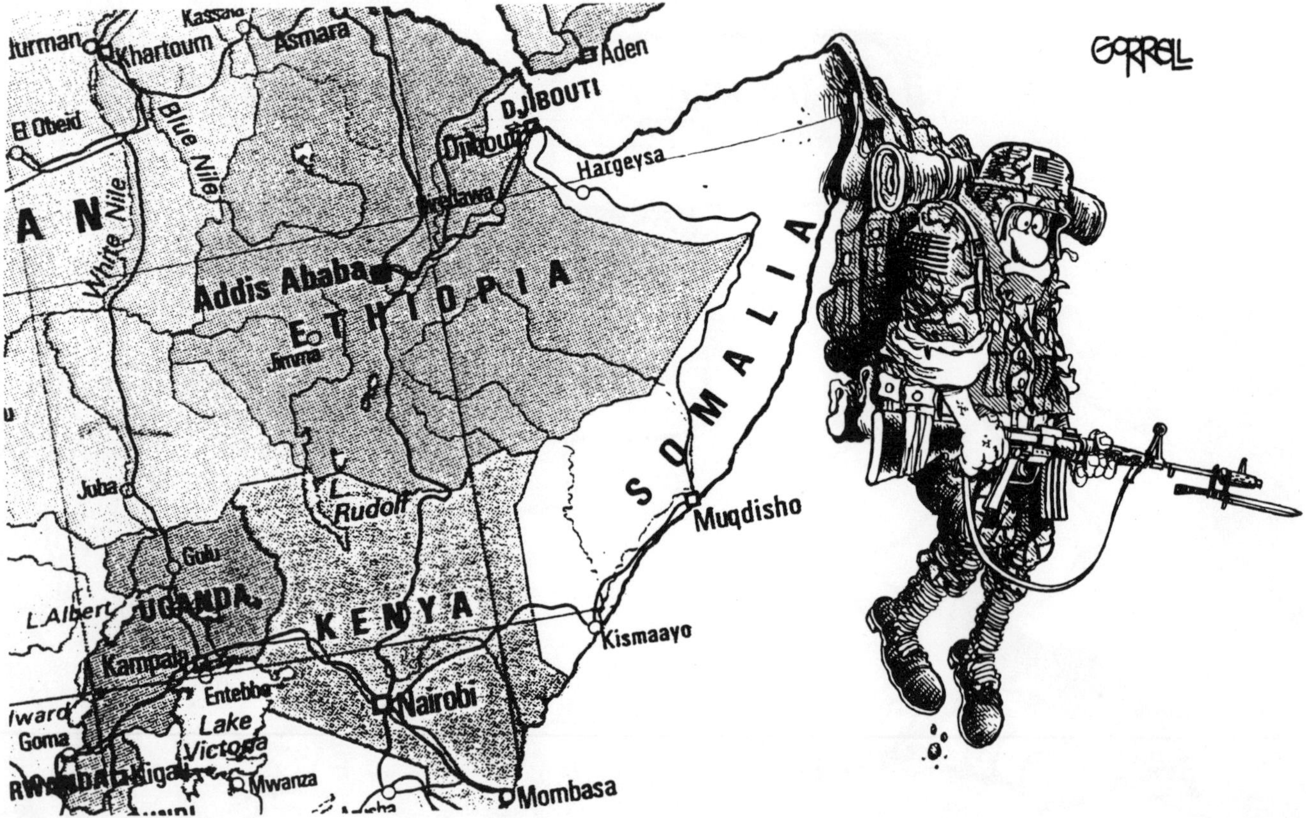

GORRELL
Khartoum
Asmara
Aden
DJIBOUTI
Djibouti
El Obeid
Blue Nile
White Nile
Hargeysa
Addis Ababa
ETHIOPIA
Jimma
SOMALIA
Juba
L. Rudolf
Muqdisho
Gulu
UGANDA
L. Albert
KENYA
Kismaayo
Kampala
Entebbe
Nairobi
Lake Victoria
Goma
Kigali
Mwanza
Mombasa

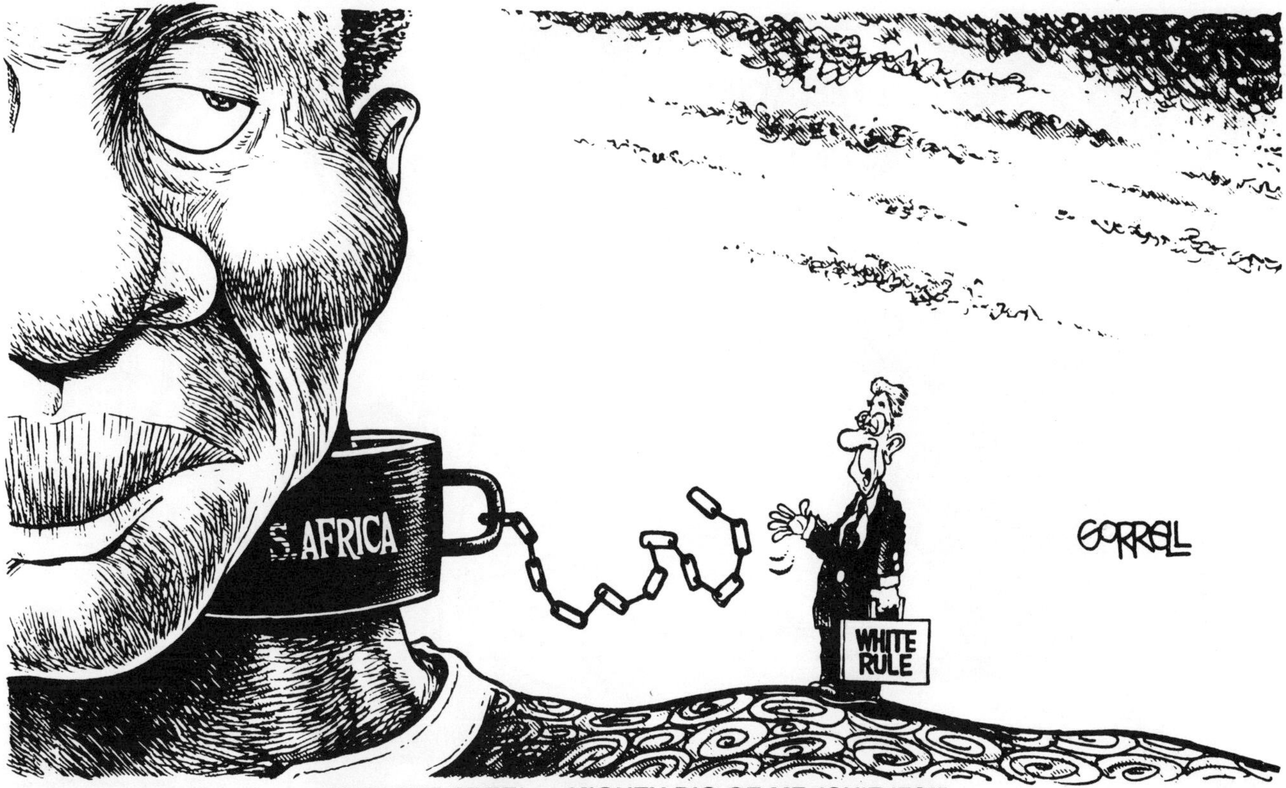
S. AFRICA
WHITE RULE
GORRELL

"YOU'RE FREE! . . . MIGHTY BIG OF ME, ISN'T IT?!"

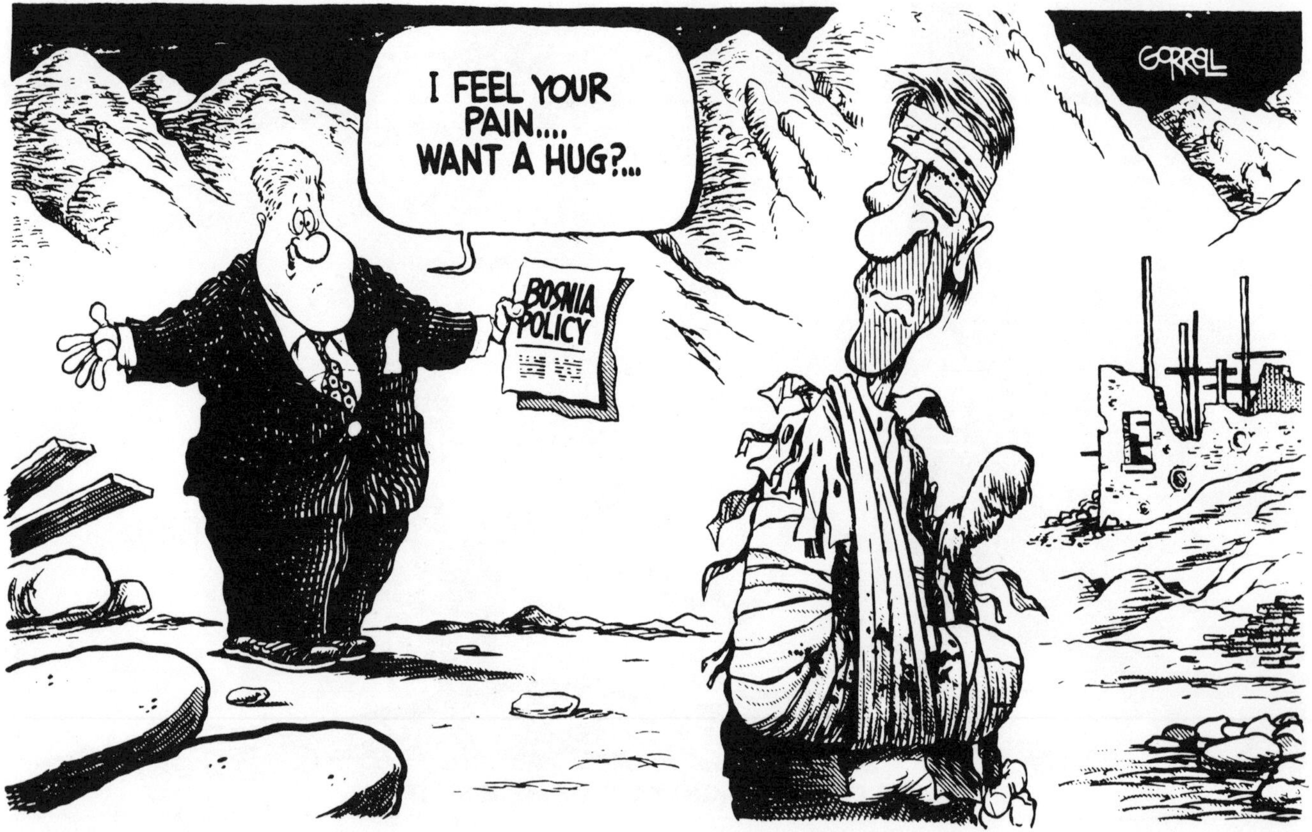
I FEEL YOUR PAIN.... WANT A HUG?...
BOSNIA POLICY
GORRELL

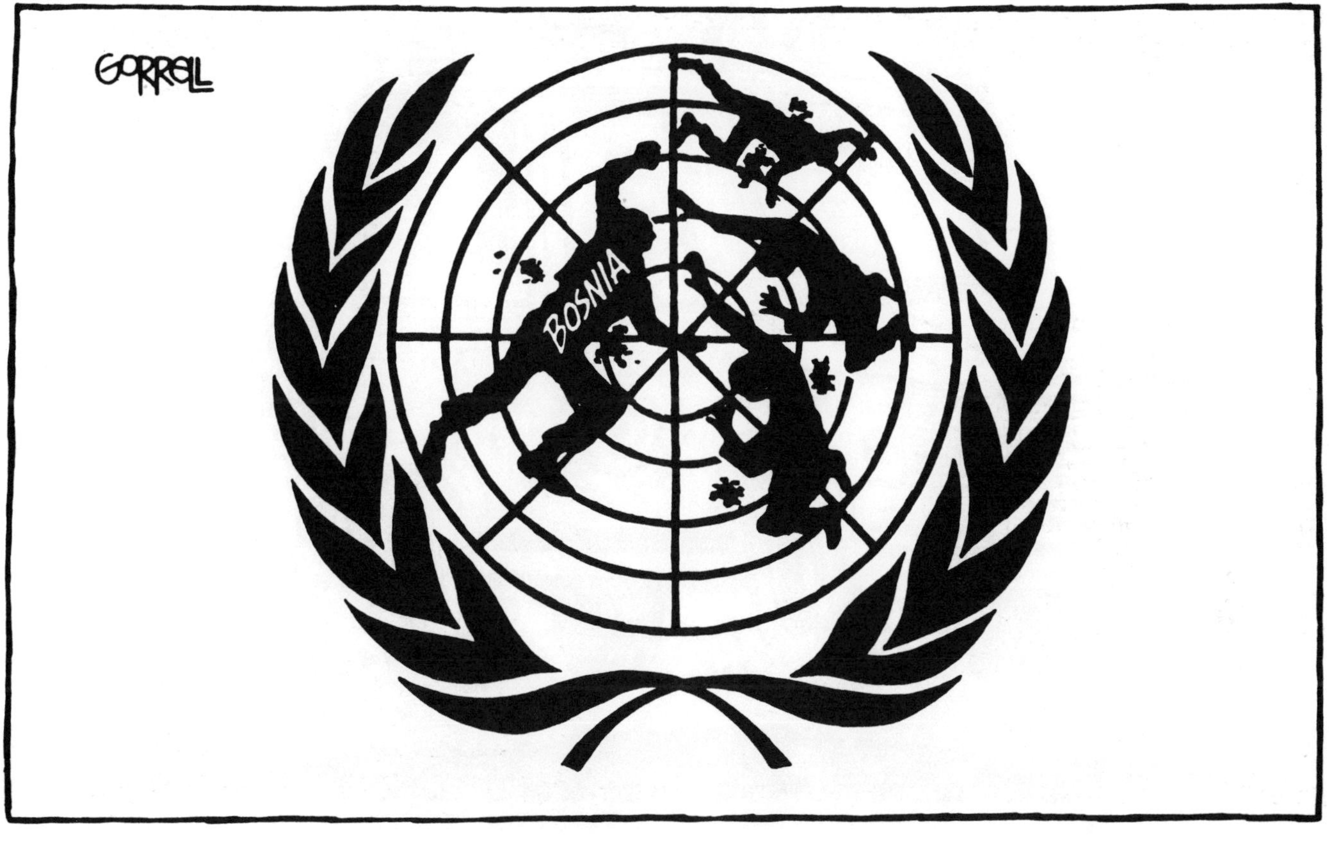
GORRELL
BOSNIA

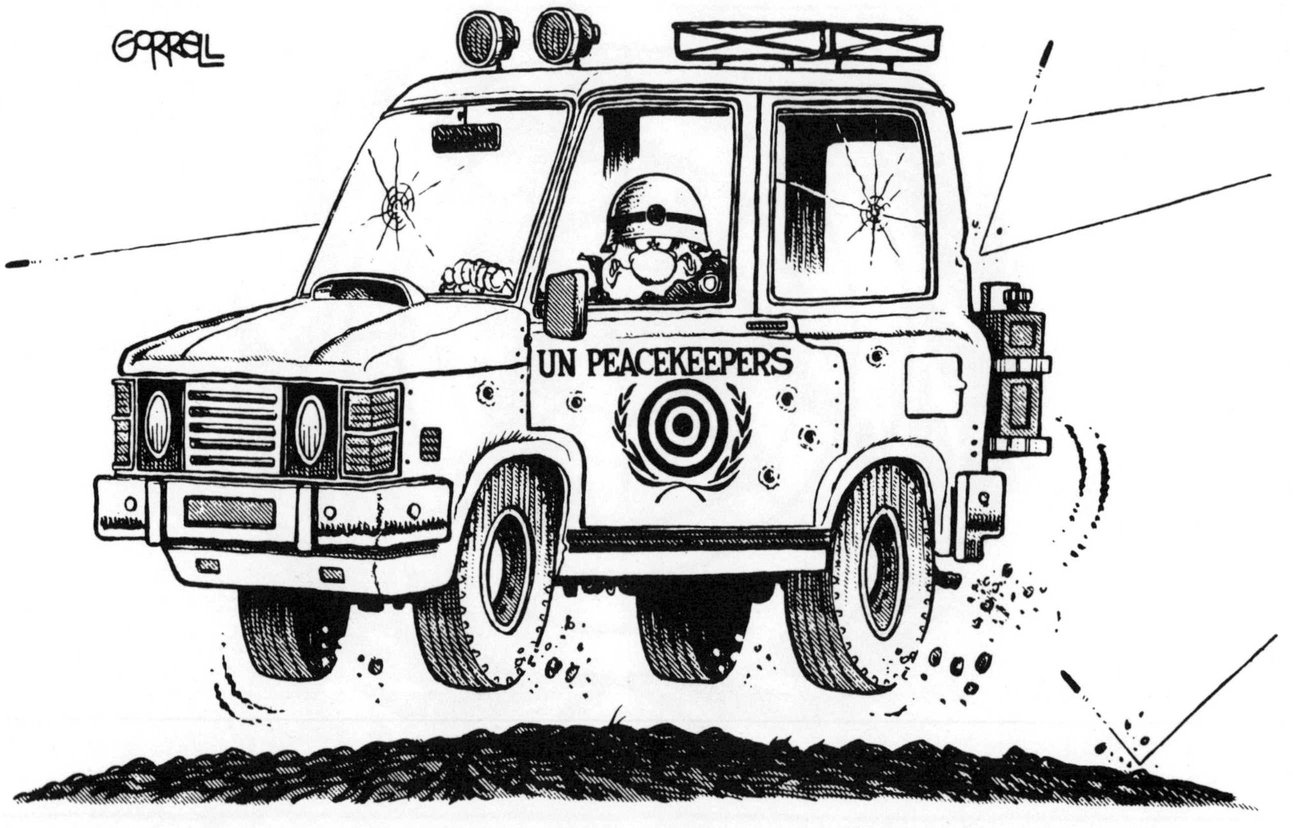
GORRELL
UN PEACEKEEPERS

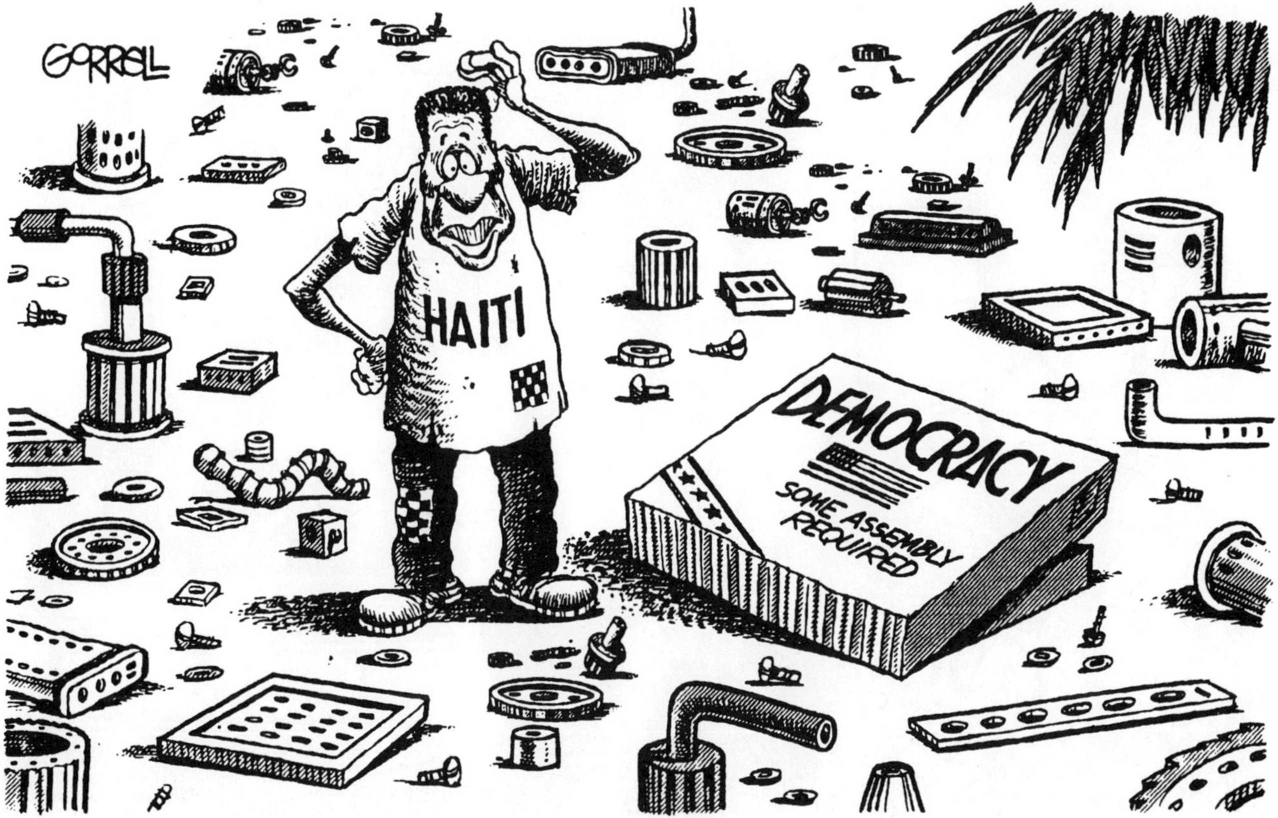
GORRELL
HAITI
DEMOCRACY
SOME ASSEMBLY REQUIRED

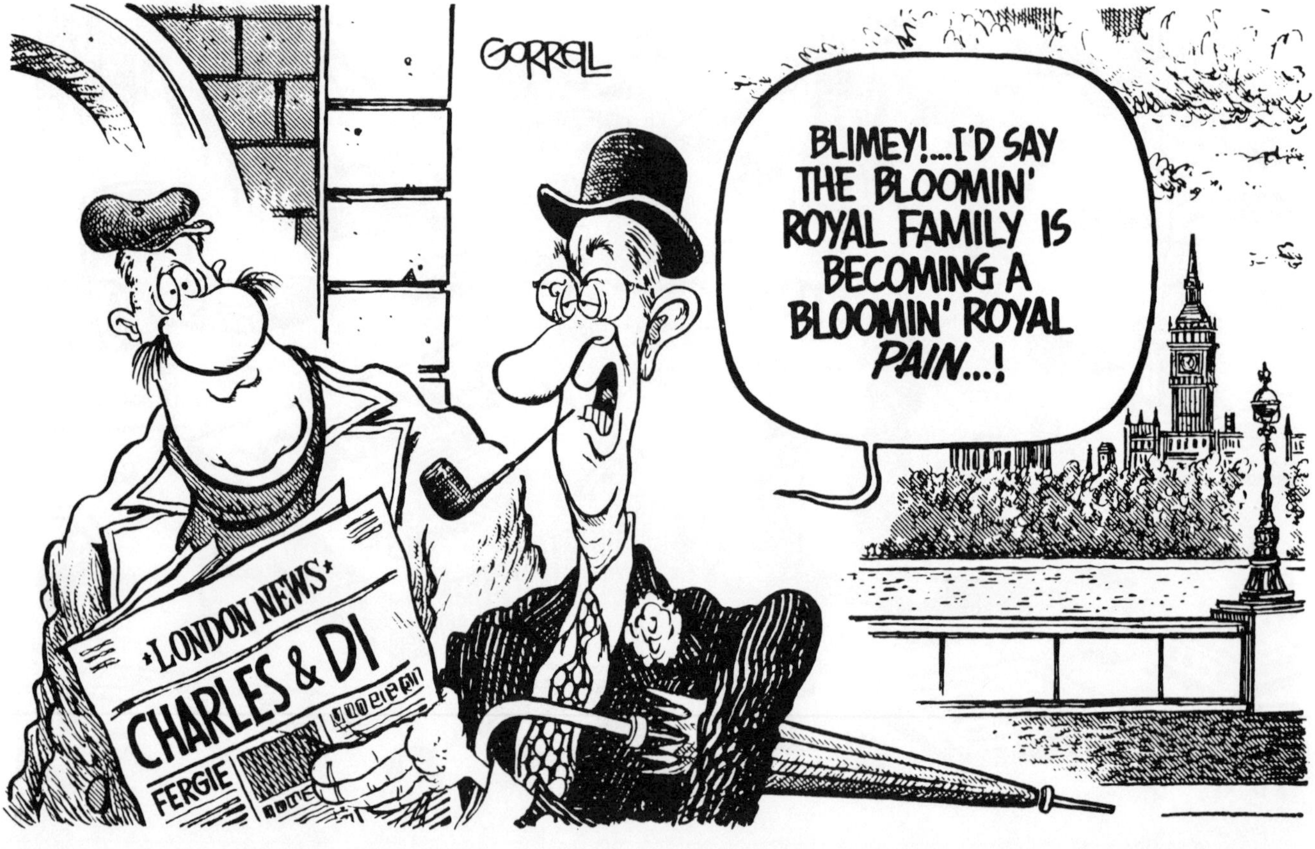
GORRELL
BLIMEY!...I'D SAY THE BLOOMIN' ROYAL FAMILY IS BECOMING A BLOOMIN' ROYAL PAIN...!
LONDON NEWS
CHARLES & DI
FERGIE

Richmond and
the Old Dominion

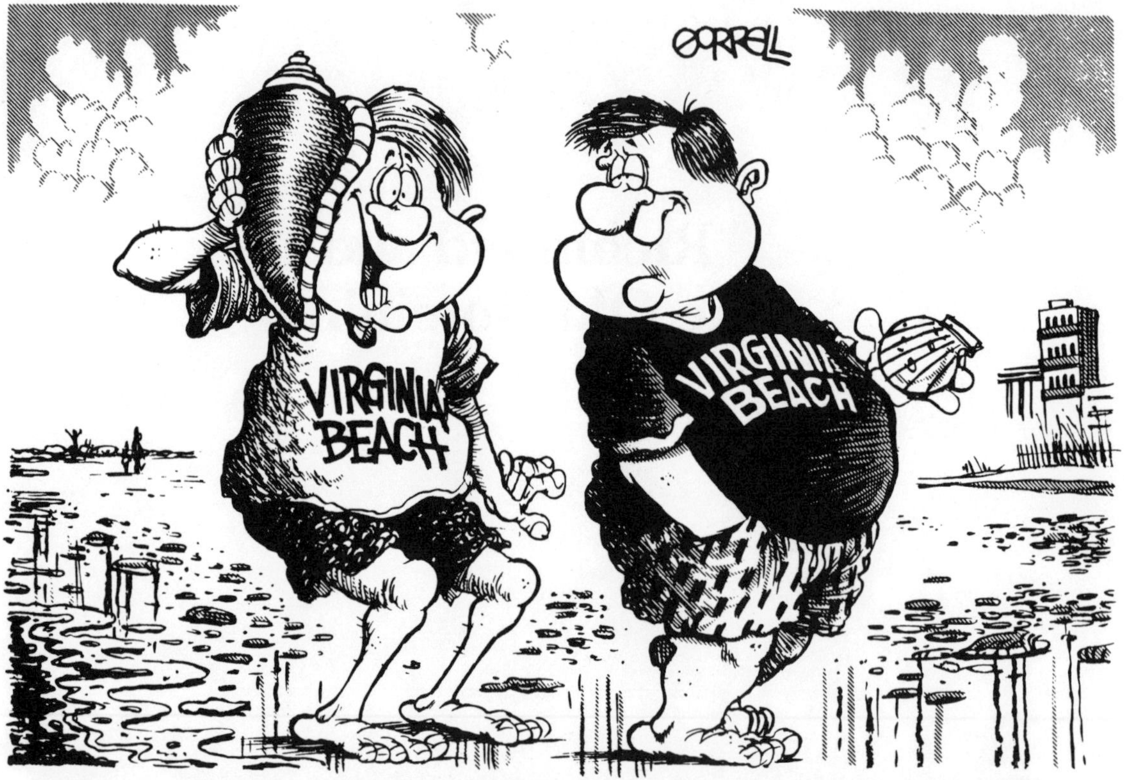
GORRELL
VIRGINIA BEACH
VIRGINIA BEACH

"COOL!... HOLD IT TO YOUR EAR, AND YOU CAN HEAR RUMORS ABOUT *CHUCK ROBB!*"

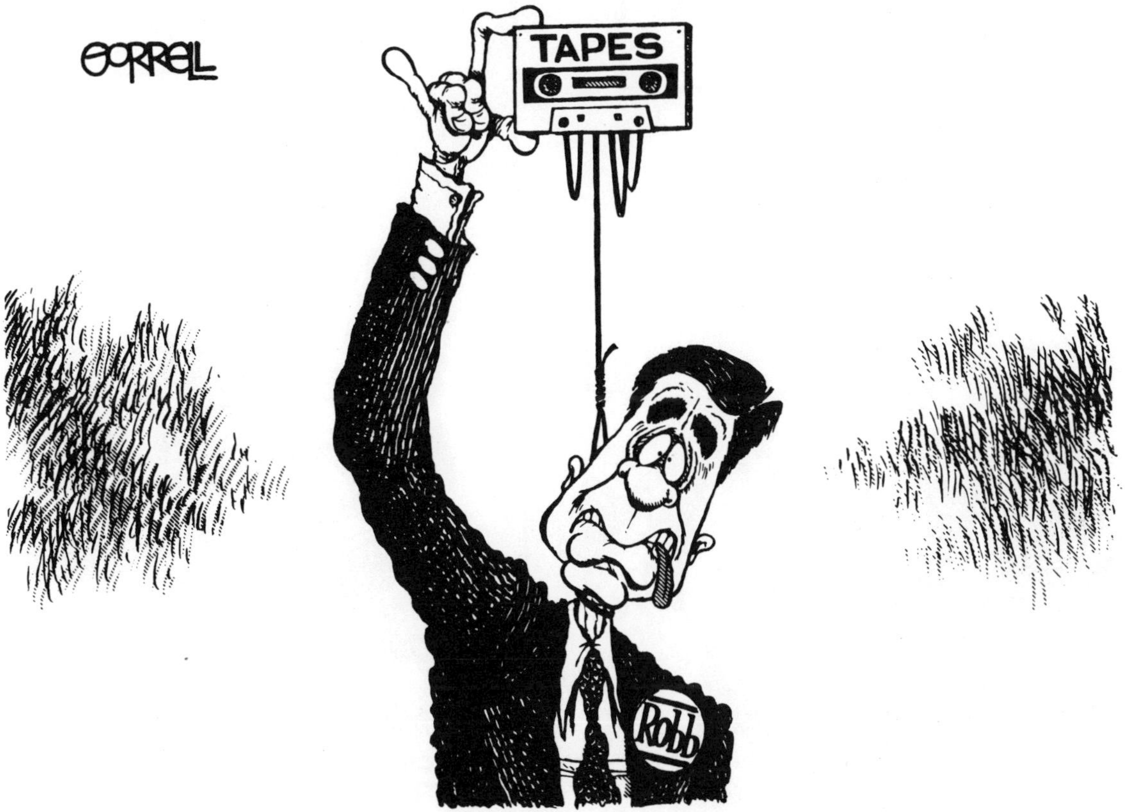
SORRELL
TAPES
Robb

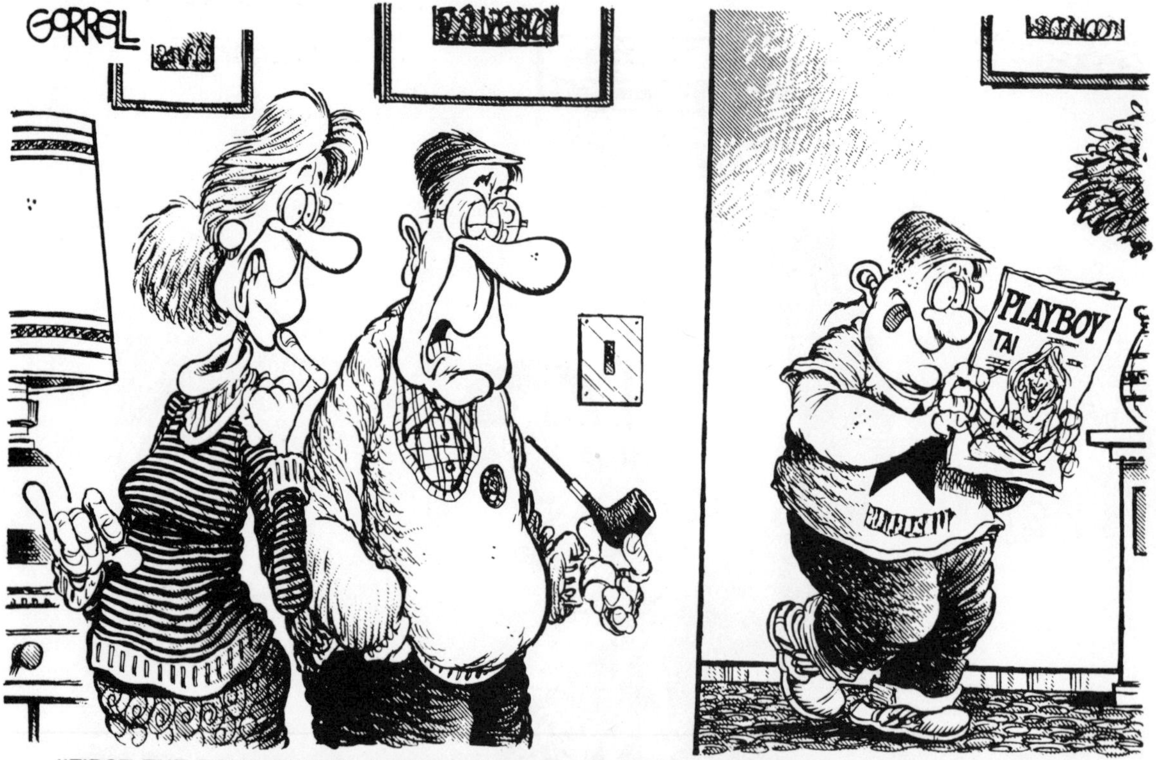
GORRELL
PLAYBOY

"FIRST THE DOUG WILDER INTERVIEW, AND NOW THE CHUCK ROBB STORY. . . . AT LEAST JUNIOR'S TAKING AN INTEREST IN *VIRGINIA POLITICS* . . . !"

ACLU PROPOSAL FOR VOTING DISTRICT IN HENRICO COUNTY THAT INSURES ELECTION OF A BLACK....

A JEW....

A CHRISTIAN....

FEMINIST....

PHARMACIST....

CARTOONIST....

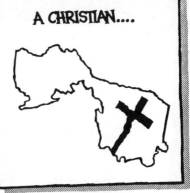

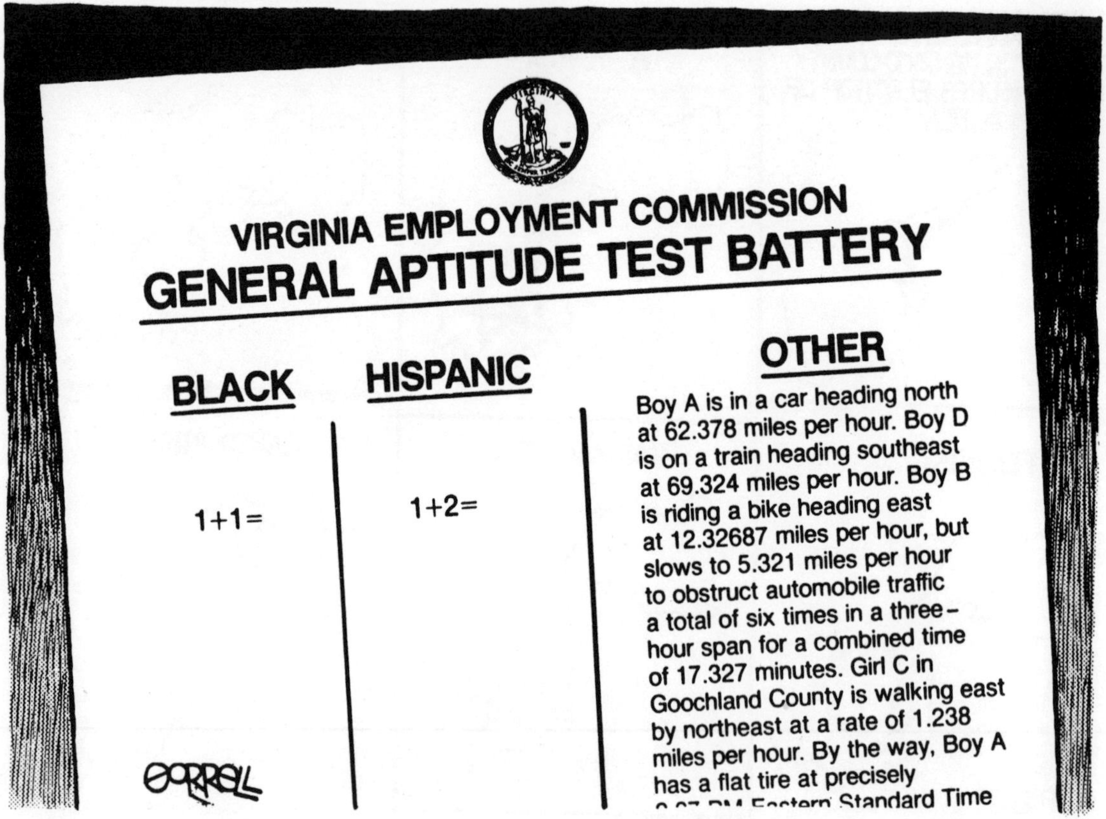

VIRGINIA EMPLOYMENT COMMISSION
GENERAL APTITUDE TEST BATTERY

BLACK

1+1=

HISPANIC

1+2=

OTHER

Boy A is in a car heading north at 62.378 miles per hour. Boy D is on a train heading southeast at 69.324 miles per hour. Boy B is riding a bike heading east at 12.32687 miles per hour, but slows to 5.321 miles per hour to obstruct automobile traffic a total of six times in a three-hour span for a combined time of 17.327 minutes. Girl C in Goochland County is walking east by northeast at a rate of 1.238 miles per hour. By the way, Boy A has a flat tire at precisely 8:07 PM Eastern Standard Time

CORRELL

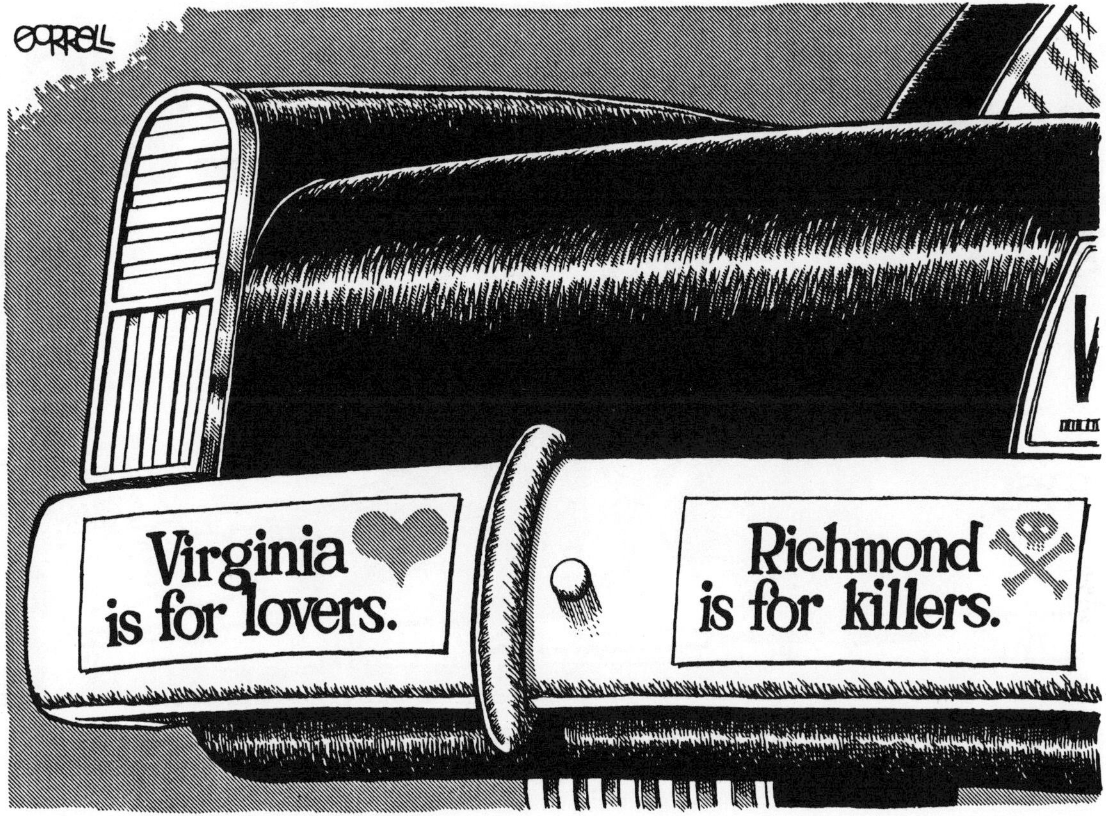
SORRELL
Virginia is for lovers.
Richmond is for killers.

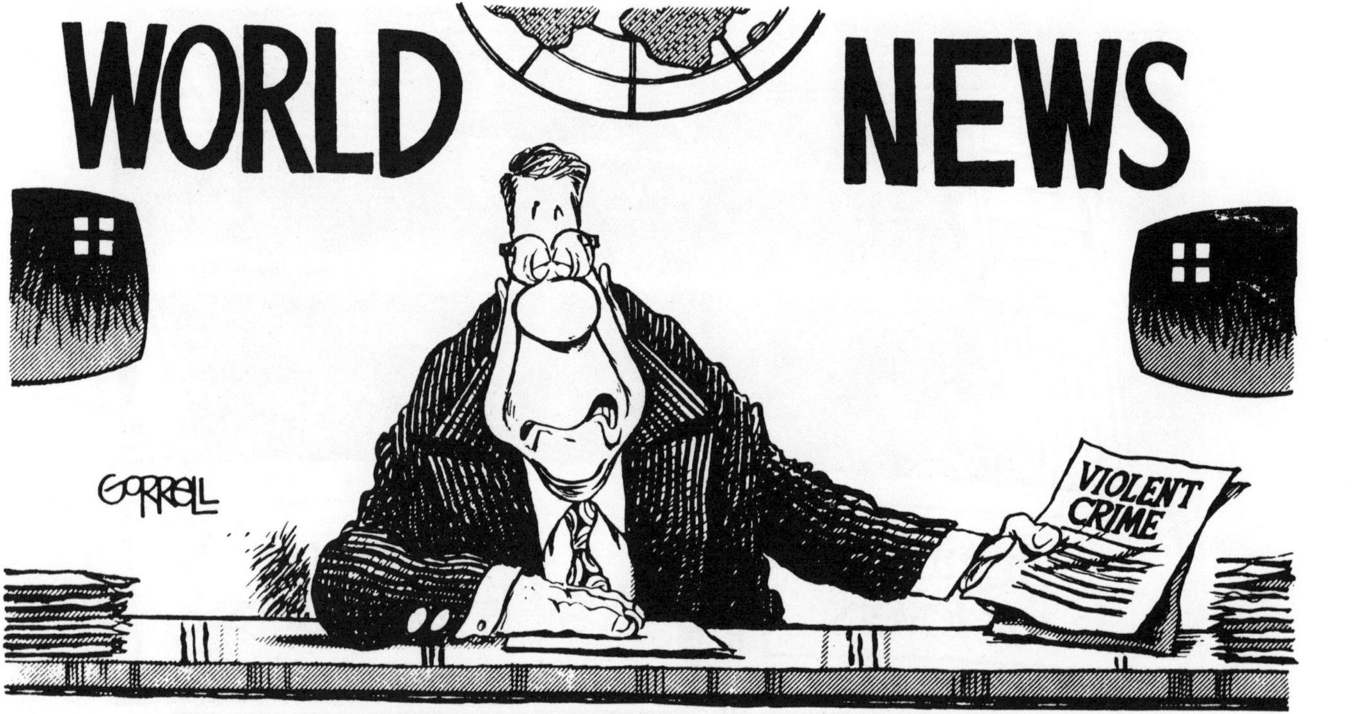
WORLD NEWS
GORRELL
VIOLENT CRIME

"IN AN EFFORT TO STEM THE RISING TIDE OF BLOODSHED, THE UNITED NATIONS TODAY ANNOUNCED ITS DEPLOYMENT OF A MULTI-NATIONAL PEACEKEEPING FORCE TO RICHMOND, VIRGINIA."

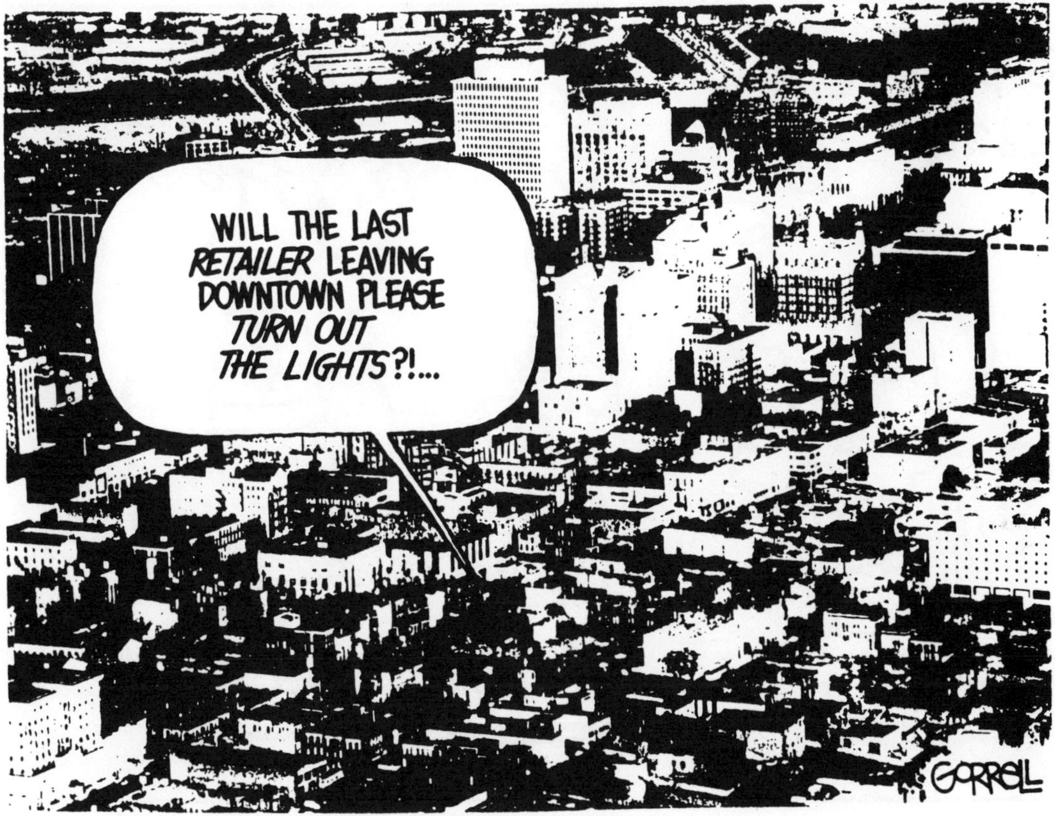
WILL THE LAST RETAILER LEAVING DOWNTOWN PLEASE TURN OUT THE LIGHTS?!...
GORRELL

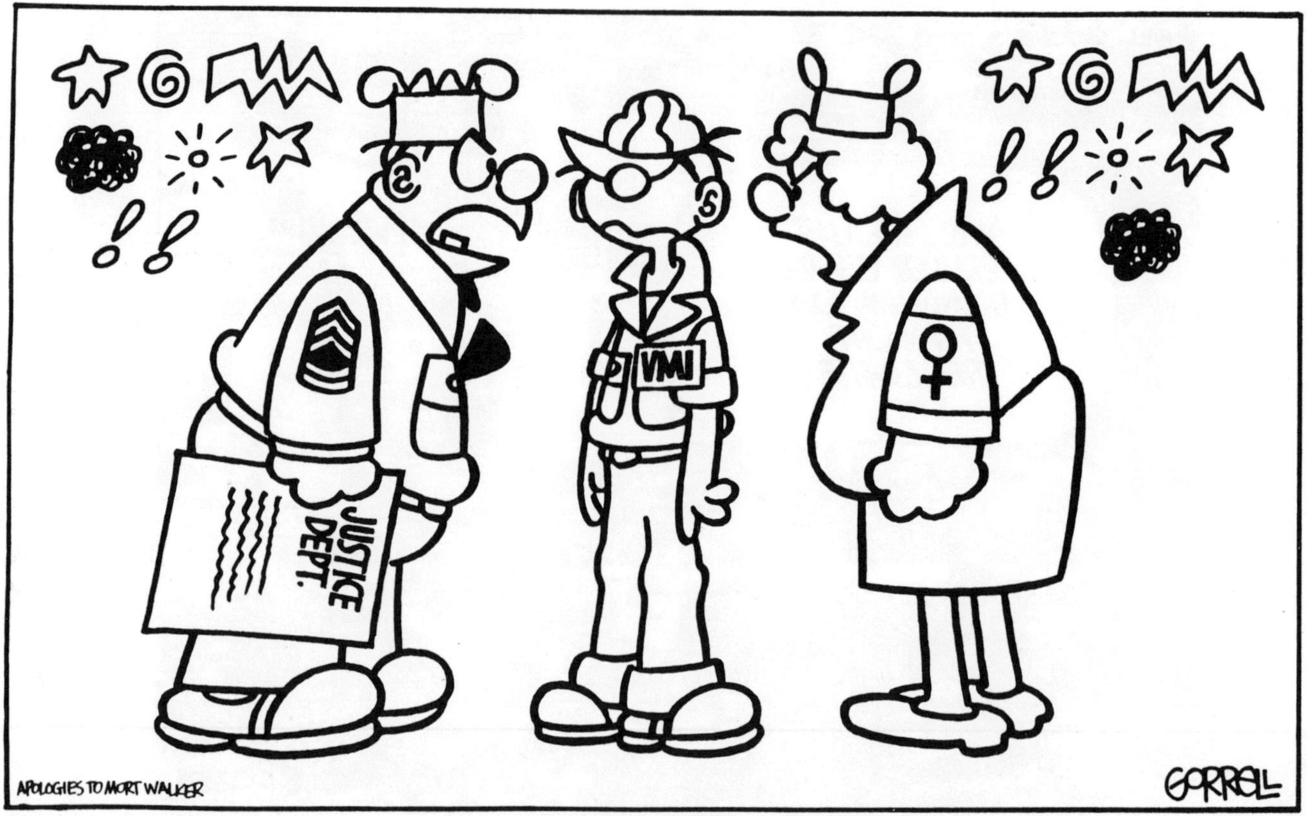
VMI
JUSTICE DEPT.
APOLOGIES TO MORT WALKER
GORRELL

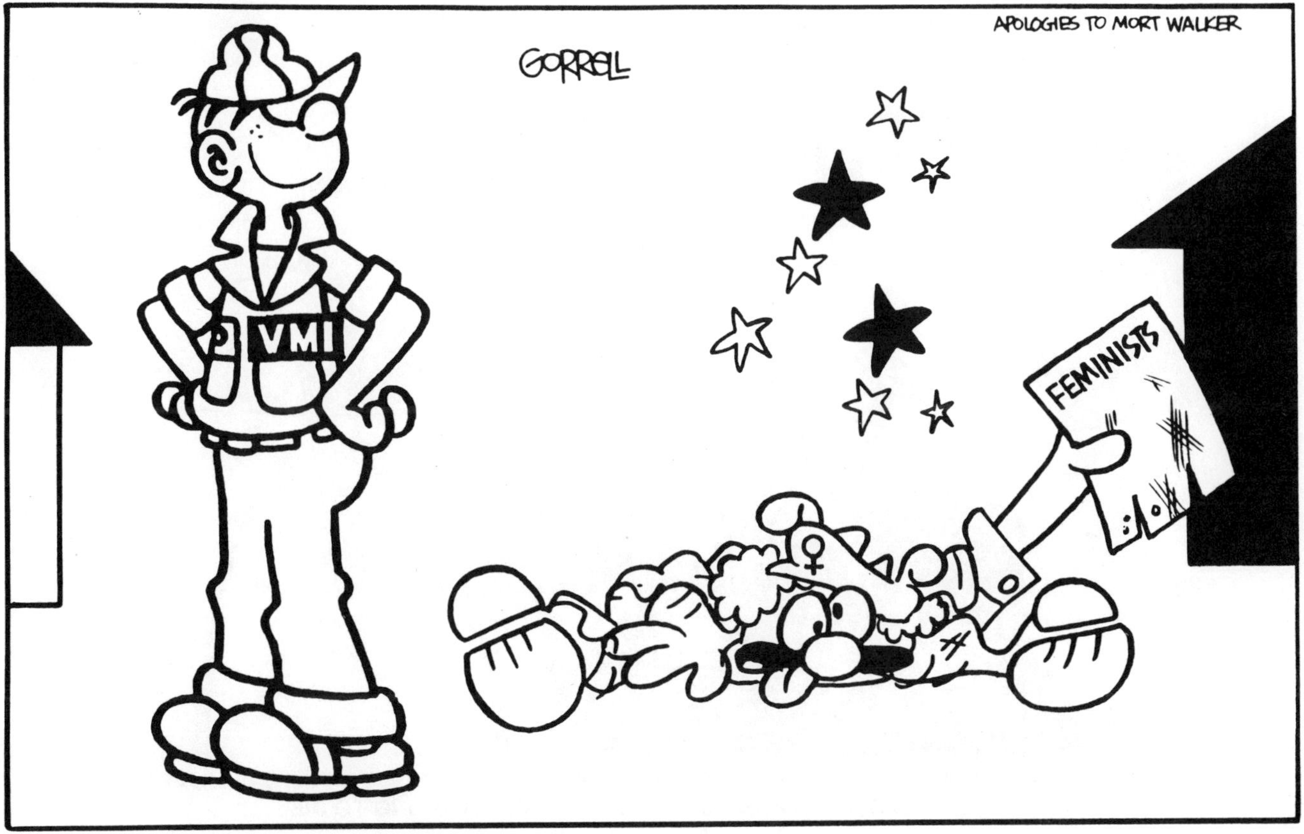
APOLOGIES TO MORT WALKER
GORRELL
VMI
FEMINISTS

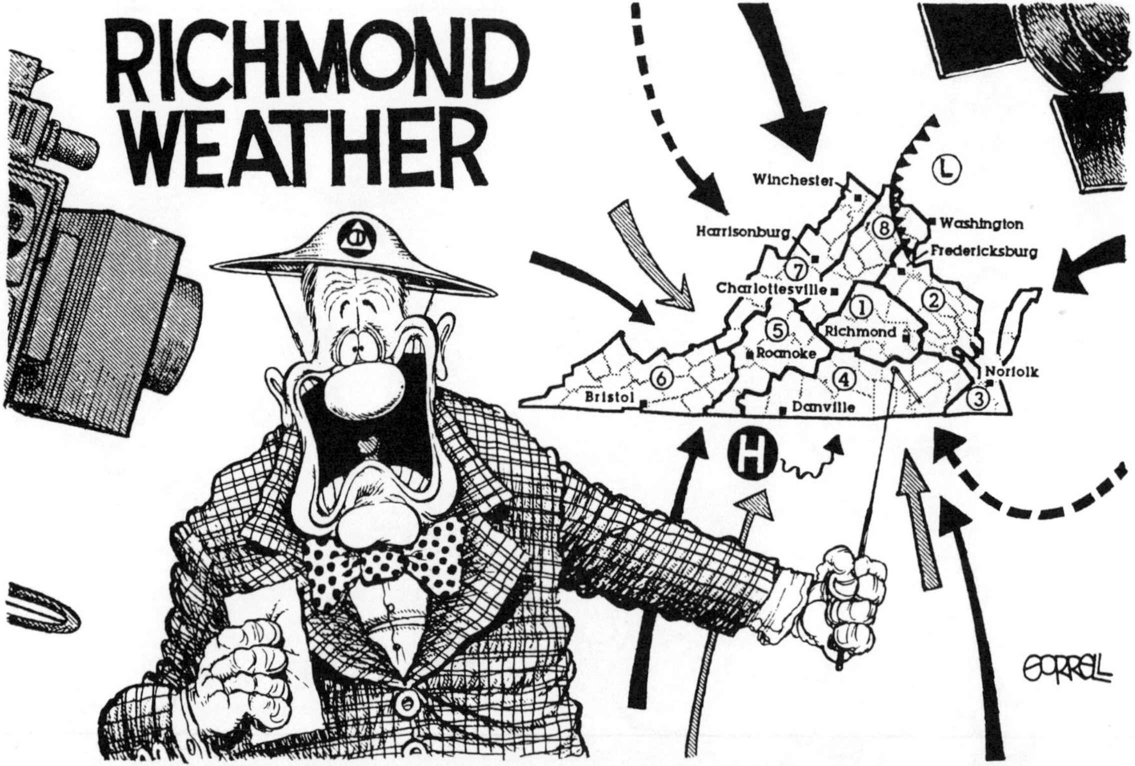
RICHMOND
WEATHER
Winchester
Harrisonburg
Washington
Fredericksburg
Charlottesville
Richmond
Roanoke
Norfolk
Bristol
Danville
L
H
SORRELL

"WE HAVE A SNOW ALERT! I REPEAT, A *SNOW ALERT!* THIS IS *NOT* A DRILL! TAKE COVER! RUN FOR YOUR LIVES! WE'RE ALL GOING TO *DIE . . .!*"

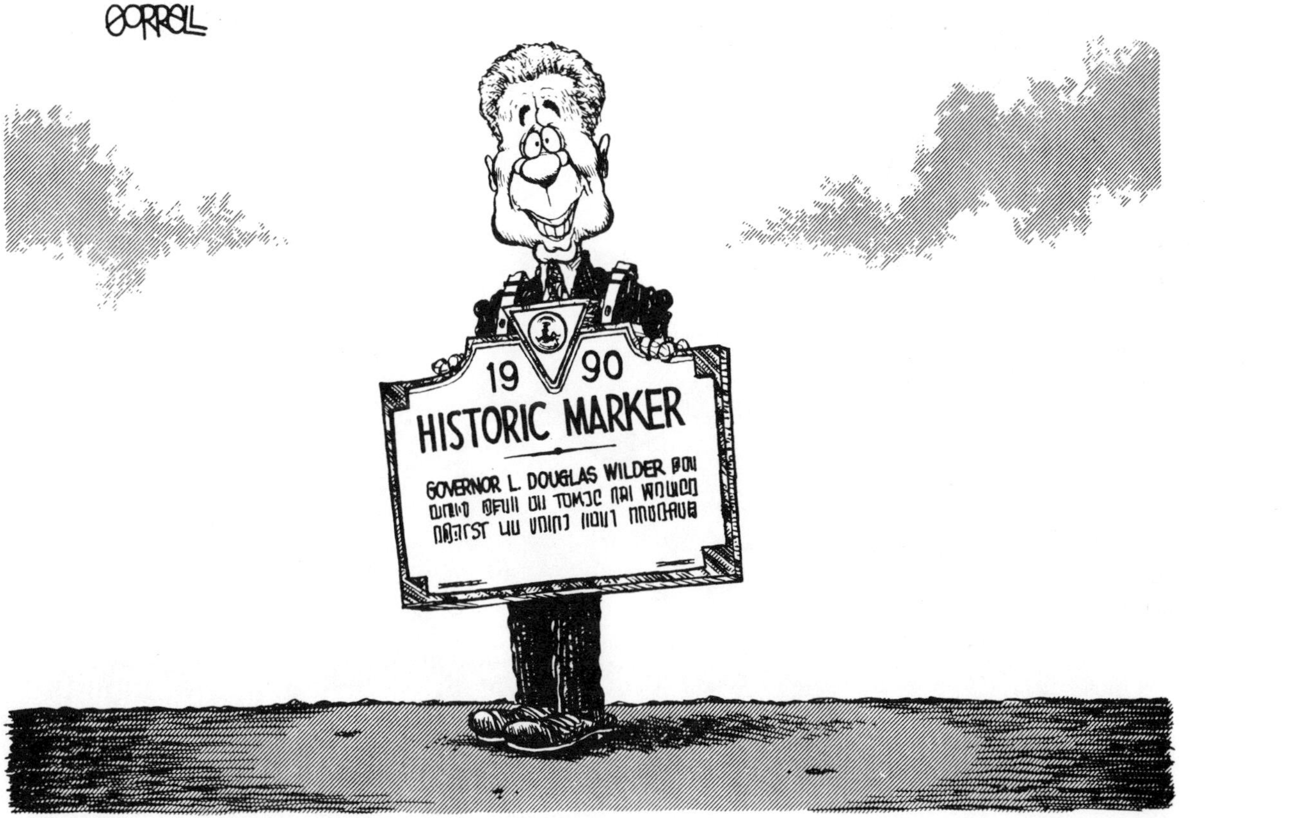
SORRELL
19 90
HISTORIC MARKER
GOVERNOR L. DOUGLAS WILDER

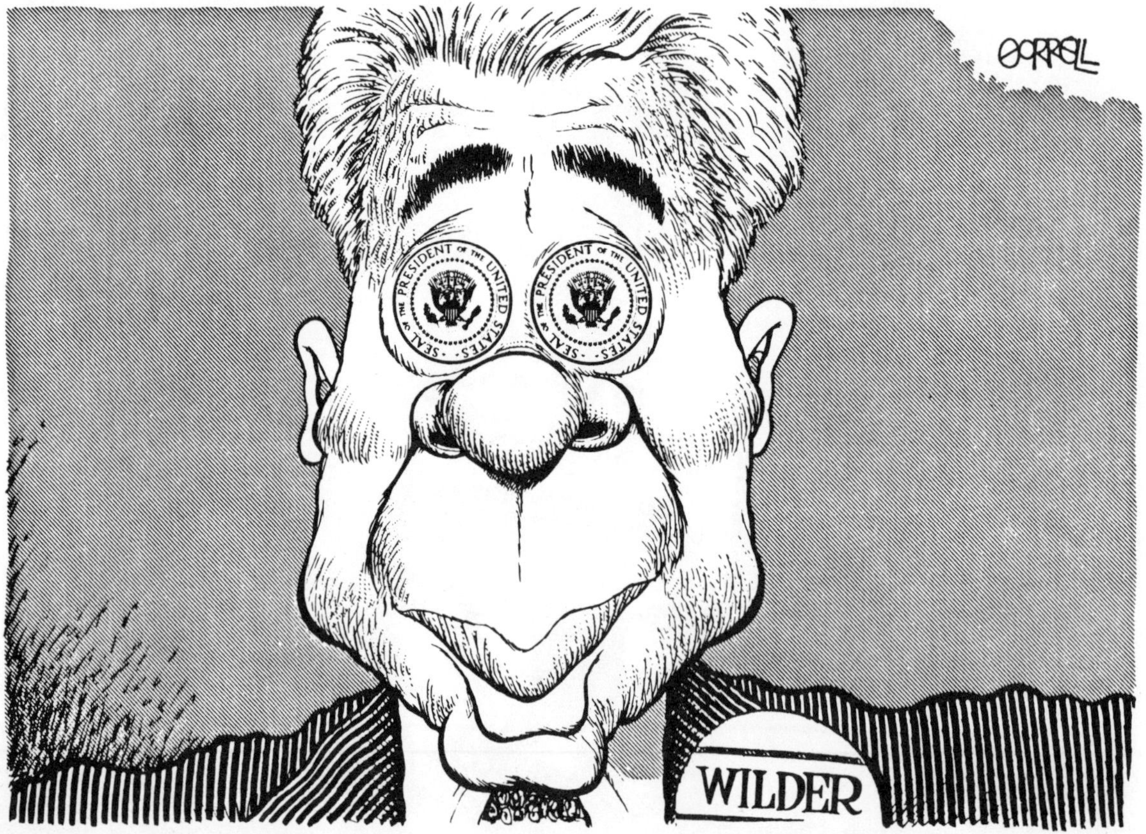
GORRELL
SEAL OF THE PRESIDENT OF THE UNITED STATES
SEAL OF THE PRESIDENT OF THE UNITED STATES
WILDER

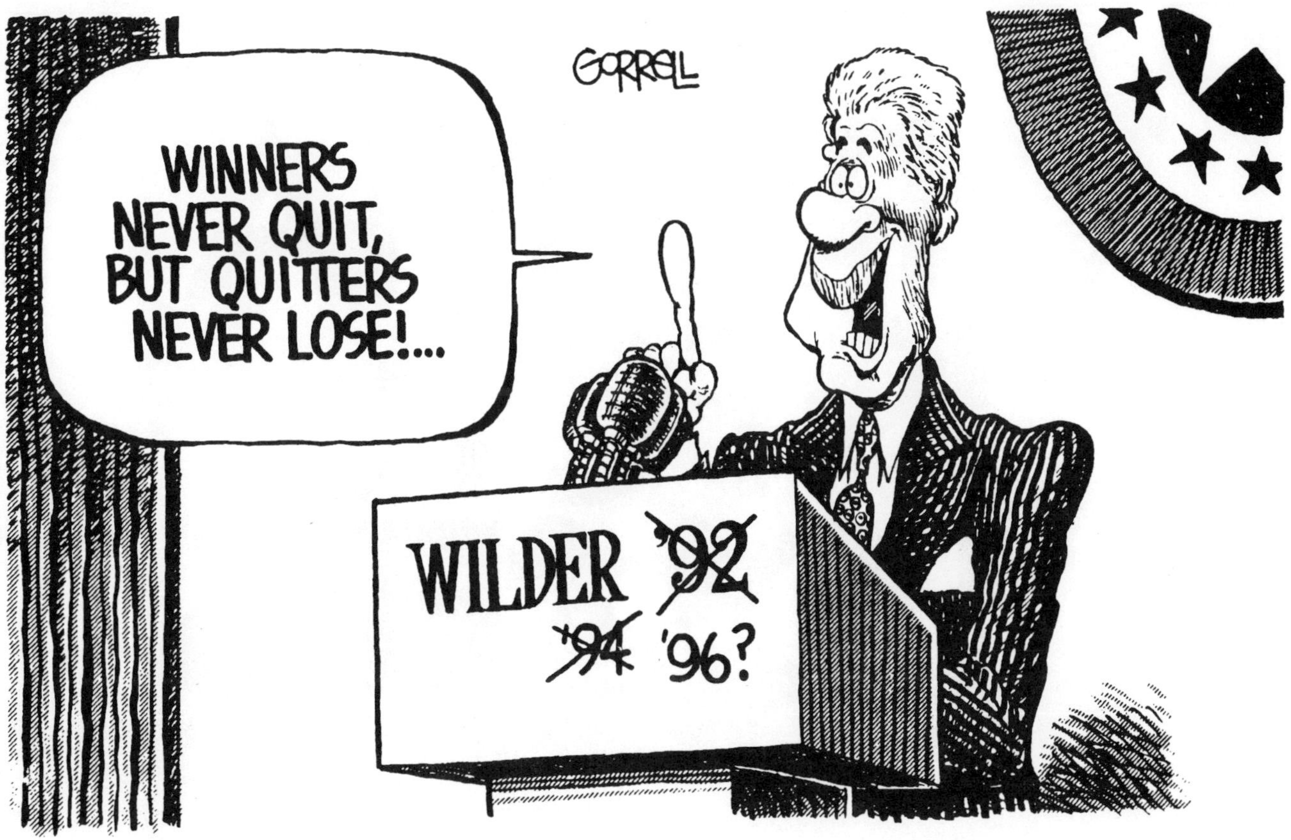
GORRELL
WINNERS NEVER QUIT, BUT QUITTERS NEVER LOSE!...
WILDER '92
'94 '96?

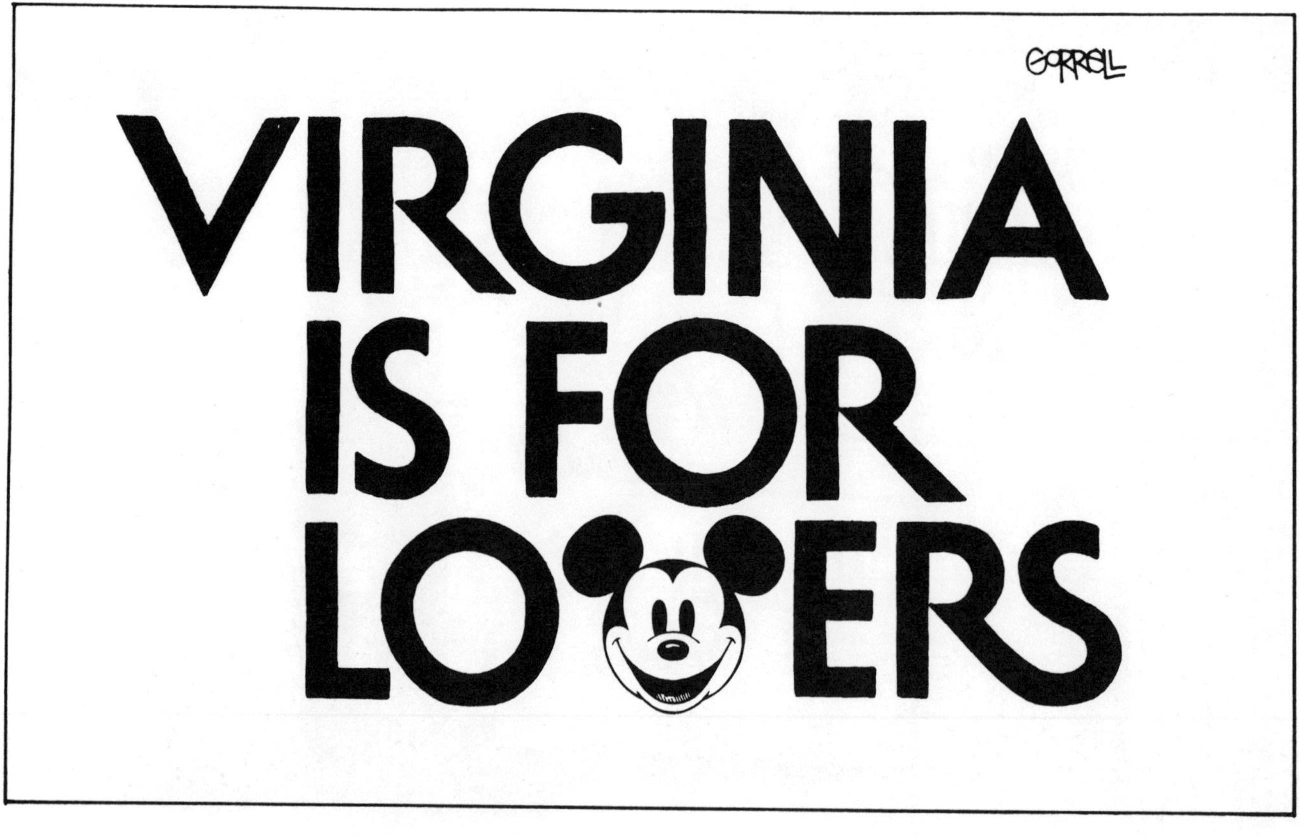
GORRELL
VIRGINIA
IS FOR
LO ERS

SA 27

BATTLE OF HAYMARKET

ON THIS SITE IN 1994, THE CITIZENS OF
NORTHERN VIRGINIA JOINED FORCES TO
SAVE THEIR TERRITORY FROM THE HORRORS
OF ECONOMIC PROSPERITY BY REPELLING
THE INVADING FORCES OF
MICKEY MOUSE.

CONSERVATION & DEVELOP- MENT COMMISSION 1981

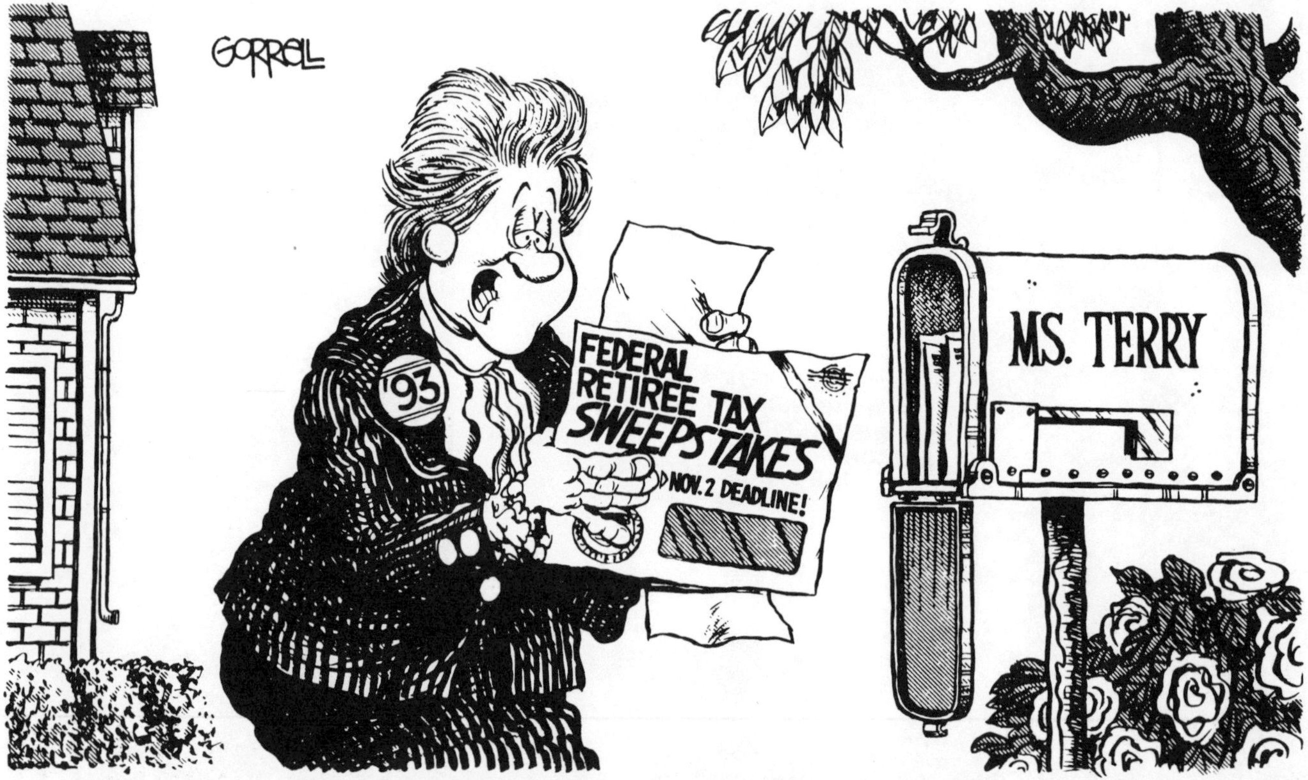
GORRELL
'93
FEDERAL
RETIREE TAX
SWEEPSTAKES
NOV. 2 DEADLINE!
MS. TERRY

"CONDOLENCES! . . . YOU MAY ALREADY BE A LOSER!"

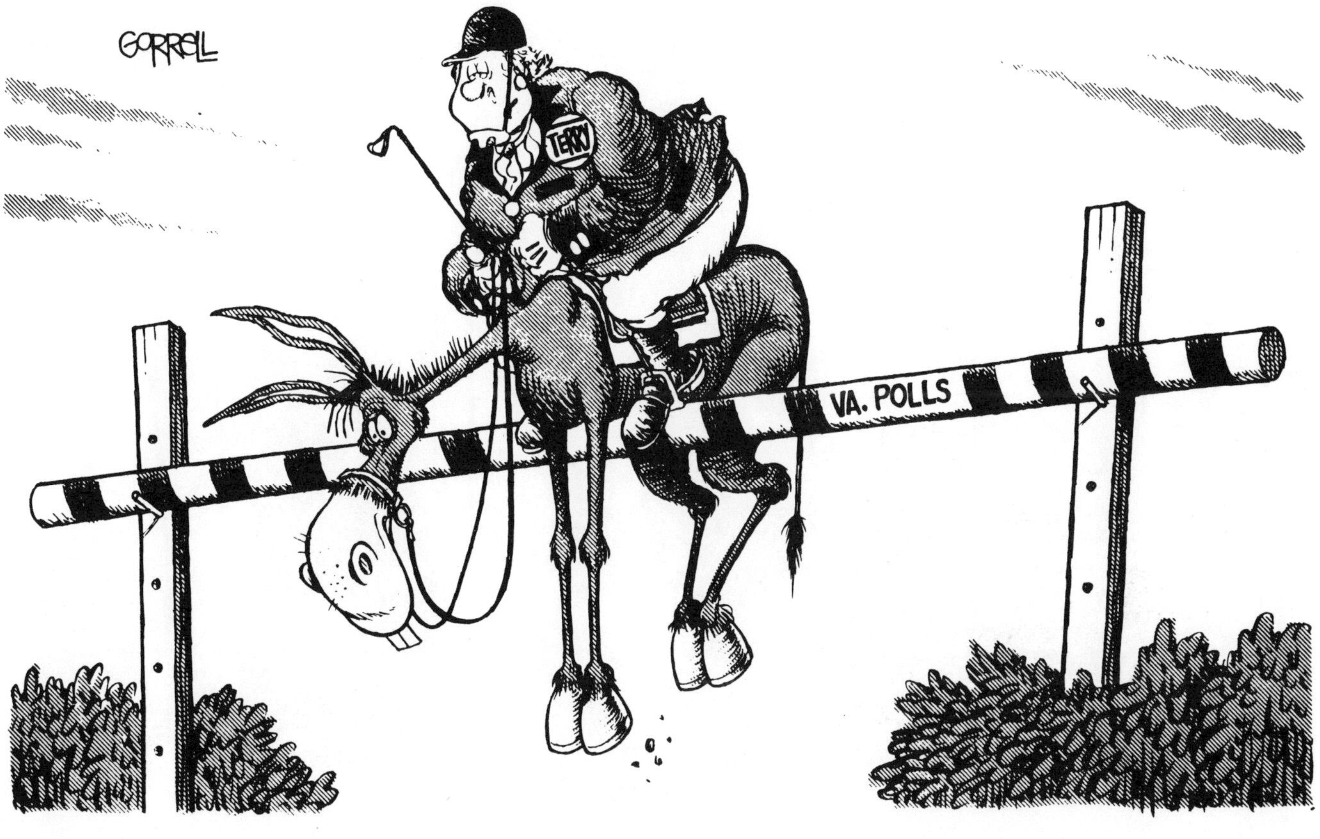
GORRELL
TERRY
VA. POLLS

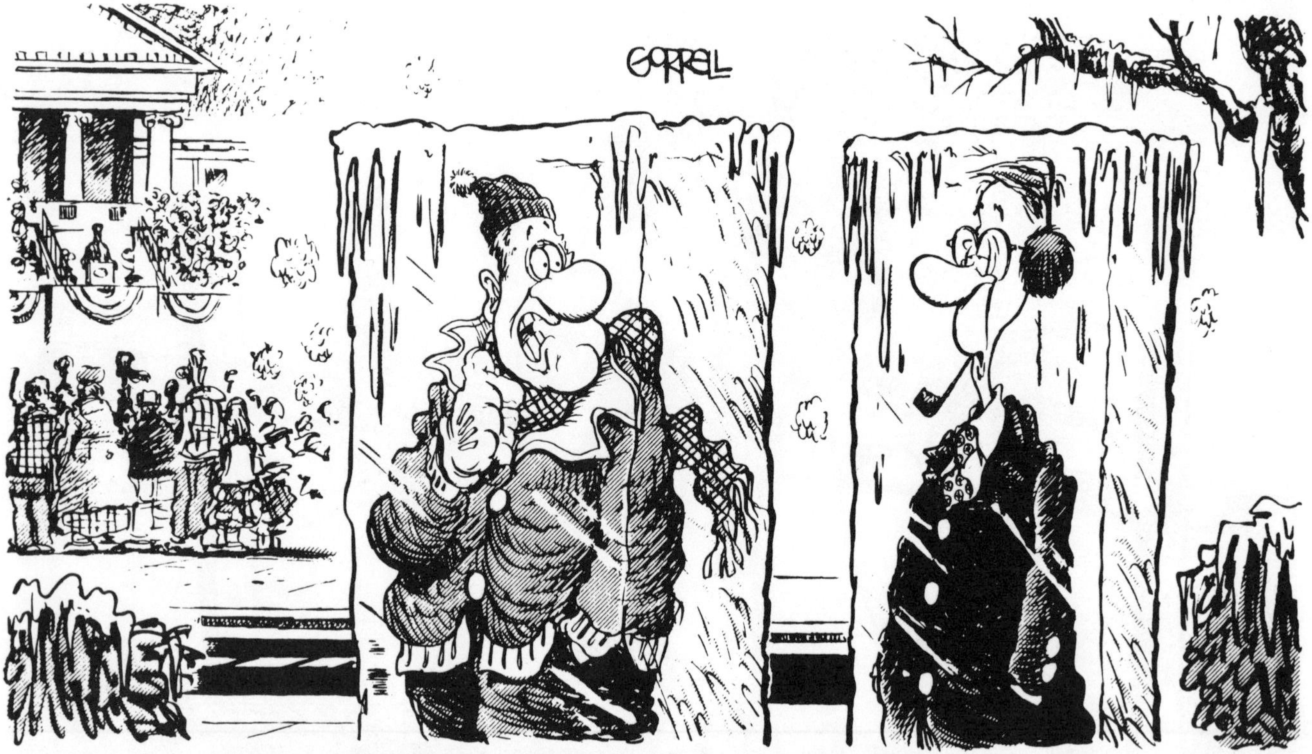
GORRELL

"WELL . . . THEY SAID IT WOULD BE A COLD DAY BEFORE VIRGINIA HAD ANOTHER REPUBLICAN GOVERNOR!"

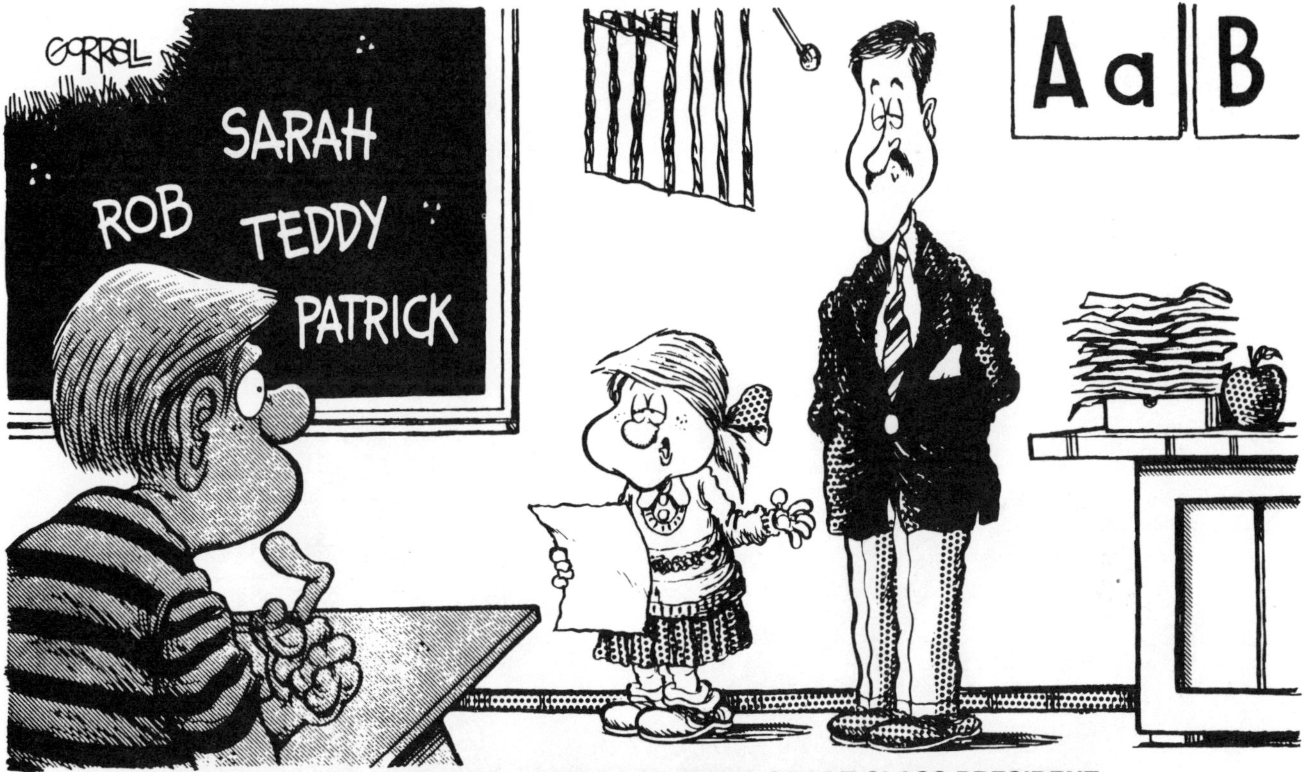
GORRELL
SARAH
ROB
TEDDY
PATRICK
Aa
B

"THAT CLOSES OUR NOMINATIONS FOR THIRD-GRADE CLASS PRESIDENT . . . .
NOW, HERE WITH HIS ANALYSIS IS LARRY SABATO."

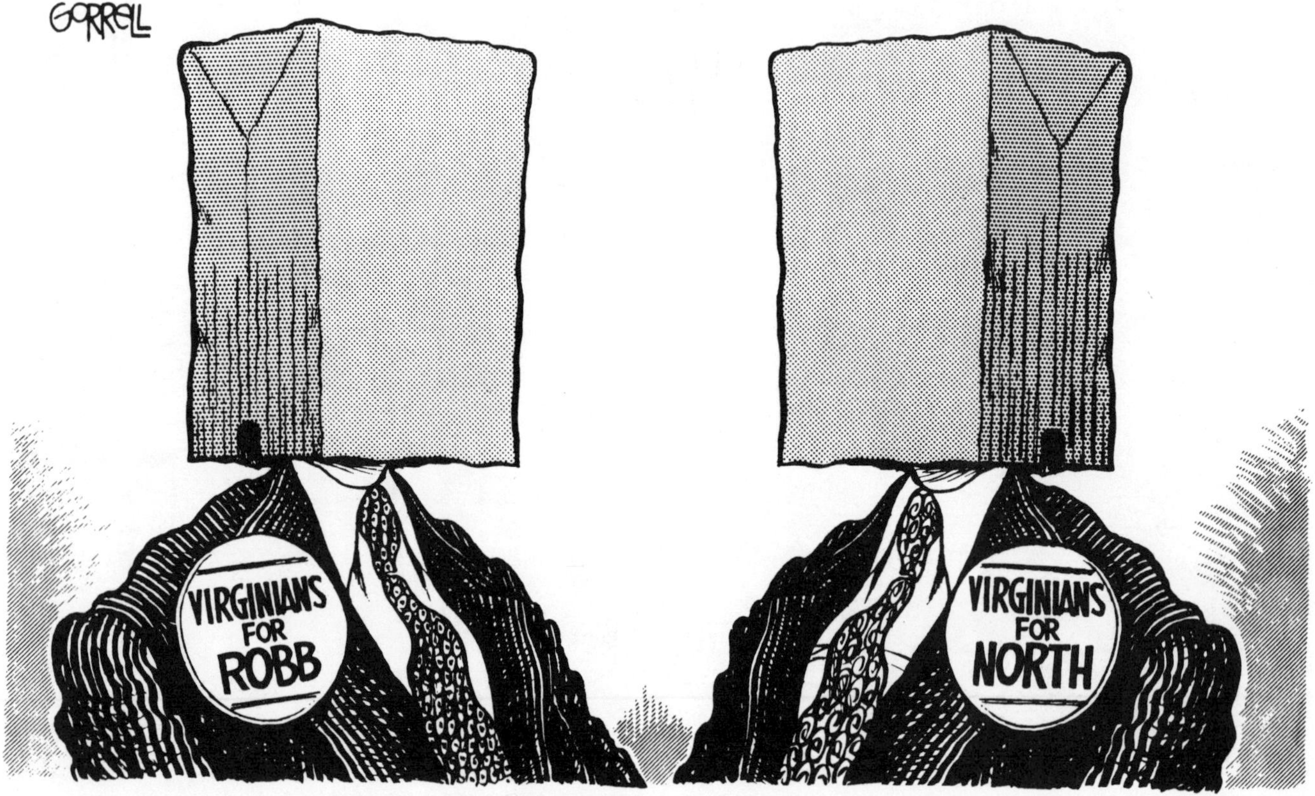
GORRELL
VIRGINIANS FOR ROBB
VIRGINIANS FOR NORTH

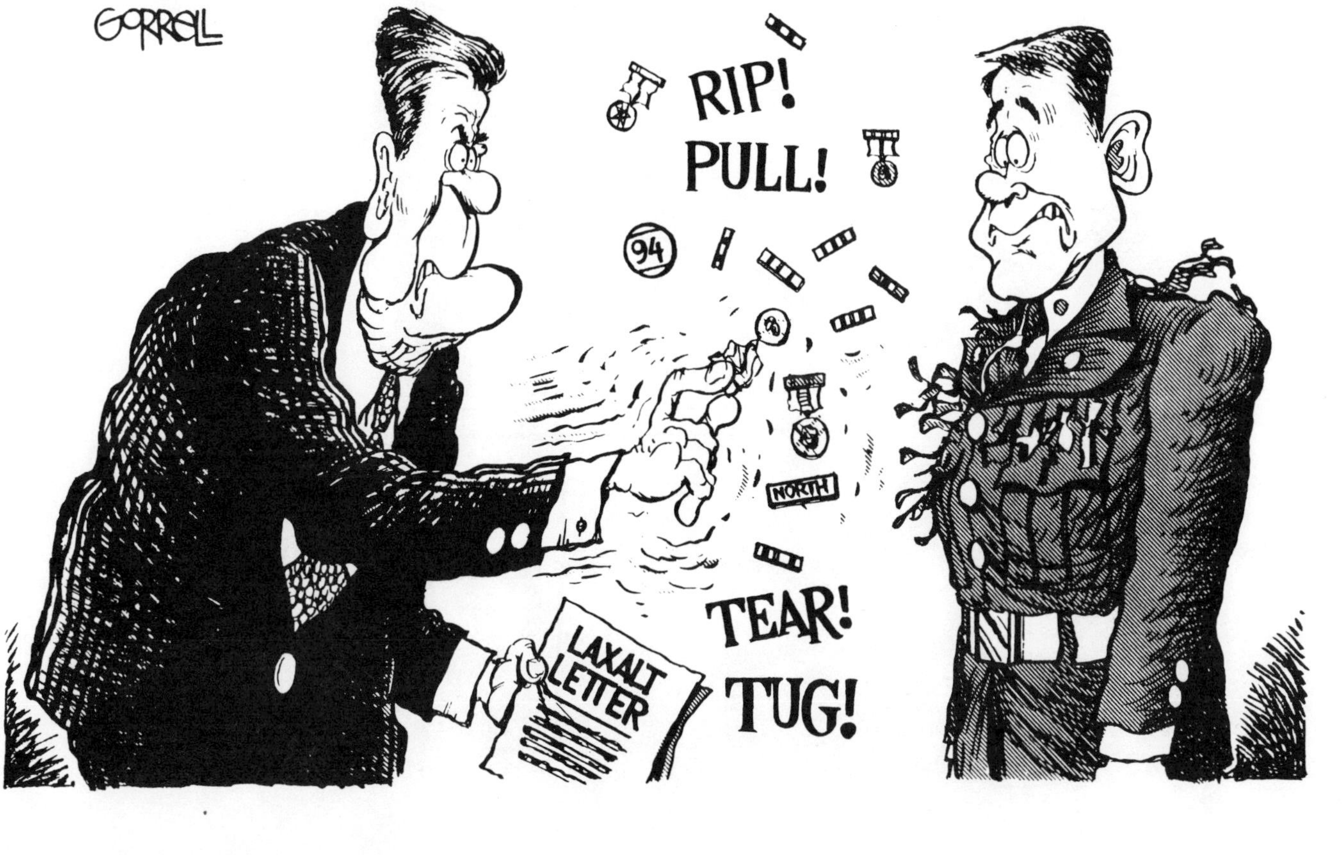
GORRELL
RIP!
PULL!
94
NORTH
TEAR!
TUG!
LAXALT LETTER

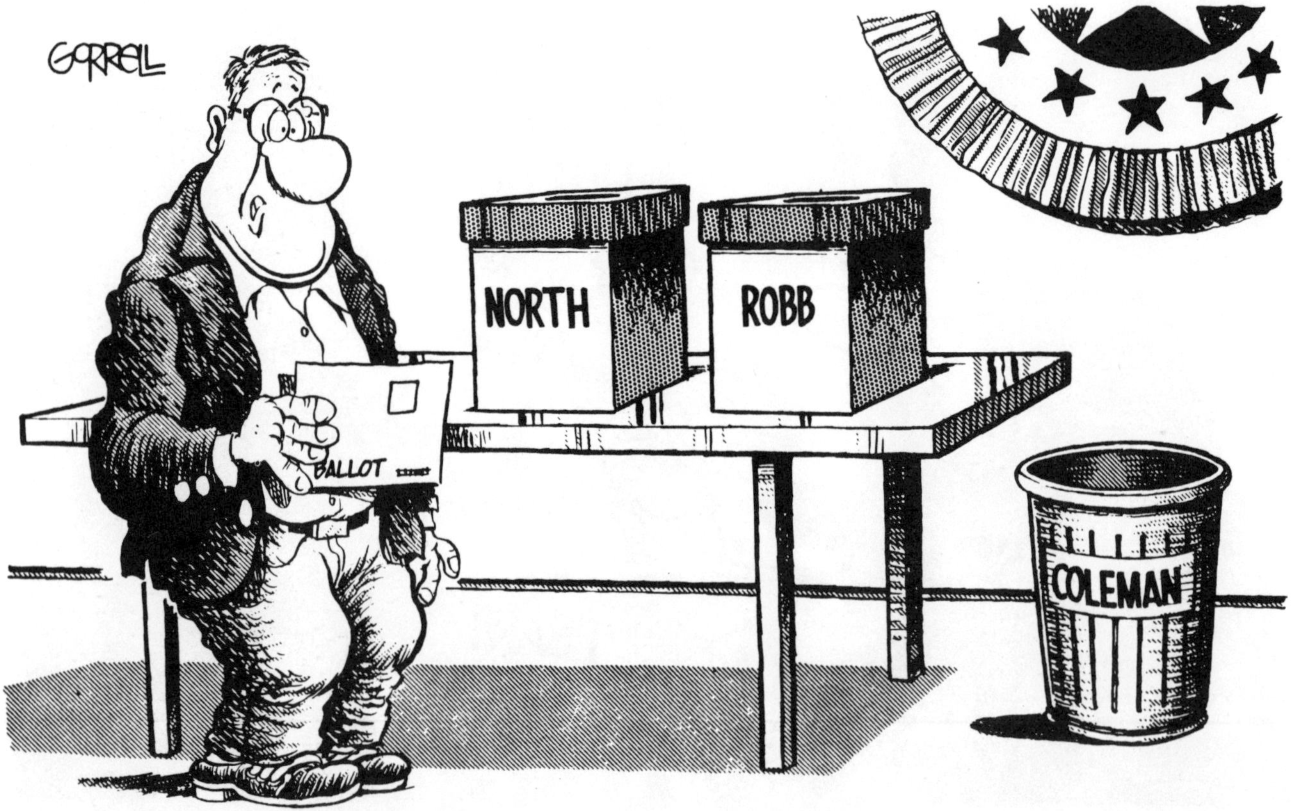
GORRELL
NORTH
ROBB
BALLOT
COLEMAN

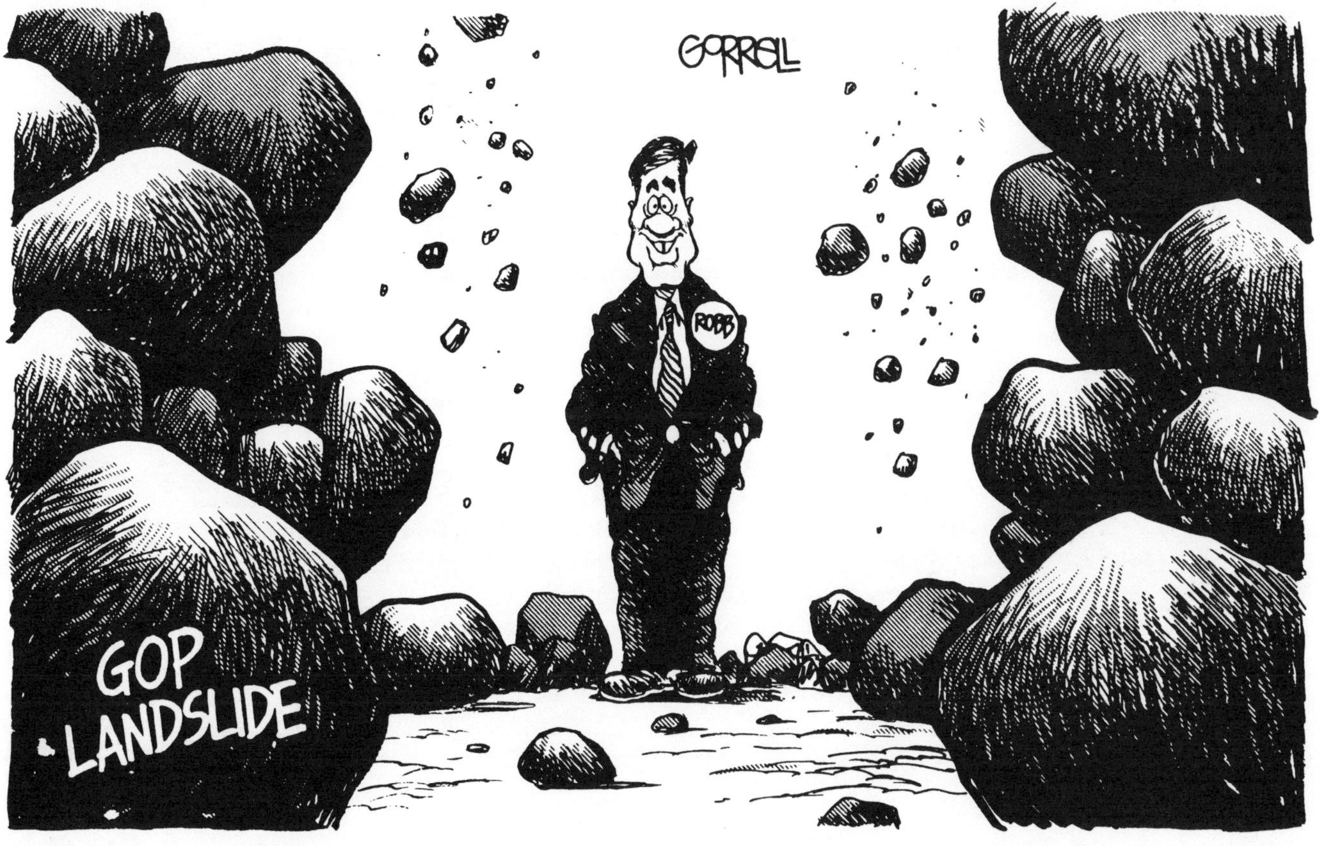
GORRELL
ROBB
GOP LANDSLIDE

About the Cartoonist

Born and raised in Greensboro, North Carolina, Bob Gorrell attended the University of Virginia as an Echols Scholar and graduated in 1977 with majors in both English literature and religious studies. Following cartooning stops in Fort Myers, Florida, and Charlotte, North Carolina, he joined *The Richmond News Leader* in 1983. Since 1992, Gorrell has contributed three to four editorial cartoons each week to the *Richmond Times-Dispatch.*

Gorrell's work is distributed by Creators Syndicate, and has appeared in hundreds of daily newspapers. *Newsweek, National Review, U.S. News & World Report,* and other periodicals frequently reprint his drawings. Among his many honors are citations from the Overseas Press Club of America, the Fischetti Editorial Cartoon Competition, the Dragonslayer Cartoon Contest, and the H. L. Mencken Awards. Gorrell has won first place for editorial cartooning in seven Virginia Press Association Award Competitions.

Gorrell lives in Goochland County, Virginia, with his wife, Pat, and their four children, Rob, Sarah, Teddy, and Patrick. He spends his time away from cartooning rooting for the UVa Wahoos and making a mockery of golf.